# SETTLEMENT OF INVESTMENT DISPUTES UNDER THE ENERGY CHARTER TREATY

The Energy Charter Treaty has come of age, with almost fifty states parties and a small but growing body of arbitral case law. In this new study of the Treaty's investment protection provisions, Thomas Roe and Matthew Happold set out to identify and explain the Treaty's principal provisions and to suggest answers to some of the difficult problems thrown up by its drafting. They discuss in detail questions such as the standards of protection granted by the Treaty and the international responsibility of states for breaches of the Treaty, the various procedures available for the vindication of rights under the Treaty and the conditions to be satisfied before a claimant's complaint may be considered on the merits. Specific issues addressed include the impact of EU law on claims under the Treaty and the Treaty's provisions concerning taxation.

THOMAS ROE is a barrister at 3 Hare Court, Temple, London specialising in commercial dispute resolution. He has extensive experience of disputes with international elements and concerning the rights and obligations of the state. He is a member of the Chartered Institute of Arbitrators.

MATTHEW HAPPOLD is Professor of Public International Law at the University of Luxembourg. He is also a member of chambers at 3 Hare Court, Temple, London. He has published extensively on a wide range of international law subjects.

JAMES DINGEMANS QC is Head of Chambers at 3 Hare Court, Temple, London. He is a recorder and Deputy High Court Judge (England and Wales), former Chairman of the International Relations Committee of the Bar Council of England and Wales, a Member of the Council of the Commonwealth Lawyers' Association and a Fellow of the Chartered Institute of Arbitrators.

LAW PRACTITIONER SERIES

The *Law Practitioner Series* offers practical guidance in corporate and commercial law for the practitioner. It offers high-quality comment and analysis rather than simply restating the legislation, providing a critical framework as well as exploring the fundamental concepts which shape the law. Books in the series cover carefully chosen subjects of direct relevance and use to the practitioner.

The series will appeal to experienced specialists in each field, but is also accessible to more junior practitioners looking to develop their understanding of particular fields of practice.

The Consultant Editors and Editorial Board have outstanding expertise in the UK corporate and commercial arena, ensuring academic rigour with a practical approach.



*Books in the series include*

*A Practical Guide to Private Equity Transactions* Geoff Yates and Mike Hinchliffe

*Stamp Duty Land Tax* Michael Thomas; Consultant Editor David Goy QC

*Accounting Principles for Lawyers* Peter Holgate

*The European Company: Volume 1* General Editors: Dirk van Gerven and Paul Storm

*The European Company: Volume 2* General Editors: Dirk van Gerven and Paul Storm

*Capital Markets Law and Compliance: The Implications of MiFID* Paul Nelson

*Reward Governance for Senior Executives* Edited by Carol Arrowsmith and Rupert McNeil

*Prospectus for the Public Offering of Securities in Europe Volume 1: European and National Legislation in the Member States of the European Economic Area* General Editor: Dirk van Gerven

*Prospectus for the Public Offering of Securities in Europe: Volume 2: European and National Legislation in the Member States of the European Economic Area* General Editor: Dirk van Gerven

*Common Legal Framework for Takeover Bids in Europe: Volume 1* General Editor: Dirk van Gerven

*Common Legal Framework for Takeover Bids in Europe: Volume 2* General Editor: Dirk van Gerven

*Accounting Principles for Non-Executive Directors* Peter A. Holgate and Elizabeth Buckley

*The Law of Charitable Status* Robert Meakin

*The Business Case for Corporate Governance* Ken Rushton

*Cross-Border Mergers in Europe: Volume 1* Edited by Dirk Van Gerven

# SETTLEMENT OF INVESTMENT DISPUTES UNDER THE ENERGY CHARTER TREATY

THOMAS ROE

AND

MATTHEW HAPPOLD

Consultant Editor

JAMES DINGEMANS QC

CAMBRIDGE
UNIVERSITY PRESS

CAMBRIDGE
UNIVERSITY PRESS

Shaftesbury Road, Cambridge CB2 8EA, United Kingdom

One Liberty Plaza, 20th Floor, New York, NY 10006, USA

477 Williamstown Road, Port Melbourne, VIC 3207, Australia

314–321, 3rd Floor, Plot 3, Splendor Forum, Jasola District Centre, New Delhi – 110025, India

103 Penang Road, #05–06/07, Visioncrest Commercial, Singapore 238467

Cambridge University Press is part of Cambridge University Press & Assessment, a department of the University of Cambridge.

We share the University's mission to contribute to society through the pursuit of education, learning and research at the highest international levels of excellence.

www.cambridge.org
Information on this title: www.cambridge.org/9780521899383



First published 2011

*A catalogue record for this publication is available from the British Library*

*Library of Congress Cataloging-in-Publication data*
Roe, Thomas, 1972–
Settlement of investment disputes under the Energy Charter Treaty / Thomas Roe and Matthew Happold ; consultant editor, James Dingemans.
p. cm. – (Law practitioner series)
Includes bibliographical references and index.
ISBN 978-0-521-89938-3 (hardback)
1. Energy Charter Treaty (1994) 2. Energy industries – Law and legislation. 3. Dispute resolution (Law) 4. Arbitration and award, International. I. Happold, Matthew. II. Dingemans, James. III. Title. IV. Series.
K3981.R64 2011
346.04′679 – dc22 2011000633

ISBN 978-0-521-89938-3 Hardback

To Helen, Alexander, Elizabeth and Theodore, and for Cassian – Ach, zu schnell erlosch'ner Freudenschein!

T.R.

'As to precedents, to be sure they will increase in course of time; but the more precedents there are, the less occasion is there for law; that is to say, the less occasion is there for investigating principles.'

Samuel Johnson

J. Boswell, *Life of Johnson*

CONTENTS

# FOREWORD

Of *The Pilgrim's Progress*, Huckleberry Finn said that he 'read considerable in it now and then', and that 'the statements was interesting, but tough'. To the quite small body of persons who have 'read in' them, the documents constituting the Energy Charter Treaty may or may not have been interesting, but they will surely have found them tough. In contrast with the ICSID Convention, which as a text is a masterpiece of multinational drafting even though as a practical source of rules it lacks spine, the Energy Charter Treaty is an uncouth thicket from which even an interested person could well recoil. Nevertheless, although the field of view is narrow and highly particular, it is important in theory as well as in practice, and calls for an informed, readable and scholarly monograph. This is what the present work supplies.

Since this is a foreword, not a review, I must with difficulty abstain from offering a personal appraisal of international energy law and practice; of dispute resolution in that field; and of the crippling inconsistencies in the jurisprudence of bilateral investment treaty disputes, now apparently incurable. The books get longer and longer, and so do the awards, whilst colloquia, study groups, task forces and the like continue to proliferate, often producing book-length records of their proceedings; yet in the absence of a doctrine of binding precedent there is currently no means of imposing order where it is needed. Although notable talents continue to be involved, the entire area of study seems to be heading for a thrombosis.

This bleak landscape offers an almost irresistible invitation to wade in with proposals for a remedy. But only 'almost', for the urge to add another pebble to the pile must be resisted, particularly in a foreword, whose writer is not given the broad licence to deploy his own ideas and personality conferred on a reviewer. A foreword must be about the book itself, not the contributor. The task is more limited, and more practical, namely to encourage a prospective reader to partake of what is on offer.

Quite often, a foreword is perfunctory, the fruits of no more than dipping into the book, or even its index, and the writer of it quite frequently contributes only as a favour to the author or publisher. Not so here. With pleasure and profit, as advertisements used to say, I read the whole book straight through. This is a tribute, not only to the clarity of the language but also to careful structuring which enables the essence of the Energy Charter regime to be perceived amidst the tangled foliage. These features make the book an ideal primer for those lacking an extensive acquaintance with the subject.

There is, however, much more to it than that, for the authors offer balanced accounts of selected practical and conceptual issues. The balance and the selection are important. A schoolgirl's celebrated review of a book, on *The Elephant*, read: 'This book tells you more about the elephant than you want to know', and one or two of the otherwise excellent works on the kindred topic of bilateral investment treaty disputes are handicapped by a similar surplus of material. In the present writer's opinion the text of this trail-blazing work avoids surfeit whilst at the same time furnishing most readers with what they require. I am glad to commend *Settlement of Investment Disputes under the Energy Charter Treaty* as an enterprising, scholarly and useful volume with a very promising future ahead of it.

Lord Mustill PC LLD FBA 24 Lincoln's Inn Fields
London WC2

# PREFACE

The difficulties which face the scholar or practitioner of international investment law in the second decade of the twenty-first century do not include a lack of reading material. The authors of a further contribution ought therefore to begin with a defence of their decision to make it.

Ours, put shortly, is that the Energy Charter Treaty's provisions on investor–state dispute settlement deserve an up-to-date study of their own. Although the Treaty is limited in its application to just one field of international investment – energy – that field is of great significance and sensitivity, and is one in which the interests of states in attracting foreign investment on the one hand and on the other in regulating the conduct of foreign investors are inevitably in a state of real or potential tension. And what it lacks in breadth of subject-matter the Energy Charter Treaty makes up for in the number of its signatories: some forty-six countries and the European Union are parties (another state applies the Treaty provisionally and Russia must apply the Treaty for twenty years to all investments made until 18 October 2009). The Energy Charter Treaty is, in short, a very important treaty whose provisions ought to be well understood by all parties and by all relevant investors. Yet in truth the Treaty is not always easy to understand and the meaning of many of its provisions remains obscure.

In writing this study we have had three main aims. First, to describe clearly the Treaty's principal investor–state dispute resolution provisions. Second, to think – in rather more detail than would be possible in a work on international investment protection law generally – about the meaning of those provisions, especially the ones which give rise to the most difficulty. When we conceived this project, we planned to fulfil this aim simply by *identifying* points of difficulty and the arguments on each side. We found this an impossible limitation to keep to and have instead felt free to state our views. Whether or not readers agree with them, we hope that we have thereby contributed to the fulfilment of our third aim: to stimulate debate and thereby contribute in a small way to the development of an area of law which in many ways is still in its infancy. For, although the corpus of arbitral case law on bilateral investment treaties is vast (and sometimes highly relevant), very few cases have yet been determined under the Treaty itself and much remains open to debate.

We gratefully acknowledge the insights into the Energy Charter Treaty, and into the field of international investment protection generally, provided by papers and discussion at conferences organised by the Energy Charter Secretariat and attended by us in Washington DC in 2007 and in Brussels in 2009. We are grateful to Liz Heathfield for her help in conceiving this book. We thank James Dingemans QC for agreeing to act as our consultant editor and for his valuable assistance both in that capacity and in discussions about real cases. The views stated in this book are, however, ours alone; nor are they put forward to represent the views of any client. Errors, too, are ours.

Kim Hughes of Cambridge University Press has given us much guidance and shown great patience when the many other pressures of our professional and academic lives got in the way. Kate Ollerenshaw has been an astute and tactful copy-editor. We are extremely grateful. Above all we thank our respective families, of whose company the Energy Charter Treaty, interesting though it is, has deprived us for an unconscionably long time.

We have tried to state the law as at 1 August 2010.

*Thomas Roe*
*London*

*Matthew Happold*
*Luxembourg*

# TABLE OF CASES

## European Court of Human Rights

*Behrami* v. *France; Saramati* v. *France, Germany and Norway* (2007) 45 EHRR SE10 181, 182

*Bosphorus Hava Yolları Turizm ve Ticaret Anonim Şirketi* v. *Republic of Ireland* (2006) 42 EHRR 1 95, 184

*Matthews* v. *United Kingdom* (1999) 28 EHRR 361 183–4

*OAO Neftyanaya Kompaniya Yukos* v. *Russia*, ECHR appl no. 14902/04, Admissibility Decision, 29 January 2010 188n

## European Court of Justice

*Commission of the European Communities* v. *Austria* (Case C-205/06) [2009] 2 CMLR 50 89–90n, 172n

*Commission of the European Communities* v. *Finland* (Case C-118/07) [2010] All ER (EC) 558 89–90n, 172n

*Commission of the European Communities* v. *Republic of Ireland* (Case C-459/03) [2006] ECR I-4635 94n

*Commission of the European Communities* v. *Sweden* (Case C-249/06) [2009] 2 CMLR 49 89–90n, 172n

*Eco Swiss China Time Ltd* v. *Benetton International NV* (Case C-126/97) [1999] ECR I-3055 103n

*European Parliament* v. *Council of the European Union* (Case C-316/91) [1994] ECR I-625 175

*France* v. *Commission of the European Communities* (Case C-327/91) [1994] ECR I-3641 179n

*Kadi* v. *Council of the European Union and Commission of the European Communities*, Opinion of Advocate General Maduro (Case C-402/05P) [2008] ECR I-635, [2009] 1 AC 1225 97

*NV Algemene Transport- en Expeditie Onderneming van Gend en Loos* v. *Netherlands Administratie der Belastingen* (Case 26–62) [1963] ECR 1 96–7, 102n

*Opinion 1/91* (Draft Treaty on a European Economic Area) [1991] ECR I-1061 96–7n

*Parti ecologiste 'Les Verts'* v. *Parliament* (Case 294/83) [1986] ECR 1339 96n

## International Court of Justice

*Case concerning Elettronica Sicula*, 20 July 1989, ICJ Rep (1989) 15 117
*Case concerning Oil Platforms (Islamic Republic of Iran* v. *United States of America)*, 1996 ICJ Rep 803 28, 43n, 45n, 46n
*Kasikili/Sedudu Island* (*Botswana* v. *Namibia*), Judgment, 1999 ICJ Rep 1045 28n
*LaGrand* (*Germany* v. *United States of America*), ICJ Rep 2001 7n, 165n
*North Sea Continental Shelf* cases (*FRG* v. *Netherlands/FRG* v. *Denmark*), ICJ Rep 1969 110–11n
*Territorial Dispute* (*Libyan Arab Jamahiriya* v. *Chad*), Judgment, 1996 ICJ Rep 6 28n

## Permanent Court of International Justice

*Jurisdiction of the Courts of Danzig*, PCIJ Series C, No. 14-I 7n
*Mavrommatis Palestine Concessions* case (*Greece* v. *United Kingdom*), PCIJ, Series A, No. 2 (1924) 1

## Arbitral Tribunals and Claims Commissions*

*AAPL* v. *Sri Lanka*, Award, 27 June 1990 53n
*ADF Group* v. *United States of America*, Award, 9 January 2003 110, 112n
*AES Corp* v. *Argentina*, Decision on Jurisdiction, 26 April 2005 36–7
*AES Summit Generation Ltd v. Republic of Hungary* (ICSID Case No. ARB/01/04) 90
*AES Summit Generation Ltd and AES-Tisza Erőmű Kft.* v. *Republic of Hungary* (ICSID Case No. ARB/07/22) 90–1, 173
*Alstom Power Italia SpA, Alstom SpA* v. *Mongolia* (ICSID Case no. ARB/04/10) (settled 13 March 2003) 59n
*Amco* v. *Indonesia*, Award, 20 November 1984 165n
*AMTO* v. *Ukraine*, Award, 26 March 2008 48, 66, 78, 79, 83n, 131n, 164n
*Asian Agricultural Products Ltd* v. *Sri Lanka*, Final Award, 27 June 1990, 30 ILM 577 115n
*Azurix* v. *Argentina*, Award, 14 July 2006 116, 126, 127
*Biloune and Marine Drive Complex Ltd* v. *Ghana Investments Centre and the Government of Ghana*, Award on Jurisdiction and Liability, 27 October 1989, 95 ILR 184 120n
*Biwater Gauff (Tanzania) Ltd* v. *Tanzania*, Award, 24 July 2008 57n
Case No. A/18 (1984) 5 Iran-US Cl Trib Rep 251 (Full Tribunal, Iran-US Claims Tribunal) 65n, 93n

* Most modern awards of arbitral tribunals constituted under bilateral and multilateral investment treaties are freely available on the internet. The authors have consulted in particular the Investment Treaty Arbitration website maintained by the Faculty of Law of the University of Victoria (http://ita.law.uvic.ca). The majority of references to arbitral awards are, accordingly, identified by name and date only.

*Malaysian Historical Salvors Sdn Bhd v. Malaysia*, Decision on Application for Annulment, 16 April 2009 55–6, 57, 58n, 153n

*Methanex Corp* v. *United States of America*, Partial Award, 7 August 2002 28n, 30n

*Mitchell* v. *Congo*, Decision on Annulment, 1 November 2006 57, 58n

*Mondev International Ltd* v. *United States of America*, Award, 11 October 2002 28n, 110–11n, 130–1n, 141n, 165n

*MOX Plant Case* (*Ireland* v. *United Kingdom*), Order on Request for Provisional Measures, 3 December 2001 33, 37

*Neer* (*United States of America* v. *Mexico*), *United States – Mexico General Claims Commission*, (1926) 4 RIAA 60 2, 108–9, 110

*Noble Ventures Inc* v. *Romania*, Award, 12 October 2005 30, 125n, 126–7n, 170n

*North American Dredging Co* v. *Mexico* (1926–7) IV RIAA 26 150, 151n

*Nykomb Synergetics Technology Holding* v. *Latvia*, Award, 16 December 2003 140–1, 165n

*Olguín* v. *Paraguay* (ICSID Case No. ARB/98/5), Award, 26 July 2001 65n

*Pan American Energy LLC and BP Argentina Exploration Company* v. *Argentina*, Decision on Preliminary Objections, 27 July 2006 124–5n

*Pantechniki SA Contractors & Engineers* v. *Albania*, Award, 28 July 2009 57n

*Petrobart Ltd* v. *Kyrgyz Republic*, Award, 29 March 2005 56, 60–3, 64, 69–70, 143n, 153n, 156n

*Plama Consortium Ltd* v. *Bulgaria*, Decision on Jurisdiction, 5 February 2005 34–5, 43, 44, 45, 54, 79, 80–2, 83–4, 85–6, 87–8n, 129n

*Pope & Talbot Inc* v. *Canada*, Award on the Merits, 10 April 2001 109, 110, 111–12n, 118n

*Romak SA* v. *Uzbekistan*, Award, 26 November 2009 56

*Ronald S Lauder* v. *Czech Republic*, Award (Final), 3 September 2001 137n

*Rumeli Telekom AS* v. *Kazakhstan*, Decision of the *ad hoc* Committee, 25 March 2010 158–9

*Salini Costruttori SpA and Italstrade SpA* v. *Jordan*, Award of 15 November 2004 43n, 45n, 129n

*Salini Costruttori and Italstrade* v. *Morocco*, Decision on Jurisdiction, 23 July 2001 57, 60, 61, 64n, 87n

*Saluka Investments BV* v. *Czech Republic*, Partial Award, 17 March 2006 28, 30–1, 59, 114n, 116n

*S. D. Myers Inc* v. *Canada*, First Partial Award, 13 November 2000 109

*Siemens AG* v. *Argentina*, Award on Jurisdiction, 3 August 2004 128n

*Siemens AG* v. *Argentina*, Award, 6 February 2007 116, 125n

*Société de Surveillance SA* v. *Pakistan*, Decision on Jurisdiction, 6 August 2003 123, 137n

*Société de Surveillance SA* v. *Philippines*, Decision of the Tribunal on Objections to Jurisdiction, 29 January 2004 28, 30, 123–4n

## Canada



## Switzerland



## United Kingdom

*Lesotho Highlands Development Authority* v. *Impregilo SpA* [2005] UKHL 43, [2006] 1 AC 221 40n

*Mutasa* v. *Attorney-General* [1980] QB 114 1n

*O'Neill* v. *Phillips* [1999] 1 WLR 1092 112n

*R (Abassi)* v. *Secretary of State for Foreign and Commonwealth Affairs* [2002] EWCA Civ 1598, [2003] UKHRR 76 1n

*Reliance Industries Ltd* v. *Enron Oil and Gas India Ltd* [2002] 1 Lloyd's Rep. 645 157n

*Rustomjee* v. *The Queen* (1876) 1 QBD 487 1–2n

*Shell Egypt West Manzala GmbH* v. *Dana Gas Egypt Ltd* [2009] EWHC 2097 (Comm), [2010] Bus LR D53 103n

*Stretford* v. *Football Association* [2007] EWCA Civ 238, [2007] 2 Lloyd's Rep 31 151n

*Thoburn* v. *Sunderland City Council* [2002] EWHC 195 (Admin), [2003] QB 151 147n, 177n

## United States

*San Juan Cellular Telephone Co* v. *Public Service Commission* 967 F.2d 683 (1st Cir.1992) 188n

1

# Introduction

## International treaty arbitration and the Energy Charter Treaty

### 1. Investment treaty arbitration: origins and characteristics

In the beginning was diplomatic protection. Modern international investment treaties seek to provide agreed rules concerning a state's conduct towards foreigners who invest in its territory and a neutral forum for the settlement of disputes between states and such investors. The aim is to promote foreign investment and thus economic development. But this is a relatively recent phenomenon. Traditionally, international law afforded private persons no rights. Only states had legal personality in international law. Only states had rights, duties and the capacity to bring claims to assert their rights. States were obliged to treat foreign investors in accordance with an 'international minimum standard' but this obligation could only be enforced by the aggrieved investor's state of nationality. Indeed, the obligation was seen as being owed not to the investor but to its state. As the Permanent Court of International Justice explained in 1924:

> by taking up the case of one of its subjects and by resorting to diplomatic action or international judicial proceedings on his behalf, a state is in reality asserting its own right, the right to ensure, in the person of its subjects, respect for the rules of international law.[1]

Diplomatic protection had three major disadvantages. First, from the perspective of the injured investor, it was unsatisfactory because it gave its state of nationality complete discretion whether to make a claim on its behalf or not, the rights in question belonging not to it but to its state. Claims could be pursued (or not), compromised or abandoned as the state thought politically expedient.[2] Even when compensation was paid, a

1 *Mavrommatis Palestine Concessions* case (*Greece* v. *United Kingdom*), PCIJ, Series A, No. 2 (1924), 12.

2 See *Mutasa* v. *Attorney-General* [1980] QB 114 and *R (Abassi)* v. *Secretary of State for Foreign and Commonwealth Affairs* [2002] EWCA Civ 1598, [2003] UKHRR 76.

state was under no obligation to pass it on to its national who had suffered the loss.[3]

Second, espousal of a claim by a state immediately politicised it, as it was elevated to the level of an inter-state dispute. Host states frequently complained that the institution of diplomatic protection was abused and that they were coerced to concede unmeritorious claims. Indeed, in the nineteenth and early twentieth centuries, European states and the US frequently used or threatened force to advance their nationals' claims, a practice which came to be known as 'gunboat diplomacy'. This problem was exacerbated by the absence of any standing neutral body to decide such disputes. States could, and frequently did, establish arbitral tribunals or claims commissions to determine disputes but, absent agreement, matters could only be decided through negotiation, with power disparities ever-present.

Third, perhaps because of the political nature of such proceedings, there was considerable disagreement as to what international law actually required. Capital-exporting states generally argued that a state was required to treat foreign nationals in accordance with an international minimum standard as regards their persons and property and access to justice. The classic formulation was given in 1926 by the United States–Mexico Claims Commission:

> the propriety of governmental acts should be put to the test of international standards, and . . . the treatment of an alien, in order to amount to an international delinquency, should amount to an outrage, to bad faith, to wilful neglect of duty, or to an insufficiency of governmental action so far short of international standards that every reasonable and impartial man would readily recognize its insufficiency.[4]

Capital-importing states, however, argued that all that was required was national treatment: foreign nationals must be treated no worse than a state treated its own nationals. This took the issue out of the ambit of international law but had one obvious drawback: if they must be treated no worse, foreign nationals need be treated no better than a state's own nationals.

Other disputes concerned the circumstances in which it was permissible to expropriate foreign-owned property and what level of compensation

3 See *Rustomjee* v. *The Queen* (1876) 1 QBD 487 and *Civilian War Claimants Association* v. *The King* [1932] AC 14.

4 *Neer (United States of America)* v. *Mexico*, General Claims Commission (Mexico and United States), (1926) 4 RIAA 60 at 61.

(if any) need be paid, with capital-exporting states arguing for the 'Hull formula', requiring 'prompt, adequate and effective' compensation on any taking of foreign-owned property,[5] while capital-importing states wished to leave matters to national law and national courts. These arguments over the applicable substantive law began in the nineteenth century in disputes between the newly-independent states of Latin America, on the one hand, and the European states and the US, on the other. However, they gained new life as a result of the Russian Revolution and the establishment of the Soviet Union after World War I and the breakup of the European colonial empires following World War II. Before the United Nations, in particular, the socialist states and the newly independent states of Africa and Asia argued for a 'new international economic order', which would sweep away the remnants of foreign domination by liberating developing countries' economies from the control of their former colonial masters.

This campaign reached its high point with the adoption by the United Nations General Assembly of the Declaration on the Establishment of a New International Economic Order and the Charter of Economic Rights and Duties of States.[6] The Declaration proclaimed that each state had '[f]ull permanent sovereignty... over its natural resources and all economic activities', including 'the right to nationalization or transfer of ownership to its nationals'. In such cases, according to the Charter, only 'appropriate compensation' need be paid, the amount being determined by the expropriating state's own courts under its own national law. As the General Assembly is not a legislative body, these resolutions only indicated what states who voted for them considered that international law should be; but the circumstances of their adoption showed that there was no consensus as to what it was.

Even before the proclamation of the 'New International Economic Order', foreign investors and their home states had developed legal techniques to protect their interests when they might conflict with host states' desires to take greater control of their economies. Indeed, the assertion in the Charter of Economic Rights and Duties of States that the forum for the settlement of disputes between foreign investors and host states should be the state's national courts was partly a response to investors' attempts to 'internationalise' such disputes. Particularly in the extractive industries, foreign investors sought to negotiate agreements with host state governments so as to avoid the application of host state law and the

5 See 'The Secretary of State of the United States (Cordell Hull) to Mexican Ambassador at Washington DC' (1938) 32 AJIL Supp 181.

6 GA res. 3201 (S-VI), 1 May 1974 and GA res. 3281 (XXIX), 12 December 1974.

settlement of disputes by the host state's national courts. The intention was to prevent the host state from unilaterally altering either the conditions of the contract or the legislative framework within which the foreign investor entered the contract, for example by increasing the tax payable by the investor. The host state's national courts were avoided because it was thought that they would consider that they had no choice but to apply national law over any conflicting provisions of the contract. Techniques utilised included choice of law clauses providing for the application of some form of non-national law, such as 'general principles of law' or public international law; 'stabilisation clauses' freezing the provisions of host state law applicable to the foreign investor as at the time the contract was entered into; and dispute settlement clauses providing for international arbitration. However, the legal effects of 'internationalisation' and 'stabilisation clauses' were hotly debated and different arbitral tribunals interpreted often very similar clauses rather differently.[7] Moreover, as developing independent states gained in experience and legal sophistication, they became much less willing to enter into contracts on such terms.

In an attempt to provide a neutral forum for the settlement of investor–state disputes, the World Bank sponsored negotiations which led to the conclusion in 1965 of the Washington Convention on the Settlement of Investment Disputes between States and Nationals of Other States ('ICSID Convention').[8] The Convention established the International Centre for Settlement of Investment Disputes ('ICSID'): an international organisation, part of the World Bank Group, headquartered in Washington DC, which provides facilities for the arbitration and conciliation of investment disputes between state parties to the ICSID Convention and nationals of other state parties to the Convention. The Convention sought to balance foreign investors' and host states' interests. Submission to international arbitration was meant to ensure that foreign investors obtained the benefit of a neutral forum, while host states gained from the Convention's prohibition of the exercise of diplomatic protection by an investor's state of nationality during arbitral proceedings.[9] ICSID arbitration is based on consent. A case may only be referred to ICSID if both parties have given written consent for its referral;[10] and the law applicable to the dispute is

7 See, especially, the three awards arising out of the nationalisation of foreign-owned oil concessions by the Libyan government discussed in R. von Mehren and P. Kourides, 'International Arbitrations Between States and Foreign Private Parties: The Libyan Nationalization Cases' (1981) 75 *American Journal of International Law* 476.

8 575 UNTS 159 (1965).

9 Article 27 of the ICSID Convention.

10 Article 25(1), *ibid.*

that agreed by the parties or, failing such choice of law, 'the law of the Contracting State party to the dispute . . . and such rules of international law as may be applicable'.[11]

Originally, it was envisaged that consent to ICSID arbitration would usually be by inclusion in a contract of a submission clause, but the majority of cases referred to the Centre have been brought under treaty dispute settlement provisions. This is an indication of the success of another post-war development: the proliferation of bilateral investment treaties ('BITs'). The first BIT was signed between Germany and Pakistan in 1959. Since then, their numbers have grown exponentially. According to UNCTAD, by the end of 2008 there were some 2,676 in existence (although not all are in force).[12]

BITs built on a number of previous initiatives. Some of the standards of treatment required by them derive from customary international law. Others derive from treaties of friendship, commerce and navigation ('FCNs'), particularly those in the US post-war FCN programme, and from various failed efforts to agree a multilateral investment agreement. The 1948 Havana Charter for an International Trade Organization included an investment chapter but, except for the GATT, never came into force; whilst the 1950s and 1960s saw other attempts, both by private groups (the Abs–Shawcross Draft Convention on Investments Abroad) and in public forums (the OECD Draft Convention on the Protection of Foreign Property).[13]

Although individual BITs vary, they have strong familial resemblances, generally containing provisions guaranteeing (to the investments they cover) fair and equitable treatment, national treatment and 'most-favoured nation' treatment; and prohibiting unreasonable and discriminatory measures and expropriation without full compensation.

But where BITs were genuinely innovative was that they began to provide for the settlement of disputes between investors and host states by international arbitration, often under the auspices of ICSID.[14] The

11 Article 42(1), *ibid.*

12 UNCTAD, *IIA Monitor No. 3 (2009): Recent Developments in International Investment Agreements (2008–June 2009)*, (UNCTAD/WEB/DIAE/IA/2009/8), p. 2.

13 OECD, Draft Convention on the Protection of Foreign Property and Resolution of the Council of the OECD on the Draft Convention (1968) 7 KM 118, 120. For more detail, see K. Vandevelde, 'BIT by BIT: A Brief History of International Investment Agreements' (2005) 12 *University of California-Davis Journal of International Law and Policy* 157.

14 The earliest such treaty is believed to be the 1972 France–Tunisia BIT.

phenomenon has been called 'arbitration without privity',[15] for BITs require no prior contractual relationship between the host state and the foreign investor. It is enough that there is a dispute between the investor and the host state of a type for which the treaty provides arbitration as the dispute-resolution method; which means generally, but not exclusively, a dispute as to whether the state has treated the investor, in relation to its investment, in a manner contrary to the standards required by the treaty. The agreement to arbitrate this dispute arises from the state's standing offer to investors of the other state party, contained in the BIT, to submit such disputes to arbitration and the investor's acceptance of that offer by its service on the state of a notice of arbitration.

It is this combination of substantive protections and dispute settlement procedures that has made BITs such a popular and effective mechanism of investment protection. Because they are treaties, governed by international law, they are not (unless the state denounces the entire treaty) subject to unilateral change by a state. Because proceedings are brought by the investor, not by its state of nationality, the pitfalls of diplomatic protection are avoided and disputes are depoliticised. And BITs have been attractive to developing states because, as treaties, they are based on consent and, being bilateral, they can be seen as bargains between particular states which do not compromise positions taken collectively by the developing states on the content of general international law.

The growing liberalisation of the global economy, beginning in the late 1980s, coincided with an acceleration in the conclusion of BITs. This period also saw attempts to conclude a number of multilateral treaties: some successful, such as the North American Free Trade Agreement (1994) ('NAFTA') between Canada, Mexico and the US, which includes an investment chapter; others not, such as the OECD's efforts to agree a Multilateral Investment Agreement. The Energy Charter Treaty ('ECT') was the product of one such initiative (itself a result of political developments in the late 1980s and early 1990s) and its investment chapter draws directly on the provisions of the existing body of investment treaties.

This shift – from reliance on diplomatic protection to protect foreign investors to permitting them to bring treaty claims on their own behalf – has led to debate over whether investment agreements confer rights on covered investors.[16] BITs and other investment agreements, including Part

15 J. Paulsson, 'Arbitration without Privity' (1995) 10 *ICSID Review – Foreign Investment Law Journal* 232.

16 See, in particular, O. Spiermann, 'Individual Rights, State Interests and the Power to Waive ICSID Jurisdiction under Bilateral Investment Treaties' (2004) 20 *Arbitration International*

III of the Energy Charter Treaty, are often framed in terms of obligations owed by states rather than rights granted to investors. This might not, however, be thought determinative. It is the effect of the provisions that counts. In contradistinction to diplomatic protection cases, under investment agreements investors prosecute their claims regardless of whether their state of nationality supports, agrees or even opposes them and they, not their state, receive any damages awarded. Certainly, there is no rule in international law preventing the conferral of legal personality on private persons.[17] Nor does it seem satisfactory to say that someone has not been granted a right because the grantor can rescind its grant. If that were the case, then no-one would have rights under any human rights treaty.[18]

At present, it suffices to state that whatever the debate over whether investment treaties confer substantive rights on covered investors, it is difficult to argue that they do not confer a right to international arbitration.

## 2. The Energy Charter Treaty: origins and negotiating history

The Energy Charter Treaty ('ECT') was opened for signature in Lisbon on 17 December 1995. Having attained the necessary thirty ratifications,[19] it came into force on 16 April 1998. At present, forty-six states, the European Union ('EU') and European Atomic Energy Community ('Euratom') are parties to the ECT.[20] Five states[21] have signed but not ratified, of which two (Belarus and Russia) originally bound themselves to apply the Treaty provisionally.[22] Russia, however, has announced that it does not intend to ratify the Treaty, meaning that its obligation provisionally to apply Parts III and V of the Treaty (with which this book is concerned) is now time-limited.[23]

179; Z. Douglas, *The International Law of Investment Claims* (Cambridge University Press, 2009), pp. 1–38; and *Ecuador* v. *Occidental Exploration and Production Co* [2005] EWCA Civ 1116, [2006] QB 432 at paragraphs 20–2.

17 See *Jurisdiction of the Courts of Danzig*, PCIJ Series C, No. 14-I, pp. 17–19; and *LaGrand* (*Germany* v. *United States of America*), ICJ Rep 2001, paragraphs 75–8.

18 See, e.g., Article 58, European Convention on Human Rights, permitting denunciation of the Convention.

19 Article 44(1) of the ECT.

20 See Appendix B.

21 Australia, Belarus, Iceland, Norway and Russia.

22 Article 45(1) of the ECT. At the time of signature, Australia, Iceland and Norway filed declarations under Article 45(2) of the ECT that they did not accept provisional application.

23 See pp. 67–77 below.

The ECT is by far the most widely ratified investment protection agreement, and though applicable only to a single, albeit immensely important, economic sector, the ECT differs from other multilateral investment treaties, which are regional in nature, in having a potentially global reach. Indeed, the ECT is far more than an investment protection agreement, covering a broad range of other issues in the energy sector, including trade, transit and the environment. It seeks to provide 'a legal framework in order to promote long-term cooperation in the energy field, based on complementarities and mutual benefits, in accordance with the objectives and principles of the [European Energy] Charter'.[24] The ECT's Contracting Parties stretch across Europe and Asia, and include states with diverse political and economic systems. It is consequently inaccurate to see the ECT as a European treaty; a perception exacerbated by a widespread, if erroneous, tendency to refer to it by the name of its precursor, the European Energy Charter.

This is not, however, to say that the ECT did not have its origins in Europe nor that it was not meant to serve, *inter alia*, European states' interests.[25] The process leading to the adoption of the ECT started in 1991 with an initiative of Ruud Lubbers, then the Prime Minister of the Netherlands, which held the presidency of the European Community ('the EC'). At the European Council summit in Dublin in June 1991, Lubbers proposed the creation of a 'European Energy Community' bringing together the EC member states, the USSR, and the countries of Central and Eastern Europe.[26] The idea behind his proposal for greater European energy cooperation was simple. The late 1980s and early 1990s had seen the lifting of the Iron Curtain, the end of Communist rule in Central and Eastern Europe and the beginning of the breakup of the Soviet Union. The new governments in Central and Eastern Europe and the former Soviet Union sought to liberalise their economies and modernise their industries, privatising state-owned enterprises and replacing state planning with free markets. A number of such countries were rich in oil and gas. Others were strategically placed to provide access to those resources.

24 Article 2 of the ECT.

25 For a more comprehensive history and analysis of the events leading up to the adoption of the ECT see J. Doré, 'Negotiating the Energy Charter Treaty' in T. Wälde (ed.), *The Energy Charter Treaty: An East–West Gateway for Investment and Trade* (London: Kluwer Law International, 1996). See also C. Bamberger, 'The Negotiation of the Energy Charter Treaty' in G. Coop and C. Ribeiro (eds.), *Investment Protection and the Energy Charter Treaty* (New York: JurisNet, 2008), p. xxxix.

26 See R. Lubbers, 'Foreword' in T. Wälde (ed.), *The Energy Charter Treaty: An East–West Gateway for Investment and Trade* (London: Kluwer Law International, 1996).

However, outside capital, technology and expertise were needed effectively to exploit them and to transport them to potential consumers. New opportunities beckoned for Western businesses, whilst European governments sought to improve their countries' 'energy security' by reducing their energy dependence on the Middle East and guaranteeing long-term access to the energy resources of the former Soviet Union. Moreover, both the EC and many of the countries of Central and Eastern Europe and the former Soviet Union were anxious to overcome the political divisions of the Cold War. Greater economic integration was seen as a means to this as well as an end in itself.

Other Western states also sought to be involved because they wished to ensure that their traders and investors were not disadvantaged by any agreement. The US in particular was concerned that access to the energy sector in the former Soviet Union might be monopolised by the EC. In consequence, although this was originally a European project, US lobbying led to the inclusion of non-European OECD members. The negotiating conference for the European Energy Charter was convened by the European Commission, but Canada, Japan, Australia, New Zealand and the US participated in the negotiations leading to its adoption in The Hague in December 1991.

The European Energy Charter ('EEC', also known as the Energy Charter Declaration) is a non-legally binding political declaration.[27] Signatories make a political commitment:

> to promote the development of an efficient energy market throughout Europe, and a better functioning global market, in both cases based on the principle of non-discrimination and on market-orientated price formation, taking due account of environmental concerns.[28]

More specifically, the signatories commit to work together to facilitate access to and the development of energy resources; to promote access to markets for energy products; to liberalise trade in energy; to protect investments in the energy sector; to develop and implement safety standards; to promote technology exchanges; and to cooperate on energy efficiency and environmental protection and on education and training in the energy industry. In addition, they agree to supplement the Charter

27 However, as will be seen, it is of legal relevance in interpreting the ECT. The Charter itself is a part of the Concluding Document of the Hague Conference on the European Energy Charter, reproduced in Energy Charter Secretariat, *The Energy Charter Treaty and Related Documents: A Legal Framework for International Energy Cooperation* (Brussels: Energy Charter Secretariat, 2004), p. 209.

28 EEC, Title 1: Objectives: see Energy Charter Secretariat, *The Energy Charter Treaty*, p. 214.

with a treaty setting out general rules on energy trade and cooperation, and protocols covering specific topics of interest: nuclear issues, energy efficiency, and oil and gas.

Negotiations were originally expected to be completed by the summer of 1992. However, consensus proved elusive and it was not until the end of 1994 that agreement was reached. The negotiations also saw considerable developments as regards both process and outcome. It had been envisaged that negotiation of the basic agreement and the protocols would proceed on parallel tracks. However, although a Protocol on Energy Efficiency and Related Environmental Aspects ('PEEREA')[29] was completed in June 1992, negotiations on the nuclear issues and oil and gas protocols had to be suspended. Effectively, they were subsumed into the negotiations on the main treaty.

In addition, ambitions for the treaty were scaled down and a two-stage approach adopted. A major objective of the negotiations was to ensure that foreign investors in the energy sector did not suffer discrimination, in comparison either to nationals of the host state (national treatment) or to nationals of other states (most-favoured nation treatment).[30] However, differences emerged as to the scope of any non-discrimination provision; specifically whether it should apply to the entry of investors into a market as well as to the treatment of investments after admission. In deference to the US's belief in the importance of market access,[31] a provision on pre-investment national treatment was included in the draft treaty, but other Western countries, notably Norway and France, opposed this. The Eastern countries also had difficulties in accepting national treatment fully and sought exceptions and transition periods. Moreover, 1993 saw relations between President Yeltsin and the Russian Duma reach their nadir, calling into question the Russian government's ability to get any agreement ratified.

In an effort to break the stalemate, the EC proposed moving to a two-stage approach. Provisions for non-discrimination at the pre-investment stage were relegated to a second treaty, to be subsequently negotiated. This was acceptable both to the EC, which, for both political and economic reasons, was anxious to keep Russia within the treaty; and to the

29 See *ibid.*, p. 139.

30 EEC, Title IV: Final provisions, paragraph 2: see Energy Charter Secretariat, *The Energy Charter Treaty*, p. 221.

31 The US Model BIT included a right to admission (subject to exceptions). Those of European states did not, focusing instead on investors' rights after admission.

Russian government, which sought to conclude a treaty so as to show its domestic constituents that its pro-Western orientation brought tangible benefits and to anchor its internal reforms externally. However, the US was unhappy with the compromise. It did not quit the negotiations but these and other concerns, together with a belief that it could extract more extensive concessions via bilateral negotiations with the states of Central and Eastern Europe and the former Soviet Union,[32] ultimately led to its decision not to sign the Treaty.[33] In the event, all other parties to the negotiations (forty-nine states plus the European Communities) did sign.

Following the adoption of the ECT[34] the Energy Charter Conference and the Energy Charter Secretariat were established in preparation for its coming into force. As also envisaged in the ECT,[35] an Amendment to the Trade-Related Provisions of the Energy Charter Treaty,[36] updating those provisions to take account of the establishment of the World Trade Organization, was adopted. However, negotiations for a supplementary treaty to bind parties to accord national and most-favoured nation treatment at the pre-investment stage were unsuccessful. It had been anticipated that such negotiations would be completed by December 1997.[37] However, when the deadline came round, a number of issues remained unresolved. The EC was unhappy about the inclusion of some OECD members in the annex to the draft treaty providing for exceptions from national treatment in cases of privatisation, whilst Australia, Iceland and Norway opposed the application of the investor–state dispute settlement provisions in the ECT to the supplementary treaty. In June 1998, following two further

32 The US and Russia concluded a BIT in 1994. However, it remains unratified by Russia: see N. Rubins and A. Nazarov, 'Investment Treaties and the Russian Federation: Baiting the Bear?' (2008) 9 *Business Law International* 100.

33 For an explanation of the US's reasons: see Doré, 'Negotiating the Energy Charter Treaty' (at pp. 149–52) and W. Fox, 'The United States and the Energy Charter Treaty: Misgivings and Misperceptions' in T. Wälde (ed.), *The Energy Charter Treaty: An East–West Gateway for Investment and Trade* (London: Kluwer Law International 1996).

34 For discussion of developments during this period, see C. Bamberger, J. Lineham and T. Wälde, 'The Energy Charter Treaty in 2000: In a New Phase' (2000) 18 *Journal of Energy & Natural Resources Law* 3. See also S. Elshihabi, 'The Difficulty behind Securing Sector-Specific Investment Establishment Rights: The Case of the Energy Charter Treaty' (2001) 35 *International Lawyer* 137 at 148–55.

35 Article 30 of the ECT.

36 Energy Charter Secretariat, *The Energy Charter Treaty*, p. 163.

37 See Article 10(4) of the ECT and the Understanding to the Final Act with respect to Article 10(4).

sessions of the formal adoption conference, the EC announced that it was unable to adopt the draft text. Negotiations were halted and have not been resumed.[38]

Another blow to the ECT regime was the failure of Russia to ratify the Treaty. The ECT had taken its final form, despite US reservations, following agreement between the EC on one side and Russia on the other. However, although Russia signed the ECT in 1995 and bound itself to apply the Treaty provisionally, the ECT was never submitted to the Duma for ratification.[39] This change in policy was a result both of political changes – in particular Boris Yeltsin's resignation and the accession of Vladimir Putin to the Russian presidency in 2000 – and economic developments – increases in oil and gas prices and the improvement of the Russian economy. As Rubins and Nazarov comment:

> With no particular need to attract foreign capital, and still relatively limited outward investment on the part of Russian companies, the [Russian] Government could see no particular benefit to limiting its freedom to act in relation to foreign investors.[40]

Indeed, in July 2009, Russia gave notice of its intention not to become a party to the ECT. Although Russia will continue to be bound to apply Parts III and V of the Treaty provisionally until 2029, there is debate about what this obligation entails.[41]

The ECT was envisaged as only one stage in a process of liberalisation of the energy sector in Eurasia; a process which, for largely political reasons, was subsequently halted and has since made little progress.[42] In addition, two of the 'pillars' of the Treaty, the US and Russia, have chosen not to continue to participate,[43] leaving the EU standing alone. However, it is more accurate to say that the now-twenty-seven EU member

38 In its first review of the ECT, the Energy Charter Conference stated that it would periodically review the possibility of making progress on non-discriminatory treatment in the pre-investment stage: see 'Conclusions of the Review Conducted under Article 34(7) of the Energy Charter Treaty', as adopted by the Energy Charter Conference at its 15th Meeting on 14 December 2004.

39 For initial Russian views, see A. Konoplyanik, 'The Energy Charter Treaty: A Russian Perspective' in T. Wälde (ed.), *The Energy Charter Treaty: An East–West Gateway for Investment and Trade* (London: Kluwer Law International, 1996).

40 Rubins and Nazarov, 'Investment Treaties and the Russian Federation', 105.

41 This is discussed in Chapter 2 below.

42 Indeed, in a similar fashion, negotiations on a transit protocol began in 2000 but have not yet reached agreement (although consultations are continuing).

43 Although, as a signatory of the ECT, Russia remains a member of the Energy Charter Conference, whilst the US has observer status.

states are Contracting Parties to the ECT together with twenty-four other states across Europe and Asia, including several countries which did not participate in the Treaty's negotiation.[44] This is a substantial number, and ECT cannot be described as a wholly European legal regime.[45] Indeed, the Treaty remains open to accession by any state willing to commit to its provisions.[46] Moreover, the achievements embodied in the Treaty itself are not minor, and its institutional aspects mean that the ECT process provides not only a legal framework but also a policy forum for wider cooperation in the energy sector in which many states which are not parties to the ECT choose to participate.[47]

## 3. Main provisions of the Energy Charter Treaty and related instruments

The wide range of issues covered and the difficulties in obtaining agreement on its content are reflected in the ECT's structure, which is complex, confusing and, at times, incoherent. The original draft was extensively reworked during the negotiations. Controversial issues were decided at the political level, often with little or no input from the legal committee.[48] The decision of the conference leadership to impose a deadline for the conclusion of the negotiations produced meaningful treaty commitments but at a cost. As Bamberger, who chaired the legal committee, writes, the result was that:

> In form, the Energy Charter Treaty is an untidy, 'user-unfriendly' package comprised of eight 'parts' and fourteen 'Annexes', which are subject to five Conference 'Decisions' and to numerous 'Understandings', 'Declarations' and interpretations that were made in connection with its adoption. It also contains various exceptions and exclusions, some fairly general while others are quite specific.[49]

44 Bosnia-Herzegovina, Croatia, the Former Yugoslav Republic of Macedonia and Mongolia. In 2009 Serbia announced that its accession to the ECT was a priority: see Energy Charter Secretariat press release, 'PM Underlines Ambition to Join Energy Charter Treaty', 29 September 2009.

45 Contracting Parties include Armenia, Azerbaijan, Georgia, Japan, Kazakhstan, Kyrgyzstan, Mongolia, Turkmenistan, Tajikistan, Turkey and Uzbekistan. In addition, in 2009 the Energy Charter Conference adopted a proposal for the accession of Jordan to the ECT.

46 Article 41 of the ECT provides that, following the expiry of the period during which it was open for signature (which ended on 16 June 1995), the Treaty is open to accession by states and Regional Economic Integration Organizations which have signed the Charter.

47 'Conclusions of the Review Conducted under Article 34(7) of the Energy Charter Treaty', as adopted by the Energy Charter Conference at its 15th Meeting on 14 December 2004, paragraph 2.

48 Bamberger, 'The Negotiation of the Energy Charter Treaty', p. xlv.

49 *Ibid.*

The ECT itself is Annex 1 to the Final Act of the European Energy Charter Conference. Its various component parts – preamble, Parts, Annexes etc. – are all integral to the Treaty and relevant to its interpretation.[50] The Treaty concentrates on five main subjects: trade in energy materials and products (Parts II and VI); the protection and promotion of investments in the energy sector (Part III); the transit of energy products and materials (Article 7); environmental protection and energy efficiency (Article 19); and the settlement of disputes (Part V).

### *(a) Trade*

Article 3 of the ECT provides that:

> The Contracting Parties shall work to promote access to international markets on commercial terms, and generally to develop an open and competitive market, for Energy Materials and Products.

Article 29 of the ECT applies GATT 1947 rules (with a few exceptions) to the Contracting Parties' trade in Energy Materials and Products.[51] It also imposes notification requirements for import and export tariffs on Energy Materials and Products, and a 'best efforts' obligation to limit increases in tariffs. At the time of the ECT's conclusion, most of the signatory states were not parties to the GATT. The trade provisions were designed to have a transitional function prior to those states becoming members of the World Trade Organization ('WTO'), importing fundamental GATT disciplines – non-discrimination, transparency and trade liberalisation – into their trade relations in the energy sector. They only apply as between ECT Contracting Parties at least one of which is not a party to the GATT (defined as referring to both GATT 1947 and GATT 1994) or a relevant Related Instrument (including the Agreement Establishing the World Trade Organization and its other Annexes). They are not meant to trespass upon activities within the purview of GATT 1947 or the WTO.

Article 29 does not incorporate the provisions of the WTO Agreements on Trade in Services ('GATS') and Trade-Related Intellectual Property Rights ('TRIPS') to Contracting Parties' energy trade relations. However, Article 5 of the ECT prohibits Contracting Parties from imposing

50 Although the preamble does not include any substantive provisions, it is part of the context in which the specific terms of the Treaty must be interpreted, as well as being relevant to determining the Treaty's object and purpose: see Article 31(1) and (2), Vienna Convention on the Law of Treaties, 1155 UNTS 331 (1969) ('VCLT').

51 As defined in Article 1 of the ECT.

trade-related investment measures ('TRIMs') that are inconsistent with Articles III and XI of the GATT, and Article 6 imposes some general obligations on Contracting Parties with regard to competition issues.

The opening of the ECT for signature, in December 1995, came soon after the signing of the Agreement Establishing the World Trade Organization on 15 April 1994, and that Agreement's coming into force and the consequent establishment of the WTO on 1 January 1995. As a consequence, the ECT anticipated further negotiations to take account of these developments. Negotiations were initiated in June 1995 and resulted in the modification of Part II of the ECT by an Amendment to the Trade-Related Provisions of the Energy Charter Treaty, adopted by the Energy Charter Conference in April 2002. The Trade Amendment applies the provisions of the WTO Agreement to trade between Contracting Parties, at least one of which is not a WTO member. It applies not only to trade in Energy Products and Materials, but also to trade in Energy-Related Equipment.[52]

The Trade Amendment came into force on 21 January 2010. However, most ECT Contracting Parties are now also WTO members, so the significance of the ECT's trade provisions and the Trade Amendment is now rather diminished.[53]

### *(b) Investment*

Part III of the ECT, with which this book is principally concerned, covers the promotion and protection of investments in the energy sector. It obliges Contracting Parties to treat investors of other Contracting Parties and their investments in accordance with certain specified standards. Part III was modelled on provisions in existing bilateral investment treaties. Indeed, it appears that the original draft was based upon the UK Model BIT,[54] although it was extensively revised during the negotiations and various provisions have their equivalents in a number of states' investment protection agreements whilst others are wholly original.[55]

Part III places particular emphasis on the principle of non-discrimination. Contracting Parties are obliged to accord national

52 As defined in Article 1 of the ECT.

53 The remaining states parties to the ECT which are not members of the WTO are Azerbaijan, Bosnia-Herzegovina, Kazakhstan, Kyrgyzstan, Turkmenistan and Uzbekistan.

54 Bamberger, 'The Negotiation of the Energy Charter Treaty', p. xl.

55 C. Bamberger, 'Overview' in T. Wälde (ed.), *The Energy Charter Treaty: An East–West Gateway for Investment and Trade* (London: Kluwer Law International, 1996) p. 8.

treatment and most-favoured nation treatment (whichever is most favourable) to nationals of other Contracting Parties which have invested in their energy sector. Part III also includes various non-contingent standards of protection, which apply regardless of how a Contracting Party might treat its own nationals or those of other states. It requires fair and equitable treatment and most constant protection and security, and prohibits expropriation (save in specific, limited circumstances) and unreasonable or discriminatory measures. Other provisions cover such issues as the transfer of funds and the employment of key personnel, as well as including an 'umbrella clause' requiring states to honour obligations entered into with an investor.

However, the binding provisions of Part III only protect investments once made. The provisions relating to the making of investments are largely hortatory. This, as already mentioned, was a major bone of contention during the negotiation of the ECT and efforts to agree a supplementary treaty covering the issue have so far been unsuccessful.

### *(c) Transit*

Article 7 of the ECT covers transit issues. Transit is defined as the carriage of Energy Materials and Products across at least two national boundaries. Consequently, Article 7 applies in several situations. It always requires that the energy be carried across the territory of a Contracting State to the ECT, but that carriage can be from one Contracting State to another Contracting State or from one part of a Contracting State to another part of the same state. The forms of carriage covered include transport through oil and gas transmission pipelines, and electricity grids and lines.

The provision is meant to ensure freedom of transit on a non-discriminatory basis. However, there is no obligation to permit mandatory third-party access to transit facilities. Article 7 also prohibits the disruption of supplies during a dispute over transit prior to the conclusion of the provision's dispute settlement procedures. However, this obligation only applies to a Contracting Party or any entity under the control of a Contracting Party. It does not apply to private parties, nor require Contracting Parties to control their behaviour. This can be seen as a weakness in the provision, as illustrated when the supply of gas to Ukraine was cut off in 2006 and 2009 during disputes over the applicable tariffs, and Russia argued, given Gazprom's independent legal personality, that Article 7 did not apply to the dispute.

As a result of perceptions of shortcomings in Article 7, in 1999 the Energy Charter Conference decided to instigate negotiations on a Transit Protocol. Multilateral negotiations began in 2000 and were concluded in 2003 with the tabling of a text for adoption by the Energy Charter Conference in December of that year. Full agreement had not been reached, however, between the EU and Russia, and bilateral consultations have continued with the aim of agreeing a complete draft text to put before all the Energy Charter member states and the conclusion of the negotiations remains an aspiration of the Energy Charter Conference.[56] The major remaining issue appears to be the extent of the applicability of the Protocol to the transport of energy within the EU.[57]

### (d) *Environmental protection and energy efficiency*

Article 19 of the ECT imposes a number of 'best endeavour' obligations on Contracting Parties regarding environmental protection and energy efficiency. In particular:

> [E]ach Contracting Party shall strive to minimize in an economically efficient manner harmful Environmental Impacts occurring either within or outside its Area from all operations within the Energy Cycle in its Area, taking proper account of safety... In its policies and actions each Contracting Party shall strive to take precautionary measures to prevent or minimize environmental degradation. The Contracting Parties agree that the polluter in the Areas of Contracting Parties should, in principle, bear the cost of pollution...

These general obligations then form the basis of a list of measures which Contracting Parties 'shall accordingly' take.

The negotiators were careful to ensure that nothing in Article 19 could provide a cause of action, either in litigation between ECT Contracting Parties or before their national courts. This is not, however, to say that the provision is legally irrelevant. It is easy to imagine a Contracting Party referring to its obligations under Article 19 to defend itself, for example, against allegations that actions taken by it with regard to foreign investments breached other provisions of the Treaty.

Article 19 is supplemented by the Protocol on Energy Efficiency and Related Environmental Aspects opened for signature at the same time as the ECT and forming Annex 3 to the Final Act. The Protocol seeks

56 Energy Charter Conference, Joint Statement, Rome, 9 December 2009, paragraph 5.

57 See G. Coop, 'The Energy Charter: More than an MIT' in C. Ribeiro (ed.), *Investment Arbitration and the Energy Charter Treaty* (New York: JurisNet, 2006), pp. 12–14.

to promote 'energy efficient policies consistent with sustainable development' and to foster cooperation in the field of energy efficiency. It sets out principles to guide Contracting Parties in implementing energy efficient policies; requires them to develop and implement programmes to improve energy efficiency; encourages parties to cooperate on energy efficiency issues; and provides a framework for the review of parties' implementation of their commitments by the Energy Charter Conference. Again, the emphasis is not on legally binding obligations but on 'best endeavours' commitments, and on encouraging compliance rather than penalising breach.

### *(e) Settlement of disputes*

Finally, the ECT provides mechanisms for the settlement of disputes with regard to the interpretation and application of its substantive provisions. This provision of mechanisms to enforce the obligations it imposes on Contracting Parties is one of the most striking features of the ECT. However, the mechanisms do vary according to their subject matter, and some are more efficient than others.

Article 27 provides for the settlement of disputes between Contracting Parties by diplomatic means and, failing that, by ad hoc arbitration. Disputes regarding compliance with provisions applicable to trade under Articles 5 and 29 are covered by Annex D to the ECT. This provides for the settlement of disputes by the establishment of panels under procedures akin to those in the WTO Dispute Settlement Understanding. Only Contracting Parties can make complaints, and such complaints are specifically excluded from the general procedures for the settlement of disputes between Contracting Parties in Article 27.[58] Similarly, disputes concerning the interpretation and application of Articles 5 (competition) and 19 (environmental aspects) are excluded from settlement by interstate arbitration under Article 27. Disputes between Contracting Parties with regard to their obligations under Article 19, unless the parties otherwise agree, can only be reviewed by the Energy Charter Conference, which has no power to impose a solution. Finally, Article 7 provides for the settlement of transit disputes by conciliation but does not exclude the application of Article 27 to them.

Article 26 of the ECT provides procedures for private persons to bring claims if they consider that Contracting Parties are in violation of their obligations under the Treaty's Part III investment provisions. Inspired

58 See Article 28 of the ECT.

by similar provisions in various states' BITs, this is perhaps the most innovative aspect of the ECT. It provides for the private enforcement of its investment provisions and permits aggrieved investors to seek monetary compensation for losses sustained by Contracting Parties' breach of their obligations under Part III of the ECT. Moreover, for the purposes of Article 26, the application of a trade-related investment measure by a Contracting Party in a manner contrary to Article 5 of the ECT to an existing investment is also deemed to be a breach of that state's Part III obligations.[59]

Under Article 26, Contracting Parties are deemed to have given unconditional consent to the submission of disputes to arbitration between them and investors of other Contracting Parties regarding investments made by the latter in the Area of the former. The investor can decide whether to submit the dispute to the International Centre for Settlement of Investment Disputes (provided that the respondent state is a party to the ICSID Convention), to ICSID's Additional Facility, to ad hoc arbitration using the UNCITRAL Arbitration Rules or to arbitration under the Arbitration Institute of the Stockholm Chamber of Commerce. There is no procedural requirement to exhaust domestic remedies before resorting to arbitration under Article 26. Moreover, claims submitted to arbitration under Article 26 are deemed to arise out of a commercial relationship or transaction for the purposes of Article I of the New York Convention on the Recognition and Enforcement of Foreign Arbitral Awards[60] (bringing any subsequent arbitral award within the scope of the Convention for enforcement purposes) and the Investor can require that the seat of the arbitration be in a state which is a party to the Convention (ensuring that the enforceability of any award is not prevented by application of the Convention's reciprocity provision).

The operation of Article 26 is covered in more detail in Chapter 3 below. However, it can immediately be seen that it provides a powerful weapon for foreign investors in the energy sector dissatisfied with their host state's conduct towards them.

### *(f) Understandings and Declarations*

In addition to adopting the text of the ECT, the Final Act also includes a number of Understandings in respect of the Treaty, both as a whole and with respect to specific provisions. These were adopted by all the

59 See Article 10(11) of the ECT. 60 330 UNTS 38 (1958).

signatories to the Final Act. The chapeau to Section IV of the Final Act states that:

> By signing the Final Act, the representatives [of the states participating in the European Energy Charter Conference] agreed to adopt the following Understandings with respect to the Treaty.

The Understandings represent interpretations of the ECT and several of its provisions agreed by all the signatories to the Treaty at the time of its adoption. Although not part of the Treaty, they are agreements 'relating to the treaty . . . made between all the parties in connection with the conclusion of the treaty', and, as such, part of the treaty's context for the purpose of interpreting its provisions.[61] Indeed, as they reflect the contemporaneous views of all the signatories at the time of the adoption of the Treaty text, it might be thought that they should be given considerable weight. They will consequently be referred to during the book when relevant to the interpretation of Treaty provisions under discussion.

The Final Act also includes a number of Declarations. One Declaration was made by all the signatory states,[62] and can accordingly be viewed in much the same manner as the Understandings; that is, as reflecting the signatories' interpretation of a particular provision of the ECT and as part of the Treaty's context. However, the other Declarations were made by particular signatories or groups of signatories setting out their interpretations of specific provisions of the ECT. Their legal effect is less apparent.

In the first instance the wording of a particular Declaration needs to be examined to determine what, if any, legal effect it is intended to have. The Declarations made by Russia with respect to Article 1(6) and by Denmark with respect to Article 40 would appear to have no general legal implications. The former simply states that Russia wanted a particular issue to be reconsidered in subsequent negotiations, whilst the latter sets out, consistently with Article 40 of the ECT, Denmark's position as regards the applicability of the Treaty to Greenland and the Faroe Islands.

Other Declarations, however, do purport to have particular legal effects. Article 46 of the ECT provides that no reservations can be made to the Treaty; so the Declarations cannot be viewed as excluding or modifying

61 Article 31(2)(a) of the VCLT.

62 This Declaration has regard to Article 18(2) of the ECT and declares that that provision 'shall not be construed to allow the circumvention of the application of the other provisions of the Treaty'. Article 18(2) provides, in relevant part, that: 'The Treaty shall in no way prejudice the rules in Contracting Parties governing the system of property ownership of energy resources.'

the legal effect of the provisions referred to in their application to the state or states making the Declaration.[63] As their name suggests, the Declarations are interpretative declarations rather than reservations.[64] Given their inclusion in the Final Act, it might be argued that they are instruments 'made by one or more of the parties in connection with the conclusion of the treaty and accepted by the other parties' as instruments related to the treaty.[65] Indeed, it might even be argued that, as no other signatories objected to the interpretations put forward by those states making Declarations, they should be seen as having tacitly accepted them. However, this would seem to go too far. Section VI of the Final Act simply states that 'the representatives noted the following Declarations that were made with respect to the Treaty'. There is no suggestion that they endorsed them, tacitly or otherwise. Accordingly, it would seem that the Declarations should be taken into account when interpreting the Treaty but they do not mandate any particular conclusion.

As between the states making a particular Declaration, however, it can be argued that the legal effect of a Declaration is decisive. The Declaration can be viewed as a binding agreement between those states, or as potentially estopping each from resiling from representations contained in it.[66] The only Declarations to which such arguments would seem to apply, however, are the six made with respect to Annex G(4) of the ECT regarding trade in nuclear materials between, on the one side, the European Communities and, on the other, respectively Russia, Ukraine, Kazakhstan, Kyrgyzstan, Tajikistan and Uzbekistan.

In practice, disputes regarding the legal effects of Declarations are likely to be uncommon, given that Australia, Canada and the US, all of which made Declarations, are not Contracting Parties to the ECT. This leaves, in addition to the Declarations already mentioned, only two more to be considered. The first, made by the European Communities and their (then) member states and Austria, Norway, Sweden and Finland, relates to Article 7, so has no implications for foreign investors. The second, made

63 See Article 2(1)(d) of the VCLT for the definition of a treaty reservation.

64 An interpretative declaration is 'a unilateral declaration, however phrased or named, made by a State or by an international organization whereby that State or that organization purports to clarify the meaning or scope attributed by the declarant to the treaty or to certain of its provisions'. International Law Commission, Third Report on Reservations to Treaties by Mr Alain Pellet, Special Rapporteur, UN Doc. A/CN.4/491/Add.4, paragraph 361.

65 Article 31(2)(b) of the VCLT.

66 For discussion of estoppel in international law, see I. Brownlie, *Principles of Public International Law* (Oxford University Press, 7th edn 2008), pp. 643–5.

by the European Communities and their member states with respect to Article 25 (economic integration agreements), will be examined in Chapter 7, where it will also be shown to have limited effects.[67]

## 4. Institutional aspects of the Energy Charter Treaty and the Energy Charter process

The ECT established two permanent bodies: the Energy Charter Conference (Article 34) and the Energy Charter Secretariat (Article 35). The Charter Conference is the governing body, whilst the Secretariat undertakes an administrative role and assists the Conference in the performance of its duties.

### *(a) The Charter Conference*

The Charter Conference comprises one representative of each of the Contracting Parties and signatories to the ECT. At present, fifty-one states, the EU and Euratom are members of the Conference. This number includes Australia, Belarus, Iceland, Norway and Russia, which are signatories, but not parties, to the Treaty. A number of states and international organisations also participate as observers.[68] Indeed, the Charter Conference has actively sought to widen participation in the Energy Charter process. Observers are entitled to attend meetings of the Charter Conference and its subsidiary groups, to participate in debates and to receive all relevant documents, but have no voting rights or any obligation to contribute to the budget of the organisation. The idea is that observer status provides an introduction to the ECT leading to accession to the Treaty.

Observer status is granted upon successful application to the Energy Charter Conference, which takes its decision on the basis of whether it considers granting observer status would be mutually beneficial. At present, twenty-two states, ten international organisations and the Palestinian National Authority have observer status.[69] The most recent state to gain observer status was Indonesia, in June 2009. Indonesia's observer status followed its signature of the Energy Charter. Similarly, the granting of observer status to Afghanistan in July 2006 was conditional upon its

67 See pp. 174ff.

68 The US, which is neither a signatory nor a party to the ECT, participates in the work of the Charter Conference as an observer.

69 See Appendix B.

signature of the Energy Charter.[70] Other observers, however, have not been required to sign. Indeed, only eight observer states have signed the Energy Charter, committing them politically to the objectives enunciated therein, whilst another's signature is pending.[71] Both classes of observer can be represented at meetings of the Charter Conference and its subsidiary bodies, albeit without a right to vote, but only observers which have signed the Energy Charter are entitled to participate in the negotiation of new Charter instruments.

The Charter Conference acts as a policy forum within the legal framework of the ECT. The Conference meets regularly to discuss issues affecting energy cooperation among its members; to review the implementation of the ECT and its related treaties; and to consider possible new agreements and activities within the Energy Charter framework. It also approves the Secretariat's annual accounts and budget and appoints the Secretary General.

Decision-making by the Conference is governed by Article 36 of the ECT and differs according to the subject-matter of the vote. Unanimity is mandated for some decisions, such as the adoption of most amendments to the ECT and the accession to the Treaty of non-signatory states, but, in general, a majority of three-fourths of Contracting States present and voting (that is, excluding abstainers) is required. However, Article 36 also provides that the Contracting Parties shall make every effort to reach agreement by consensus on matters not requiring unanimity and that is how the Conference has, in practice, proceeded.

The Conference has established a number of subsidiary bodies to assist it in its work: the Investment Group, the Trade and Transit Group, the Working Group on Energy Efficiency and Related Environmental Aspects, the Strategy Group, the Budget Committee and the Legal Advisory Committee. The Conference has also created two other bodies: an Industry Advisory Panel and a Legal Advisory Task Force.

The Investment Group is the Conference's policy forum for the discussion of investment-related issues. In particular, since 2004, in a series of in-depth country reviews it has scrutinised member countries' progress in improving their investment climate and restructuring their energy markets. Reports are drafted by the Secretariat, in cooperation with the relevant member country, before scrutiny by the Working Group. The Group

70 See Energy Charter Secretariat press release, 'Afghanistan Becomes Latest Energy Charter Observer', 4 August 2006.

71 The most recent state to sign the Energy Charter was Syria: see Energy Charter Secretariat press release, 'Syria Signs Energy Charter', 29 June 2010.

can issue draft recommendations for adoption by the Charter Conference. The Investment Group also regularly reviews the register of ECT Contracting Parties' measures which do not conform to the best endeavours obligation in Article 10(2) of the Treaty to accord non-discriminatory treatment at the pre-investment stage and publishes its findings.[72]

The Trade and Transit Group deals with cross-border energy flows covered by the Treaty. It monitors and assists implementation of the trade and transit provisions of the ECT, and facilitates discussions among the membership with the aim of improving cross-border energy flows and promoting open, competitive and sustainable energy markets. In 2005, the Trade and Transit Group launched a consultative initiative for information on cross-border pipeline projects, and it has since published several reports on the subject. In 2008, the Trade and Transit Group, at the request of the Charter Conference, held consultations on the draft Transit Protocol but nothing seems to have come of them.

The Working Group on Energy Efficiency and Related Environmental Aspects discusses issues relating to energy efficiency under the Treaty and national strategies on energy efficiency. It seeks to provide members, particularly transitional economies, with information and advice on improving their legislation and policies on energy efficiency. It also monitors member countries' policies on energy efficiency through regular and in-depth reviews. Regular reviews, based on a formula agreed by the Working Group, seek to monitor members' compliance with the ECT and the PEEREA. In-depth reviews are conducted of member countries that volunteer to undertake the exercise. They are based on peer review by representatives of three or four other members and the Secretariat. The reviewers issue recommendations that are discussed by the Working Group and the Charter Conference. Members report back on the progress they have made in implementing the recommendations.

The Strategy Group is the most recent creation of the Energy Charter Conference, having been established in March 2010 to promote the modernisation of the Charter process.[73] The Strategy Group is tasked with fostering the acceptance and implementation of the ECT (in particular through the expansion of the number of parties to the Treaty) and the development of the Energy Charter process generally. It replaces the

72 See Energy Charter Secretariat, *The Blue Book: Making Investments in Energy Charter Member Countries: Exceptions to the Principle of Non-discriminatory Treatment* (Brussels: Energy Charter Secretariat, 2009).

73 See Energy Charter Secretariat press release, 'Energy Charter Establishes Strategy Group to Promote Modernisation', 30 March 2010.

Ad hoc Group on Strategy, a temporary informal forum for the discussion of strategic issues related to the Energy Charter and the ECT, established by the Charter Conference at its November 2006 meeting.

The mandates of the Budget Committee and the Legal Committee are obvious. Unlike the three bodies covering the main areas of the ECT, they have no regular schedule.

The Industry Advisory Panel is a consultative body, formed by the Charter Conference in 2004 to formalise its existing links with the energy private sector and to provide advice to the Conference and its Working Groups, in particular with regard to risk mitigation and improving the business climate. Its members are selected by nomination by the Conference member countries and invitation by the Secretariat. The Panel's membership is meant to be representative, both geographically and in terms of the different sectors in the energy industry.

The Legal Advisory Task Force has a narrower mandate. It was established in 2001 by the Charter Secretariat to assist it in drafting Model Agreements – state–state and investor–state – for cross-border oil and gas pipelines. As a result, although composed of private practitioners and in-house counsel, its meetings are chaired by the Secretariat's Legal Counsel. Thus far the Task Force has produced two editions of the Model Agreements; the first was published in 2003 and the second in 2007, after each had been endorsed by the Charter Conference.[74] They seek to balance all participants in a cross-border pipeline project's interests and to provide a starting-point for negotiations between potential partners. For example, it appears that the First Edition Model Intergovernmental Agreement helped provide a basis for negotiations between Azerbaijan and Kazakhstan in 2004 on the trans-Caspian Aktau–Baku transport system. The Task Force has now been invited to advise on the drafting of Model Agreements on trans-border electricity projects.

It can be seen that the Energy Charter process is far wider, both in terms of its membership and its ambit, than is the ECT. It is a process, with regular reviews of member countries' activities so as to encourage them to liberalise their energy sectors (including through privatisation of their energy industries), to remove barriers to and cooperate on cross-border energy flows, and to increase energy efficiency. It is also outward-looking, with the Conference seeking actively to engage with other states and

74 The Second Edition Model Intergovernmental and Host Government Agreements for Cross-Border Pipelines may be found on the Energy Charter's Secretariat's website at: www.encharter.org/fileadmin/user_upload/document/ma-en.pdf

international organisations interested in cooperating with it in pursuit of its objectives.

### *(b) The Energy Charter Secretariat*

The Secretariat assists the Charter Conference in carrying out its functions. It is located in Brussels and has a staff of 'the minimum [number] consistent with efficient performance' (which in November 2009 meant thirty-two persons).[75] It is deliberately small because it was not intended to duplicate the functions of other international organisations active in the energy field. The present Secretary General is Ambassador André Mernier, a Belgian national. The Deputy Secretary General is Ambassador Vladimir Rakhmanin, who is of Russian nationality. The main functions of the Secretariat are to staff meetings of the Charter Conference and its subsidiary bodies; to monitor and review Contracting Parties' obligations under the ECT; to provide advice on all matters related to the Treaty; and to establish and develop contacts with interested non-member states and organisations.

### *(c) The Energy Charter process review*

Article 34(7) of the ECT provides that in 1999 and thereafter at intervals of not more than five years, the Charter Conference must conduct a review of its functions in the light of the extent to which the provisions of the Treaty and its Protocols have been implemented. The most recent review was held in 2009, and its report and conclusions were presented to the 20th Meeting of the Energy Charter Conference in Rome in December 2009, as a result of which the Conference agreed to the creation of a standing Strategy Group to guide the modernisation of the Charter process[76] and to launch a process of modernisation, in particular by focusing on expanding the membership of the ECT in Asia, the Middle East and Latin America.[77]

75 Article 35(1) of the ECT.

76 See Energy Charter Secretariat press release, 'Energy Charter Conference Adopts Rome Statement', 10 December 2009.

77 Energy Charter Conference, Joint Statement, Rome 9 December 2009.

# 2

# The applicable law

## 1. Introduction

Article 26 of the ECT sets out the rules governing the settlement of disputes between investors and Contracting Parties concerning alleged breaches by the latter of their obligations under Part III of the ECT. The law governing such disputes is provided for in Article 26(6):

> A tribunal established under paragraph (4) shall decide the issues in dispute in accordance with this Treaty and applicable rules and principles of international law.

Article 26(4) provides for the submission of disputes to international arbitration: either to ICSID (under the ICSID Convention or the Additional Facility Rules), the Arbitration Institute of the Stockholm Chamber of Commerce, or ad hoc arbitration under the UNCITRAL Arbitration Rules. In all cases, the relevant arbitration rules also provide that the tribunal shall decide the dispute in accordance with the rules of law designated by the parties.[1] It is consequently clear that an arbitral tribunal deciding a dispute under Article 26 of the ECT must apply not only the Treaty itself but also any applicable rules of international law. This is not to say that the national law of the respondent state or, indeed, of the claimant's state of nationality, is irrelevant, simply that issues of that law are to be approached as matters of fact, the consequences and characterisation of which are determined by the application of international law.

## 2. Interpreting the Energy Charter Treaty

The ECT is a treaty, an agreement concluded between states in written form governed by international law.[2] As a treaty, it is itself a creature

1 See Article 42(1) of the ICSID Convention; Article 53(1) of the ICSID Additional Facility Rules; Article 22(1) of the SCC Arbitration Rules; and Article 33(1) of the UNCITRAL Arbitration Rules.

2 Article 1(a) of the Vienna Convention on the Law of Treaties, 1155 UNTS 331 (1969).

of international law. In the first instance, this means that it has to be interpreted applying the international law rules on the interpretation of treaties. Second, it means that the ECT has to be interpreted in the context of the whole body of applicable international law rules. This is made explicit by Article 26(6) of the ECT, as well as being itself a rule of treaty interpretation as codified in Article 31(3)(c) of the Vienna Convention on the Law of Treaties (1969) ('VCLT'). Indeed, Article 31(3)(c) of the VCLT is said to refer to a more general principle pervading international law: the 'principle of systemic integration'.[3]

The international law rules on treaty interpretation are generally considered to have been codified in Articles 31 and 32 of the VCLT, which, as a result, apply as a matter of customary international law,[4] even though the VCLT is not directly applicable because not all the parties to the ECT are also parties to the VCLT.[5]

Articles 31 and 32 VCLT read as follows:

> Article 31: General rule of interpretation
>
> 1. A treaty shall be interpreted in good faith in accordance with the ordinary meaning to be given to the terms of the treaty in their context and in the light of its object and purpose.
> 2. The context for the purpose of the interpretation of a treaty shall comprise, in addition to the text, including its preamble and annexes:
>    (a) any agreement relating to the treaty which was made between all the parties in connexion with the conclusion of the treaty;
>    (b) any instrument which was made by one or more parties in connexion with the conclusion of the treaty and accepted by the other parties as an instrument related to the treaty.

3 See International Law Commission, 'Conclusions of the Work of the Study Group on the Fragmentation of International Law: Difficulties arising from the Diversification and Expansion of International Law' (2006) II(2) *Yearbook of the International Law Commission*, at paragraph 19; C. McLachlan, 'The Principle of Systemic Integration and Article 31(3)(c) of the Vienna Convention' (2005) 54 *International and Comparative Law Quarterly* 279.

4 This has been recognised by the International Court of Justice: see *Territorial Dispute* (*Libyan Arab Jamahiriya* v. *Chad*), Judgment, 1996 ICJ Rep 6 at paragraph 41; *Case concerning Oil Platforms* (*Islamic Republic of Iran* v. *United States of America*), Preliminary Objections, Judgment, 1996 ICJ Rep 803 at paragraph 23; and *Kasikili/Sedudu Island* (*Botswana* v. *Namibia*), Judgment, 1999 ICJ Rep 1045 at paragraph 18; and by numerous investment treaty arbitral tribunals: see, e.g., *CME Czech Republic BV* v. *Czech Republic*, Partial Award, 13 September 2001, paragraph 284; *Mondev International Ltd* v. *United States of America*, Award, 11 October 2002, paragraph 43; *Methanex Corp* v. *United States of America*, Partial Award, 7 August 2002, paragraph 97; *Société Générale de Surveillance SA* v. *The Philippines*, Decision on Jurisdiction, 29 January 2004, paragraph 99, and *Saluka Investments BV* v. *Czech Republic*, Partial Award, 17 March 2006, paragraph 296.

5 At present, Azerbaijan, France, Malta, Romania and Turkey are not parties.

3. There shall be taken into account, together with the context:
   (a) any subsequent agreement between the parties regarding the interpretation of the treaty or the application of its provisions;
   (b) any subsequent practice in the application of the treaty which establishes the agreement of the parties regarding its interpretation;
   (c) any relevant rules of international law applicable in the relations between the parties.
4. A special meaning shall be given to a term if it is established that the parties so intended.

Article 32: Supplementary means of interpretation
Recourse may be had to supplementary means of interpretation, including the preparatory work of the treaty and the circumstances of its conclusion, in order to confirm the meaning resulting from the application of article 31, or to determine the meaning when the interpretation according to article 31:
   (a) leaves the meaning ambiguous or obscure; or
   (b) leads to a result which is manifestly absurd or unreasonable.

These provisions will be referred to subsequently in order to help elucidate some of the provisions of the ECT. However, a number of preliminary points can be made at this stage.

### *(a) Article 31 of the VCLT*

The rule set out in Article 31(1) is the 'general rule of interpretation'. Primacy is given to the treaty text: to the terms of the treaty, which must be interpreted in their context and in the light of the treaty's object and purpose. The first aspect of this injunction is simple: the treaty must be read as a whole. The various provisions need to be read together and (if at all possible) harmoniously. This suggests not only that the particular provisions of Part III of the ECT cannot be interpreted in isolation but also that Part III itself needs to be considered in relation to the other provisions of the ECT, such as, for example, Articles 18 (sovereignty over natural resources) and 19 (environmental aspects). Article 31(2) VCLT, however, defines the context more widely than simply the other operative provisions of a treaty. It includes the preamble, which in the case of the ECT refers back at several points to the European Energy Charter and the objectives and principles enunciated therein (see Chapter 1). It also includes 'any agreement relating to the treaty which was made between all the parties in connexion with the conclusion of the treaty' and 'any instrument which was made by one or more parties in connexion with the conclusion of the treaty and accepted by the other parties as an instrument related to the treaty'. As has already been observed, the ECT is peculiarly rich in Understandings and Declarations.

What the VCLT does not do, however, is provide any guidance as to how to determine the 'object and purpose' of a treaty. The parties to a treaty may have entered into it for a variety of reasons, so that its object and purpose can only be described in such general terms as to detract from its utility as an interpretative tool. Indeed, it has been argued that the concept serves little or no useful purpose.[6] The concept has, however, been extensively used in the interpretation of BITs. Claimants have argued that as BITs are intended to promote and protect foreign investment, they should be interpreted expansively, with the benefit of the doubt in cases of dispute being given to the investor. With rather less success, respondent states have countered that restrictions on sovereignty should not be presumed, so BITs should be interpreted restrictively.[7] Arbitral tribunals have taken different views. In *Société Générale de Surveillance SA* v. *The Philippines*, the tribunal held that:

> The [Philippines–Switzerland] BIT is a treaty for the promotion and reciprocal protection of investments. According to the preamble it is intended 'to create and maintain favourable conditions for investments by investors of one Contracting Party in the territory of the other'. It is legitimate to resolve uncertainties in its interpretation so as to favour the protection of covered investments.[8]

In *El Paso Energy International Co* v. *Argentina*, however, the tribunal stated that:

> This Tribunal considers that a balanced interpretation is needed, taking into account both State sovereignty and the State's responsibility to create an adapted and evolutionary framework for the development of economic activities, and the necessity to protect foreign investment and its continuing flow.[9]

Similarly, the tribunal in *Saluka Investments BV* v. *Czech Republic* concluded that:

6 J. Klabbers, 'Some Problems Regarding the Object and Purpose of Treaties' (1997) 8 *Finnish Yearbook of International Law* 138.

7 See *Methanex Corp* v. *United States of America*, Partial Award, 7 August 2002, paragraphs 103–5.

8 *Société Générale de Surveillance SA* v. *The Philippines*, Decision on Jurisdiction, 29 January 2004, paragraph 116. For the contrary view, see *Noble Ventures Inc* v. *Romania*, Award, 12 October 2005, paragraph 52.

9 *El Paso Energy International Co* v. *Argentina*, Decision on Jurisdiction, 27 April 2006, paragraph 70.

> The protection of foreign investments is not the sole aim of the [Netherlands–Czechoslovakia] Treaty, but rather a necessary element alongside the overall aim of encouraging foreign investment and extending and intensifying the parties' economic relations. That in turn calls for a balanced approach to the interpretation of the Treaty's substantive provisions for the protection of investments, since an interpretation which exaggerates the protection to be accorded to foreign investments may serve to dissuade States from admitting foreign investments and so undermine the overall aim of extending and intensifying the parties' mutual economic relations.[10]

The ECT is not a BIT but a multilateral treaty of far wider scope, encompassing trade, transit, environmental protection and energy efficiency as well as investment. Its complex structure and its balancing of diverse interests would seem to argue for the application of the approach adopted by the *Saluka* tribunal. It is clear, however, that the object and purpose of a BIT has generally been ascertained by looking at the treaty itself, particularly its preamble, which is part of the context for the purposes of its interpretation. The extent to which the concept has any independent utility might therefore be doubted.

### *(b) Article 32 of the VCLT*

Article 32, permitting recourse to supplementary means of interpretation, only applies when the application of Article 31 leads to an interpretation which is ambiguous, obscure, manifestly absurd or unreasonable. As a matter of policy, this is sensible, particularly with regard to multilateral treaties where not all of the parties to the treaty may have been involved in its negotiation. This is the case with the ECT, although not yet to any large extent.[11] More importantly, however, several of the participating states played only minor roles in the negotiations and most contentious issues were hammered out in discussions within a smaller group of states: the European Communities, Norway, Russia and the US. As with legislation at the national level, the best evidence of what a large group of persons meant might be thought to be found in the written record

10 *Saluka Investments BV* v. *Czech Republic*, Partial Award, 17 March 2006, paragraph 300.

11 Mongolia, which did not participate in the negotiations, has since acceded to the ECT, and a number of other states which did not participate in the negotiations are considering whether to accede.

of what they agreed, not the various statements made prior to their agreement.[12]

Another, practical, difficulty in seeking to rely on a treaty's *travaux préparatoires* is that they are frequently difficult to access, obscure and unhelpful. The lack of a published record can particularly disadvantage private persons. The ECT *travaux*[13] are available for consultation by the public at the Energy Charter Secretariat's Brussels offices, although there are some restrictions on their copying. Questions nevertheless remain concerning the value of particular documents, such as papers produced by individual delegations or informal working groups. Moreover, there is a general tendency in negotiations for the most difficult issues to be agreed in 'off the record' discussions. In such cases, the *travaux* will say nothing. For these reasons, the approach taken in this study has been to concentrate on the ECT text and to avoid relying on the views of its negotiators as to its meaning.[14]

### *(c) Language issues*

Article 50 of the ECT ('Authentic Texts') provides that the English, French, German, Italian, Russian and Spanish texts of the Treaty are equally authentic. There exists a tendency for arbitral tribunals only to refer to the English-language text. However, Article 50 makes it clear that it is no more authentic than any of the other versions. Unsurprisingly, given the drafting history of the ECT, discrepancies between the different official language texts exist. When such differences have implications for the interpretation of provisions of the Treaty, reference will be made to them subsequently when appropriate.[15]

12 See the arguments with regard to the interpretation of domestic statutes in J. Waldron, 'Legislators' Intentions and Unintended Legislation' in A. Marmor (ed.), *Law and Interpretation: Essays in Legal Philosophy* (Oxford University Press, 1995), pp. 329–56.

13 Or, at least, the documentary record and those audio recordings of proceedings that have been digitalised.

14 It might be noted here that although Article 32 of the VCLT gives a role to the *travaux préparatoires* in the interpretation of treaties, no value is placed on the subsequent, subjective recollections of the negotiators.

15 Article 33 of the VCLT deals with the interpretation of treaties authenticated in two or more languages. Article 33(3) provides that: 'when a comparison of the authentic texts discloses a difference of meaning which the application of articles 31 and 32 does not remove, the meaning which best reconciles the texts, having regard to the object and purpose of the treaty, shall be adopted'.

### *(d) Other treaties and general international law*

Another controversial issue has been the extent to which treaties are 'self-contained regimes' or, to put it another way, to what extent the provisions of other treaties – and the decisions of courts and tribunals interpreting such provisions – or general international law should be used as aids to interpretation. One view is that taken by the International Tribunal for the Law of the Sea in the *MOX Plant* case:

> [E]ven if the OSPAR Convention, the EC Treaty and the Euratom Treaty contain rights or obligations similar or identical with the rights or obligations set out in the [1982] Convention [on the Law of the Sea], the rights and obligations under those agreements have a separate existence from those under the Convention . . . [T]he application of international law rules on interpretation of treaties to identical or similar provisions of different treaties may not yield the same results, having regard to, *inter alia*, differences in the respective contexts, objects and purposes, subsequent practice of parties and *travaux préparatoires*[.][16]

Scepticism has already been expressed as to the utility of resort to the *travaux* or the object and purpose of a treaty. It might be thought, however, that the *MOX Plant* approach fails to take account of how treaties build upon each other and how negotiators 'recycle' provisions, something that is particularly apparent with regard to investment agreements, not least because many states now have model agreements which they use as starting-points in negotiations and which regularly lead to uniformities in language. Indeed, we are now at the stage where several states have revised their Model BITs in order to take account of the jurisprudence of arbitral tribunals in investor–state treaty disputes.

Article 31(3)(c) ('there shall be taken into account, together with the context . . . any relevant rules of international law applicable in the relations between the parties') has been seen as particularly relevant in this context, reflecting what has been called the principle of systemic integration that exists in international law. This principle provides that two presumptions should be applied when interpreting a treaty:

(i) according to the *positive presumption*, parties are taken 'to refer to general principles of international law for all questions which [the treaty] does not itself resolve in express terms or in a different way';

16 *MOX Plant* case (*Ireland* v. *United Kingdom*), Order on Request for Provisional Measures, 3 December 2001, paragraphs 50–1.

(ii) according to the *negative presumption*, in entering into treaty obligations, the parties intend not to act inconsistently with generally recognised principles of international law or with previous treaty obligations towards third states.[17]

The first presumption seems uncontentious; the second may be more controversial. It is, however, only a presumption and can be rebutted by clear treaty language.

Indeed, the ECT includes a provision specifically covering its relationship with other treaties. Article 16 of the ECT regulates the relationship between Parts III and V of the ECT and other treaties concerning the same subject matter, i.e., the promotion and protection of investments in the energy sector, and the settlement of disputes between investors and ECT Contracting Parties. Article 16 provides that:

> Where two or more Contracting Parties have entered into a prior international agreement, or enter into a subsequent international agreement, whose terms in either case concern the subject matter of Part III or V of this Treaty,
>
> (1) nothing in Part III or V of this Treaty shall be construed to derogate from any provisions of such terms of the other agreement or from any right to dispute resolution with respect thereto under that agreement; and
> (2) nothing in such terms of the other agreement shall be construed to derogate from any provision of Part III or V of this Treaty or from any right to dispute resolution with respect thereto under this Treaty,
>
> where any such provision is more favourable to the Investor or Investment.

Article 16 would appear designed to avoid disputes as to whether one such agreement had displaced the other by application of the maxims *lex posterior derogat priori* or *lex specialis derogat generali*. Instead, each treaty continues to apply equally, unaffected by the other[18] and an investor may seek to rely on the substantive or procedural provisions of either. Indeed, given that the two treaties continue to apply in parallel, an investor could bring proceedings under both agreements. In *Plama Consortium Ltd* v. *Bulgaria*, the claimant filed a request for arbitration with ICSID claiming breaches of both the ECT and the Cyprus–Bulgaria BIT, arguing that the 'most-favoured nation' ('MFN') provision of the

17 See International Law Commission, 'Conclusions of the Work of the Study Group on the Fragmentation of International Law', paragraph 19.

18 Although the provisions in one treaty can arguably be 'incorporated' into the other by virtue of a most-favoured nation clause in the latter treaty: see p. 128 below.

latter treaty imported the ICSID arbitration provisions in other BITs entered into by Bulgaria into the treaty. The claim was registered by ICSID and an arbitral tribunal constituted, although the tribunal subsequently held that it had no jurisdiction over the claim under the Cyprus–Bulgaria BIT on the ground that the treaty's MFN clause did not have the effect which the claimant claimed.[19] However, the constitution of one tribunal to determine the claims under both treaties would seem entirely appropriate.[20]

It might, however, also be argued that Article 16 indicates that Parts III and V of the ECT are intended to be interpreted in isolation, unaffected by interpretations given to similar or identical provisions in other treaties. Such an interpretation would be unwarranted. Article 16 refers to derogations from Part III and V; it does not cover how their provisions are to be interpreted in the first place.

### *(e) Decisions of other investment arbitration tribunals*

As regards the decisions of other investment arbitration tribunals, international law knows no doctrine of binding precedent. Article 38(1) of the Statute of the International Court of Justice only mentions 'judicial decisions' as a 'subsidiary source' of international law.[21] Nor is there anything in the ECT providing for application of the doctrine of *stare decisis* to the decisions of tribunals established under Article 26. This does not mean, however, that such tribunals do not refer to the decisions of their predecessors (as they do to the judgments of other courts and tribunals, when they consider them relevant). They frequently do. However, those decisions are not binding but persuasive. Tribunals have considered that they should take due account of previous jurisprudence but need not follow it. This has meant that on some issues different tribunals have come to different conclusions.[22]

19 *Plama Consortium Ltd* v. *Bulgaria*, Decision on Jurisdiction, 5 February 2005.

20 More problematic would be the situation where a claimant utilised the different dispute settlement mechanisms in different treaties to bring separate claims with regard to the same treatment, or brought consecutive claims under different treaties before the same forum.

21 Indeed, Article 59 specifically provides that the International Court of Justice is not bound by its own decisions.

22 For a list of such instances, see C. Schreuer and M. Weiniger, 'A Doctrine of Precedent?' in P. Muchlinski, F. Ortino and C. Schreuer (eds.), *The Oxford Handbook of International Investment Law* (Oxford University Press, 2008), pp. 1196–8.

Parties to investment treaty arbitrations are thus able to make the same arguments in successive arbitrations, even if the arbitration is under the same investment treaty and the arguments have previously failed. A practice by Argentina of making the same jurisdictional objections to ICSID arbitral tribunals led to the issue being the subject of in-depth analysis in *AES Corp* v. *Argentina*.[23] The tribunal agreed with Argentina that:

> each BIT has its own identity; its very terms should consequently be carefully analyzed for determining the exact scope of consent expressed by its two Parties. This is in particular the case if one considers that striking similarities in the wording of many BITs often dissimulate real differences in the definition of some key concepts . . .[24]

For the tribunal, this meant that 'findings of law made by one . . . tribunal in one case in consideration, among others, of the terms of a determined BIT, are not necessarily relevant for other . . . tribunals'.[25] Argentina, consequently, was entitled to continue to make the same arguments in successive cases. However, the tribunal went on to make some more general points:

> . . . the Tribunal would nevertheless reject the excessive assertion which would consist in pretending that, due to the specificity of each case and the identity of each decision on jurisdiction or award, absolutely no consideration might be given to other decisions on jurisdiction or awards delivered by other tribunals in similar cases.
>
> In particular, if the basis of jurisdiction for these other tribunals and/or the underlying legal dispute in analysis present either a high level of similarity or, even more, an identity with those met in the present case, this Tribunal does not consider that it is barred, as a matter of principle, from considering the position taken or the opinion expressed by these other tribunals.[26]

The tribunal distinguished between cases where tribunals considered questions relating to the interpretation of the same treaty and cases where tribunals considered questions relating to the interpretation of provisions of different treaties. Even in the first instance, however:

> An identity of the basis of jurisdiction of these tribunals, even when it meets with very similar if not even identical facts at the origin of the disputes, does not suffice to apply systematically to the present case positions or solutions already adopted in these cases. Each tribunal remains sovereign and may retain, as it is confirmed by ICSID practice, a different solution for

23 *AES Corp* v. *Argentina*, Decision on Jurisdiction, 26 April 2005, paragraphs 24–5.
24 *Ibid.*, paragraphs 24–5. 25 *Ibid.*, paragraph 26. 26 *Ibid.*, paragraphs 27–8.

> resolving the same problem; but decisions on jurisdiction dealing with the same or very similar issues may at least indicate some lines of reasoning of real interest; this Tribunal may consider them in order to compare its own position with those already adopted by its predecessors and, if it shares the views already expressed by one or more of these tribunals on a specific point of law, it is free to adopt the same solution.
>
> One may even find situations in which, although seized on the basis of another BIT as combined with the pertinent provisions of the ICSID Convention, a tribunal has set a point of law which, in essence, is or will be met in other cases whatever the specificities of each dispute may be. Such precedents may also be rightly considered, at least as a matter of comparison and, if so considered by the Tribunal, of inspiration.
>
> The same may be said for the interpretation given by a precedent decision or award to some relevant facts which are basically at the origin of two or several different disputes, keeping carefully in mind the actual specificities still featuring each case. If the present Tribunal concurs with the analysis and interpretation of these facts as they generated certain special consequences for the parties to this case as well as for those of another case, it may consider this earlier interpretation as relevant.[27]

This approach seems sensible and has been largely adopted. It avoids the isolationism of the *MOX Plant* case, whilst retaining a due regard for the distinctiveness of different treaties.

## 3. The role of national law

The general rule is that a state may not plead its own national law in order to justify or excuse a breach of its international legal obligations. This rule is codified in both the VCLT and the International Law Commission's Articles on State Responsibility.[28] However, this is not to say that the legal characterisation of a particular situation under a state's national law is always irrelevant. As is discussed in more detail in Chapter 3, the definition of 'investment' in the ECT encompasses various forms of property interests owned by investors. The Treaty, however, does not define the existence, nature or extent of such interests; nor does customary international law. Resort for this purpose must be had to the national law of the host state. However, once national law has recognised a particular

27 *Ibid.*, paragraphs 30–2.

28 Article 27 of the VCLT; ILC Articles on State Responsibility (International Law Commission, *Responsibility of States for Internationally Wrongful Acts* (2001) (GA res. 56/83 (2002), Annex)), Articles 3 and 32. See V. Heiskanen, 'May a State Invoke its Domestic Law to Evade its International Obligations?' (2005) 2(5) *Transnational Dispute Management.*

property right, provided that it amounts to an Investment as defined in Article 1(6) of the ECT it will benefit from the protections accorded in Part III. Subsequent changes of national law or conduct of host state organs or agents, even if lawful under national law, affecting an investor's property rights need to conform to the international standards set out in Part III.

Several tribunals, deciding cases under investment agreements, have not utilised such an approach, focusing instead on claimants' expectations of the respondent state, without considering the nature and extent of any property rights they held under host state law.[29] As will be seen, this is an incorrect approach: only claimants' *legitimate* expectations as regards their investments (that is, in relation to property rights covered by the relevant treaty) are protected in investment agreements.

Another issue with regard to which there is a *renvoi* to national law is the determination of an investor's nationality. As international law grants states a very wide discretion with regard to whom they may grant nationality,[30] in most cases an investor's nationality will be decided by application of the law of the state the nationality of which the investor claims, although an arbitral tribunal may not consider itself bound by prior determinations of the state's authorities if the tribunal considers, on the facts as found by it, that the premises on which those decisions were based were erroneous.[31]

29 See Z. Douglas, 'Nothing if Not Critical for Investment Treaty Arbitration: *Occidental*, *Eureko* and *Methanex*' (2006) 22 *Arbitration International* 27.

30 For discussion of the issues involved, see I. Brownlie, *Principles of Public International Law* (Oxford University Press, 7th edn 2008), pp. 382–418.

31 See *Soufraki* v. *United Arab Emirates*, Award, 7 July 2004, paragraph 55.

# 3

# Availability of dispute settlement under Article 26

## 1. Introduction – jurisdiction and admissibility

In an arbitration under the Energy Charter Treaty, as in any arbitration, two preliminary issues must logically be determined by the arbitral tribunal before it embarks upon consideration of the merits of a dispute (though whether determination of these preliminary issues requires a preliminary *hearing* is a different matter which is discussed below[1]). The first is whether or not the claim on which the claimant asks the tribunal to adjudicate is one in respect of which the tribunal has jurisdiction. The second is whether the claim is admissible. The distinction between the two has been explained as follows:

> Objections to the jurisdiction, if successful, stop all proceedings in the case, since they strike at the competence of the Tribunal to give rulings as to the merits or admissibility of the claim. An objection to the substantive admissibility of a claim invites the Tribunal to reject the claim on a ground distinct from the merits . . . [2]

As Paulsson has put it, one can answer the question, 'Is an objection one of jurisdiction or admissibility?' by asking, 'Is the objecting party taking aim at the tribunal [(jurisdiction)] or at the claim [(admissibility)]?'[3] In the context of a treaty arbitration, the issue of jurisdiction may be said to comprise the question whether the dispute is one in respect of which the host state, by becoming a party to the Treaty, has given its consent to

1 P. 42.

2 I. Brownlie, *Principles of Public International Law* (Oxford University Press, 7th edn, 2008), p. 475. It is not clear that the word 'substantive' adds anything to the word admissibility, though it is often used in the literature. See also I. Laird, 'A Distinction Without a Difference?' in T. Weiler (ed.) *International Investment Law and Arbitration: Leading Cases from the ICSID, NAFTA, Bilateral Treaties and Customary International Law* (London: Cameron May, 2005), pp. 201ff.

3 J. Paulsson, 'Jurisdiction and Admissibility', in *Liber Amicorum in Honour of Robert Briner, Global Reflections on International Law, Commerce and Dispute Resolution* (Paris: ICC Publishing, 2005), pp. 601ff at p. 616.

arbitration.[4] If it has not, it can be argued, the tribunal has no business adjudicating on the merits of the dispute.

The distinction between jurisdiction and admissibility is potentially of great practical importance since a tribunal's decisions on matters other than jurisdiction are not generally subject to review either (in the case of most modern national laws governing arbitration) by the domestic courts at the seat of the arbitration or, where the arbitral tribunal is constituted under the ICSID Convention, by an ad hoc Committee established under the annulment procedure created by Article 52 of that Convention.[5]

The issue of jurisdiction breaks down into three questions: does the tribunal have jurisdiction over the subject-matter of the dispute (sometimes called jurisdiction *ratione materiae*); does the tribunal have jurisdiction to determine the claim between these particular parties (jurisdiction *ratione personae*); and does the tribunal have jurisdiction to determine the claim in the light of the dates on which the relevant events occurred (jurisdiction *ratione temporis*)? In relation to claims sought to be brought under the ECT, these are questions to be determined principally by applying the rules set out in Article 26. The first part of this Chapter is concerned with these rules. Since both jurisdiction *ratione personae* and jurisdiction *ratione temporis* are potentially complicated by the question of 'provisional application' of the Treaty, this subject is also discussed here.

The second part of this Chapter is concerned with an issue which is argued by some to concern admissibility rather than jurisdiction, namely the 'denial of advantages' provision in Article 17. This part is also concerned with the effect (if any) of misconduct on the part of the investor:

4 Z. Douglas, *The International Law of Investment Claims* (Cambridge University Press, 2009), rightly complains at pp. 141–3 of the way in which jurisdiction, admissibility, consent to arbitration and other terms are misused in the case law. He adopts at p. 142 the French terminology which offers a more precise, if more complex, 'taxonomy'. The present work will stick to using 'jurisdiction' to refer to the question whether the tribunal is entitled to adjudicate at all and 'admissibility' to refer to the tribunal's exercise of jurisdiction to decide those issues which are logically prior to the merits of the dispute.

5 In relation to domestic courts at the seat of the arbitration, see Lord Steyn's account of the modern trend towards non-reviewability except on grounds of jurisdiction in *Lesotho Highlands Development Authority* v. *Impregilo SpA* [2005] UKHL 43, [2006] 1 AC 221; see also, as to the right to resist enforcement of an arbitral award on the ground of lack of jurisdiction, *Dallah Estate and Tourism Holding Company* v. *Ministry of Religious Affairs, Government of Pakistan* [2009] EWCA Civ 755, [2010] 2 WLR 805, per Moore-Bick LJ at paragraph 18 (affirmed [2010] UKSC 46, [2010] 3 WLR 1472). As to the enforcement of ICSID awards, see E. Baldwin, M. Kantor and M. Nolan, 'Limits to Enforcement of ICSID Awards', (2006) 23 *Journal of International Arbitration* 1.

it will be argued that this is an issue which may, depending on the facts, be one either of jurisdiction or of admissibility.

This Chapter does not deal with the procedural preliminaries to arbitration of an investor–state dispute under Article 26 of the Treaty, nor with various specific exceptions to states' consent to such arbitration. These are dealt with in Chapter 6.

## 2. Jurisdiction

The dispute settlement provisions of the Energy Charter Treaty (concerning claims by investors against states) apply to:

> Disputes between a Contracting Party and an Investor of another Contracting Party relating to an Investment of the latter in the Area of the former, which concern an alleged breach of an obligation of the former under Part III . . . (Article 26(1)).

Thus there are five conditions to be satisfied in order for a dispute to be one which a tribunal has jurisdiction under the Treaty to determine:[6]

(1) There must be a dispute concerning an alleged breach of an obligation under Part III of the Treaty by a Contracting Party.
(2) The dispute must relate to an Investment as defined by the Treaty. This condition breaks down into two subsidiary conditions:
 (i) the Investment must be one associated with an Economic Activity in the Energy Sector;
 (ii) the Investment must by its nature qualify as such within the meaning of the term as defined in Article 26.
(3) The Investment must be in the Area of the Contracting Party.
(4) The claimant must be an Investor of a Contracting Party.
(5) The events with which the claim is concerned must have occurred at a date such as to give the tribunal jurisdiction.

In the terms of the analysis of jurisdictional issues mentioned above, conditions (1), (2) and (3) concern jurisdiction *ratione materiae*, condition (4) concerns jurisdiction *ratione personae* and condition (5) concerns jurisdiction *ratione temporis*.

6 In addition, if the claimant seeks, under Article 26(4)(a)(i) of the ECT, to advance the claim by way of arbitration under the ICSID Convention, it will need to be established that the dispute is a 'legal dispute arising directly out of an investment' within the (undefined) meaning of that term in Article 25(1) of that Convention.

### *(a) Procedure for resolving issues of jurisdiction*

It is trite that an arbitral tribunal has jurisdiction to determine the extent of its own jurisdiction.[7] Tribunals frequently do so, where such issues arise, by way of a separate hearing leading to a preliminary award on jurisdiction, the rest being left for a later phase which will take place only if a respondent's jurisdictional objections fail. Where the claimant has submitted the dispute (under ECT Article 26(4)(c)) to a sole arbitrator or ad hoc tribunal established under the UNCITRAL Arbitration Rules, this is the course which, under those rules, the arbitrator or tribunal should '[i]n general' follow.[8] Alternatively, the issue of jurisdiction may be joined to the merits, i.e., decided alongside the issue of the merits after a hearing dealing with both issues. In the latter case, 'the respondent contracting party waits, as a practical matter, for the merits stage of the proceedings for a substantive determination of whether the arbitral tribunal was genuinely seized of the dispute'.[9]

An arbitral tribunal ought to consider at an early stage which course to follow. Where the claimant has elected (under ECT Article 26(4)(a)) to submit the dispute to the International Centre for Settlement of Investment Disputes, the tribunal is positively obliged to consider which course to follow.[10] Its decision will generally depend on its view, taking into account the questions raised by the jurisdictional and non-jurisdictional issues and the extent to which they are either discrete or intertwined, as to which course best reconciles the desirability of establishing clearly at the outset whether the tribunal has jurisdiction to entertain the dispute at all with the desirability of minimising the expense to both parties.

If a preliminary hearing on jurisdiction does take place, the question arises as to how the tribunal ought to approach disputed allegations of

7 See Article 41(1) of the ICSID Convention; Article 21 of the UNCITRAL arbitration rules; Section 2 of the Arbitration Act (Sweden); Section 30 of the Arbitration Act 1996 (England and Wales). The principle is often expressed in French (*compétence de la compétence*) or German (*Kompetenz-Kompetenz*). A tribunal's decision as to its own jurisdiction may, of course, be challenged, either before an ad hoc Committee constituted under Article 52(1)(b) in the case of an arbitration under the ICSID Convention or, in other cases, by the courts at the seat of the arbitration or in the place where a substantive award is sought to be enforced: see *Dallah Estate and Tourism Holding Company* v. *Ministry of Religious Affairs, Government of Pakistan* [2009] EWCA Civ 755, [2010] 2 WLR 805, per Moore-Bick LJ, paragraphs 55–6 (affirmed [2010] UKSC 46, [2010] 3 WLR 1472).

8 Article 21(4) of the UNCITRAL Arbitration Rules.

9 L. Shore, 'The Jurisdiction Problem in Energy Charter Treaty Claims', (2007) 10 *International Arbitration Law Review* 58 at 59.

10 Article 41(2) of the ICSID Convention; Article 45(5) of the Additional Facility Rules.

fact at this stage. It has been said that the tribunal should assume the claimant's allegations of fact to be true and ask (as it has been variously expressed, in language taken from the jurisprudence of the International Court of Justice (ICJ)) whether 'the assumed facts are capable of coming within those provisions of the [Treaty] which have been invoked';[11] and whether, on those facts, 'there could occur a violation [of the Treaty]', whether 'the . . . actions complained of might violate the Treaty articles'.[12] If so, the case must go to the merits phase. All of these formulations were approved and adopted in the context of jurisdictional issues arising under the ECT in *Plama Consortium* v. *Bulgaria*.[13]

However, some care is needed in this context. The tribunal should be clear about what precise issue is to be determined using this 'assumed facts' approach. If the claimant is an Investor who has made an Investment, but the issue is whether there really is a '[D]ispute . . . concerning an alleged breach of an obligation under Part III of the Treaty' – what has here been called condition (1) – then this approach is undoubtedly correct. The tribunal is in the same position as the ICJ in the *Oil Platforms* case,[14] where the US and Iran could not agree whether their dispute about the lawfulness of the former's attacks on the latter's oil platforms constituted a 'dispute . . . as to the application or interpretation' of their Treaty of Amity and thus one which they had given the ICJ jurisdiction to determine: it was necessary for the Court to determine whether the dispute was one which fell within the scope of the Treaty of Amity, and this could only sensibly be done by assuming the claimant's factual allegations to be true and asking whether, if true, they might amount to a breach of the Treaty.[15] (Condition (1), in particular the requirement that the claimant's allegations be characterised objectively, is considered further below.)

However, it does not follow that the 'assumed facts' approach is the correct one when considering the other jurisdictional conditions. On the contrary, it is submitted that it is not. For while condition (1) is concerned only with whether there is a dispute concerning an '*alleged* breach' of an obligation under Part III, the other conditions are concerned

11 *Salini Costruttori SpA and Italstrade SpA* v. *Jordan*, Award 15 November 2004.

12 *Case concerning Oil Platforms (Islamic Republic of Iran* v. *United States of America)*, 1996 ICJ Rep 803 at 810 (separate Opinion of Judge Higgins at paragraphs 32–4).

13 Decision on Jurisdiction, 8 February 2005 at paragraphs 118–19.

14 1996 ICJ Rep 803.

15 Although the fact that this is what the Court was doing emerges more clearly from Judge Higgins's separate Opinion than from the Court's holding.

with the actuality: for the tribunal to have jurisdiction to determine the substantive dispute, there must actually *be* an Investment by an Investor in the Area of the Contracting Party. A finding as to whether, *if* the facts alleged by the claimant are true, the claimant is (or might be) an Investor which has made such an Investment is worthless for the purpose of determining whether the tribunal has jurisdiction to determine the claimant's substantive complaint.[16] A hearing which merely determines this issue is no more than the hearing, in effect, of an application to strike the claim out as disclosing no reasonable grounds[17] (or, in US terms, a 'motion to dismiss'). Nothing in the Treaty itself gives an arbitral tribunal the power to make such an order (though in the case of an arbitration under the ICSID Convention there is an express general power under the Arbitration Rules to dismiss a claim at an early stage where it is 'manifestly without legal merit').[18] It has been suggested that the decision of the tribunal in *Plama Consortium* v. *Bulgaria*[19] is authority for the adoption of such an approach to claims under the Treaty.[20] However, although the tribunal in *Plama Consortium* wrote in broad terms about the correct approach to 'jurisdictional objections',[21] in its actual decision it was careful to identify each of the conditions which had to be satisfied in order for it to have jurisdiction over the dispute, and to apply the approach of assuming the claimant's factual allegations to be true only to the question whether the dispute concerned an alleged breach of Part III of the Treaty.[22] All of the other jurisdictional conditions were, rightly, ruled upon definitively.[23]

16 See Douglas, *The International Law of Investment Claims*, at pp. 273–4; *Inmaris Perestroika Sailing Maritime Services GmbH* v. *Ukraine*, Decision on Jurisdiction, 8 March 2010 at paragraphs 56–9 and the cases there cited.

17 Analogous to the English court's powers under rule 3.4(2)(a) of the Civil Procedure Rules 1998.

18 Rule 41(5) of the Rules of Procedure for Arbitration Proceedings (ICSID). See also *Trans-Global Petroleum Inc* v. *Jordan*, Decision on the Respondent's Objection under Rule 41(5) of the ICSID Arbitration Rules, 12 May 2008.

19 Decision on Jurisdiction, 8 February 2005 at paragraphs 118–19.

20 Shore, 'The Jurisdiction Problem in Energy Charter Treaty Claims', 58 (though Shore by no means approves of it).

21 See, e.g., paragraph 119.

22 At paragraph 132.

23 See paragraphs 123 ('Contracting Party'), 124 ('Investor') and 125–31 ('Investment'). Likewise in *Kardassopoulos* v. *Georgia*, Decision on Jurisdiction, 6 July 2007, the tribunal, though stating in general terms (at paragraph 103) that the 'assumed facts' approach was 'the standard applicable to jurisdictional challenges', went on to make firm findings of fact on the decisive jurisdictional issues.

### *(b) The five conditions for establishing jurisdiction*

The five conditions will now be considered in more detail.

#### (i) There must be a dispute concerning an alleged breach of an obligation under Part III of the Treaty by a Contracting Party – Condition (1)

An arbitral tribunal's jurisdiction under the ECT is limited to disputes concerning alleged breaches of Part III of the Treaty, i.e. the substantive investor-protection provisions found there. In this respect the ECT differs from many bilateral investment treaties which give jurisdiction to an arbitral tribunal to determine 'all' or 'any' disputes between the parties relating to investments.[24]

As noted above, the tribunal in *Plama Consortium* v. *Bulgaria*[25] correctly applied the 'assumed facts' approach in determining whether this condition was satisfied:

> It is self-evident from the Claimant's written and oral submissions to date that it is 'alleging' violations by the Respondent of several provisions in Part III of the ECT.... In the Tribunal's view, it is not necessary, at this jurisdictional stage of the proceedings, for the Claimant to prove positively actual violations by the Respondent: the unambiguous wording in Article 26 ECT is met by the Claimant's allegations of such violations....[I]f on the facts alleged by the Claimant, the Respondent's actions might violate the ECT, then the Tribunal has jurisdiction to determine exactly what the facts are and see whether they do sustain a violation of that Treaty.

What is required of the claimant is not simply that he allege a breach of an obligation under Part III of the Treaty but that he allege facts which, if true, might amount to such a violation.[26]

But should a tribunal, in determining whether this condition is satisfied, invariably require no more of a claimant than that his allegations of fact, if true, 'might' constitute a breach of the Treaty? It is submitted not. The complexity of the substantive law of investment protection and, in most cases, of the facts mean that a tribunal can often determine no

24 See, e.g., United Kingdom Model BIT (2005/6); Germany Model BIT (2005); Netherlands Model BIT (1997); France Model BIT (2006).

25 Decision on Jurisdiction, 8 February 2005 at paragraph 132, referring again to the *Case concerning Oil Platforms (Islamic Republic of Iran* v. *United States of America)*.

26 See *Salini Costruttori SpA and Italstrade SpA* v. *Jordan*, Decision on Jurisdiction, 15 November 2004, at paragraph 163 where the tribunal held that it had no jurisdiction to entertain a claim based on a mere assertion of the breach of an obligation in the relevant BIT.

more at a jurisdictional phase than this: only after a full hearing on the merits can the tribunal 'determine what exactly the facts are, whether as finally determined they do sustain a violation of... [the Treaty] and if so, whether there is a defence to that violation'.[27] But the tribunal ought also to bear in mind the often colossal expense of 'determin[ing] what exactly the facts are'. In a suitably clear case (and provided that the parties are given fair warning), the tribunal should not shy away from determining at the jurisdictional phase that the claimant's allegations, even if true, do not amount to a violation of the Treaty, so that there is in truth no real 'dispute concerning an alleged breach of an obligation under Part III of the Treaty' and hence no entitlement to arbitration under Article 26.

The breach relied on by the claimant must, of course, be a breach by a Contracting Party. The rules applicable where the breach alleged is that of some entity other than the central government of a Contracting Party are discussed in Chapter 7.

### (ii) The dispute must relate to an Investment – Condition (2)

As mentioned above, this has two aspects. First, is the subject-matter of the alleged investment such that it falls within the scope of the Treaty, limited as the Treaty is to the energy sector? Second, is the nature of the alleged investment such that it does in fact amount to an 'Investment' as defined in the Treaty?

**The Investment must be one associated with an Economic Activity in the Energy sector – Condition (2)(i)** Article 1(6) provides that:

> 'Investment' refers to any investment associated with an Economic Activity in the Energy Sector...[28]

Article 1(5) defines 'Economic Activity in the Energy Sector' as:

> an economic activity concerning the exploration, extraction, refining, production, storage, land transport, transmission, distribution, trade, marketing, or sale of Energy Materials and Products except those included in Annex NI, or concerning the distribution of heat to multiple premises.

27 *Case concerning Oil Platforms (Islamic Republic of Iran* v. *United States of America)*, 1996 ICJ Rep 803 per Judge Higgins at 810.

28 The term 'Investment' also applies to 'investments or classes of investments designated by a Contracting Party in its Area as "Charter efficiency projects" and so notified to the Secretariat' (Article 1(6), concluding words). At the date of publication no such projects had been notified to the Secretariat.

'Energy Materials and Products' are (by Article 1(4)) those listed in Annex EM of the Treaty (which adopts the harmonised system of the Customs Cooperation Council[29] and the Combined Nomenclature of the European Communities).

The second of the Treaty's Understandings expands on what is meant by 'Economic Activity in the Energy Sector':

> ...
>
> (b) The following activities are illustrative of Economic Activity in the Energy Sector:
>
> (i) prospecting and exploration for, and extraction of, e.g., oil, gas, coal and uranium;
> (ii) construction and operation of power generation facilities, including those powered by wind and other renewable energy sources;
> (iii) land transportation, distribution, storage and supply of Energy Materials and Products, e.g., by way of transmission and distribution grids and pipelines or dedicated rail lines, and construction of facilities for such, including the laying of oil, gas, and coal-slurry pipelines;
> (iv) removal and disposal of wastes from energy related facilities such as power stations, including radioactive wastes from nuclear power stations;
> (v) decommissioning of energy related facilities, including oil rigs, oil refineries and power generating plants;
> (vi) marketing and sale of, and trade in Energy Materials and Products, e.g., retail sales of gasoline; and
> (vii) research, consulting, planning, management and design activities related to the activities mentioned above, including those aimed at Improving Energy Efficiency.

Thus the Treaty is potentially applicable to any 'Investment' (a term whose meaning is considered below) which is associated with an economic activity concerning the exploration, extraction, refining, production, storage, land transport, transmission, distribution, trade, marketing or sale of any of the things listed in Annex EM and not listed in Annex NI, or with an economic activity concerning the distribution of heat to multiple premises.

In broad outline the effect of Annexes EM and NI is what one would expect of an instrument called the *Energy* Charter Treaty: investments associated with an economic activity concerning the exploration, extraction, etc. of nuclear fuels, coal, natural and coal gas, petroleum and

29 Also known as the World Customs Organization.

petroleum products and electrical energy are within the scope of the Treaty; but not investments associated with an economic activity concerning oils used for purposes other than energy, e.g., paints, perfumes etc.

The question arises, however, as to how closely the investment must be 'associated with' an Economic Activity in the Energy Sector. In *AMTO v. Ukraine*[30] a Stockholm Chamber of Commerce arbitral tribunal had to decide whether the ownership of shares in a company whose business was that of a contractor carrying out 'electrical installation, repairs and technical reconstruction or upgrading'[31] at a nuclear power plant was an 'investment associated with an Economic Activity in the Energy Sector'. The tribunal held that:

> the interpretation of the words 'associated with' involves a question of degree, and refers primarily to the factual rather than legal association between the alleged investment and an Economic Activity in the Energy Sector. A mere contractual relationship with an energy producer is insufficient to attract ECT protection where the subject matter of the contract has no functional relationship with the energy sector. The open-textured phrase 'associated with' must be interpreted in accordance with the object and purpose of the ECT, as expressed in Article 2. The associated activity of any alleged investment must be energy related, without itself needing to satisfy the definition in Article 1(5) of an Economic Activity in the Energy Sector.[32]

The tribunal noted that the services provided by the company in which the claimant had its investment directly related to the production of energy and that these services had been provided through multiple contracts over a substantial period of time. In these circumstances the claimant's investment qualified as one 'associated with an Economic Activity in the Energy Sector'.[33]

**The Investment must by its nature qualify as such – Condition (2)(ii)** In international investment law generally, the question of what constitutes an 'investment' arises in various different ways: under national foreign investment laws; under the ICSID Convention; and under bilateral and multilateral investment treaties.[34] What may constitute an investment for

30 Award, 26 March 2008. 31 See the tribunal's finding at paragraph 40.

32 Paragraph 42. 33 Paragraph 43.

34 See, e.g., C., Schreuer, L. Malintoppi, A. Reinisch and A. Sinclair, *The ICSID Convention: A Commentary* (Cambridge University Press, 2nd edn, 2009), pp. 71 ff.; E. Schlemmer 'Investments, Investor, Nationality and Shareholders' in P. Muchlinski, F. Ortino and C. Schreuer (eds.), *The Oxford Handbook of International Investment Law* (Oxford University Press, 2008), pp. 51–69; R. Dolzer and C. Schreuer, *Principles of International*

the purposes of one of these regimes may not necessarily constitute one for another. Thus where a claimant contends that an alleged investment has been the subject of prohibited treatment under a treaty, and seeks to advance this claim by way of arbitration under the ICSID Convention, the claimant must persuade the tribunal both that the alleged investment qualifies as such under the treaty – so as to qualify for protection from the prohibited treatment – and that it qualifies as such under the ICSID Convention – so as to give the Centre jurisdiction to entertain the claim.[35] Each issue ought to be distinctly considered.

However, before any question arises as to whether an alleged 'investment' qualifies as such under the relevant treaty, a tribunal charged with answering this question should, it is suggested, address a prior one: what are the claimant's rights as a matter of the law of the host state; or, in a case where the claimant complains of changes in that law to its detriment, what would those rights have been but for the matters complained of? For a tribunal cannot ask whether the alleged 'investment' falls within the relevant international instrument's definition of an 'investment' without first asking what it consists of (or consisted of) in terms of rights in the host state.

This is primarily a matter to be determined by the law of the host state. As the American–Turkish Claims Commission put it in the *Hoachoozo Palestine Land and Development Co* case:

> In a case in which complaint is made that governmental authorities have confiscated contractual property rights, the preliminary question is one of domestic law as to the rights of the claimant under a contract in the light of the domestic proper law governing the legal effect of the contract.[36]

*Investment Law* (Oxford University Press, 2008), pp. 60–71; C. McLachlan, L. Shore and M. Weiniger, *International Investment Arbitration: Substantive Principles* (Oxford University Press, 2007), pp. 163–96; Douglas, *The International Law of Investment Claims*, pp. 161–232; E. Gaillard, 'Identify or Define? Reflections on the Evolution of the Concept of Investment in ICSID Practice' in C. Binder, U. Kriebaum, A. Reinisch and S. Wittich (eds.), *International Investment Law for the 21st Century: Essays in Honour of Christoph Schreuer* (Oxford University Press, 2009), pp. 403–16.

35 See, e.g., *CSOB* v. *Slovak Republic*, Decision on Jurisdiction, 24 May 1999, at paragraph 68. For more detail on what constitutes an 'investment' under the ICSID Convention, see C. Schreuer *et al.*, *The ICISD Convention: A Commentary*, pp. 71 ff.

36 F. Nielsen, *American–Turkish Claims Settlement under the Agreement of 24 December 1923* (Washington: US Department of State, 1937), p. 254, cited in Z. Douglas, 'The Hybrid Foundations of Investment Treaty Arbitration' (2004) 74 *British Yearbook of International Law* 151 at 195 (himself citing K. Lipstein, 'Conflict of Laws before International Tribunals (ii)' (1949) 29 *Transactions of the Grotius Society* 51, 54). See now Douglas, *The International Law of Investment Claims*, p. 41.

As Douglas argues, there is

> a clear distinction between the law applicable to the investment contract, . . . municipal law, and the law applicable to an assessment of whether the *conduct* of the host state [of which the claimant complains] is violative of the treaty standards, . . . the treaty and international law.[37]

Thus, it is submitted, in determining whether the claimant has made an 'investment' a tribunal ought to ask itself two distinct questions: (i) by virtue of the matters said to constitute an investment, what rights, considered as a matter of the law of the host state, does the claimant have, or did the claimant have but for the events complained of;[38] (ii) do those rights constitute an 'investment' under the terms of the relevant international instrument?

In a simple case, the first question may be shortly answered, or indeed overlooked altogether if no point is taken about it by the respondent.[39] For where the content of the claimant's rights under, for example, the relevant contract appears clear, a tribunal may have little difficulty taking the contract at face value rather than investigating whether it might have some different meaning under the relevant domestic law. Indeed, where a host state contends that an apparently clear agreement does not give the claimant the rights which one might expect from its terms, the tribunal is likely to scrutinise this contention closely, recognising that 'the principle *pacta sunt servanda* is, in HLA Hart's provocative phrase, "the minimum content of Natural Law"'.[40]

In any more complex case, however, it is submitted that the first task of the tribunal is to ascertain the claimant's rights as a matter of the law of the host state. Only then is it appropriate to turn to the second

37 Douglas, 'The Hybrid Foundations of Investment Treaty Arbitration', 196 (emphasis in original). See also A. Newcombe and L. Paradell, *Law and Practice of Investment Treaties: Standards of Treatment* (Alphen aan den Rijn: Kluwer Law International, 2009), pp. 92–8.

38 It may be, of course, that the parties have agreed that some law other than the law of the host state should govern the contract. If such a choice of law is recognised by the law of the host state, then plainly the claimant's rights will be those under the chosen law.

39 Douglas, *The International Law of Investment Claims*, pp. 201–12, shows that the question of the claimant's rights as a matter of the law of the host state has often been overlooked in cases which are far from simple. See also Z. Douglas, 'Nothing if Not Critical for Investment Treaty Arbitration: *Occidental*, *Eureko* and *Methanex*' (2006) 22 *Arbitration International* 27.

40 O. Spiermann, 'Applicable Law' in P. Muchlinski, F. Ortino and C. Schreuer, *The Oxford Handbook of International Investment Law* (Oxford University Press, 2008) p. 94, citing H. L. A. Hart, *The Concept of Law* (Oxford University Press, 2nd edn, 1994), p. 193.

question, namely whether those rights may properly be characterised as an 'investment' within the meaning of the relevant international instrument. This is a question of international law.

The above analysis might at first blush be thought to be undermined, in the case of a claim under the Energy Charter Treaty, by its Article 26(6), which provides that the tribunal 'shall decide the issues in dispute in accordance with this Treaty and applicable rules and principles of international law'.

Does this mean that all questions, including those as to the nature and extent of the rights said to constitute the 'Investment', fall to be determined by international, rather than domestic, law? It is submitted not. The rule or principle that a tribunal must first determine as a matter of national law what the claimant's rights are (or were until the matters complained of) is itself an applicable rule or principle of international law. And an approach which begins by analysing the content of the alleged 'Investment' under the law of the host state is entirely 'in accordance with' the ECT since (as will be discussed below) the ECT requires the tribunal to analyse whether what the claimant alleges to be an 'Investment' constitutes an 'asset' as defined in Article 1(6), a question which cannot sensibly be answered without reference to the law of the host state.

A qualification to the analysis discussed above is illustrated by the decision in *Kardassopoulos* v. *Georgia*.[41] The claimant's alleged investment consisted of a concession granted by a Georgian state-owned enterprise. Georgia challenged the tribunal's jurisdiction on the ground (*inter alia*) that the state-owned enterprise had acted outside the scope of its powers in granting the concession and that consequently the concession was void *ab initio* as a matter of Georgian law. Hence, Georgia argued, the claimant had no 'Investment' capable of protection.[42] The tribunal rejected this argument, essentially on two grounds. First, if one read the treaty purposively, even if a Georgian court would find the concession void as a matter of Georgian law, this did not deprive the concession of its quality as an 'investment' as a matter of international law when the reason for that invalidity was the actions of the Georgian state-owned enterprise, not the investor.[43] Second, the state-owned enterprise had represented that

41 Decision on Jurisdiction, 6 July 2007. The claim was brought under both the ECT and the Greece–Georgia BIT.

42 See paragraphs 42–57.

43 Paragraphs 174–84. The tribunal deals in this part of its decision solely with the claim under the BIT, but it is submitted that exactly the same is true of the claim under the ECT.

the concession was valid and the investor had reasonably relied on this. Since, by the principle codified in the Articles on Responsibility of States for Internationally Wrongful Acts,[44] the representation was attributable to Georgia regardless of any excess of authority by the state-owned enterprise in making it, Georgia was estopped from denying the concession's validity. The tribunal thus rightly recognised that the principle of looking first at the claimant's rights in the law of the host state may have to give way when those rights have been impaired at the outset by the state's own actions.

Article 1(6) of the ECT provides that '"Investment" means every kind of asset, owned or controlled directly or indirectly by an Investor'. Article 1(6) then lists various assets which the definition 'includes':

> (a) tangible and intangible, and movable and immovable, property, and any property rights such as leases, mortgages, liens, and pledges;
> (b) a company or business enterprise, or shares, stock, or other forms of equity participation in a company or business enterprise, and bonds and other debt of a company or business enterprise;
> (c) claims to money and claims to performance pursuant to contract having an economic value and associated with an Investment;
> (d) Intellectual Property [which, by Article 1(12), 'includes copyrights and related rights, trademarks, geographical indications, industrial designs, patents, layout designs of integrated circuits and the protection of undisclosed information'];
> (e) Returns [defined in Article 1(9) as 'the amounts derived from or associated with an Investment, irrespective of the form in which they are paid, including profits, dividends, interest, capital gains, royalty payments, management, technical assistance or other fees and payments in kind'];
> (f) any right conferred by law or contract or by virtue of any licences and permits granted pursuant to law to undertake any Economic Activity in the Energy Sector [i.e. to undertake any economic activity concerning the exploration, extraction, refining, production, storage, land transport, transmission, distribution, trade, marketing, or sale of Energy Materials and Products except those included in Annex NI, or concerning the distribution of heat to multiple premises: see Article 1(5)].

Article 1(6) further provides that: 'A change in the form in which assets are invested does not affect their character as investments.'

44 GA res. 56/83 (2002), Annex, Article 7.

Two questions thus arise: first, what constitutes being 'owned or controlled directly or indirectly'; second, what amounts to an 'Investment'.

The first question is the subject of the third of the 'Understandings' adopted by the parties to the Treaty:

> For greater clarity as to whether an Investment made in the Area of one Contracting Party is controlled, directly or indirectly, by an Investor of any other Contracting Party, control of an Investment means control in fact, determined after an examination of the actual circumstances in each situation. In any such examination, all relevant factors should be considered, including the Investor's
>
> (a) financial interest, including equity interest, in the Investment;
> (b) ability to exercise substantial influence over the management and operation of the Investment; and
> (c) ability to exercise substantial influence over the selection of members of the board of directors or any other managing body.
>
> Where there is doubt as to whether an Investor controls, directly or indirectly, an Investment, an Investor claiming such control has the burden of proof that such control exists.

This is largely self-explanatory. The reference to 'doubt' in the final sentence must refer, it is suggested, to the position either where the respondent has denied that the claimant does control the Investment or where the tribunal of its own motion has taken the point that the claimant's control is not clear. In either case the burden lies on the claimant to prove control.

The Treaty, in common with many BITs,[45] seeks to protect not only the interests of an investor whose investment is held directly but the interests of one who holds it through a series of shareholdings etc.[46] Moreover, by including in the definition of 'Investment' 'shares, stock, or other forms of equity participation in a company or business enterprise', the Treaty, again like many BITs,[47] allows for the possibility that a *minority* shareholder might advance a claim in respect of a company incorporated in the host state, towards which the host state has allegedly behaved in breach of Part III of the Treaty. This imports into ECT arbitration the same conceptual difficulties which bedevil such claims in investment arbitration generally.

45 See, e.g., the long list of cases cited in Dolzer and Schreuer, *Principles of International Investment Law*, p. 57, n. 77.

46 See *Kardassopoulos* v. *Georgia*, Decision on Jurisdiction, 6 July 2007, paragraphs 121–4.

47 See, e.g., *Genin* v. *Estonia*, Award, 25 June 2001; *AAPL* v. *Sri Lanka*, Award, 27 June 1990; *CMS* v. *Argentina*, Decision on Jurisdiction, 17 July 2003; *GAMI* v. *Mexico*, Award, 15 November 2004.

In particular, what, if anything, shields a host state from a series of treaty claims by different shareholders in the same company; and what ought to be the consequence for shareholders' treaty claims of steps which may be taken, or ought to be taken, by the locally-incorporated company by means of local litigation or arbitration of the dispute or issues related to it? It is beyond the scope of this work to tackle this issue save to note that international investment law generally is very far from working out a principled approach to the problems which arise.[48]

As to the question of what constitutes an 'Investment', in defining the term in the way it does, the ECT follows the approach and much of the wording of a number of bilateral investment treaties.[49] As with such treaties, the list of assets may be broadly said to include: (i) traditional property rights, (ii) participation in companies, (iii) money claims and rights to performance, (iv) intellectual and industrial property rights and (v) concession or similar rights.

However, it is not altogether clear how widely the drafters of the ECT intended the concept of 'Investment' to stretch. The drafting of Article 1(6), as with the other instruments which it resembles, is somewhat obscure.[50] The expression 'every kind of asset', which is what 'Investment' is said to 'mean', is wide enough to denote almost any legal right enjoyed as a result of some obligation owed by a subject of a host state. And the non-exclusive list of assets included within the definition of 'Investment' is one which 'encompass[es] virtually any right, property or interest in money or money's worth'.[51] Many such rights could be of a nature quite unlike anything which in ordinary language might be regarded as an investment. The list is much more broadly drawn than (for example) the NAFTA's Article 1139,[52] with its focus on 'enterprises' and the commitment of capital; and there is no equivalent of the NAFTA's stipulation that 'investment does not mean [*inter alia*] . . . claims to money that arise solely from . . . commercial contracts for the sale of goods or

48 For perhaps the most comprehensive attempt to date to impose some order on this area, see Douglas, *The International Law of Investment Claims*, pp. 363–457.

49 See, e.g., United Kingdom Model BIT (2005/6), Article 1; Germany Model BIT (2005), Article 1; Netherlands Model BIT (1997), Article 1; France Model BIT (2006), Article 1 ('*Le terme "investissement" désigne tous les avoirs, tels que les biens, droits et intérêts de toutes natures et, plus particulièrement mais non exclusivement . . .* ').

50 See A. Turinov, '"Investment" and "Investor" in Energy Charter Treaty Arbitration: Uncertain Jurisdiction', (2009) 26 *Journal of International Arbitration* 1.

51 *Plama Consortium* v. *Bulgaria*, Decision on Jurisdiction, 8 February 2005, paragraph 125.

52 See North American Free Trade Agreement, Part Five: Investment, Services and Related Matters, Chapter 11: Investment, Article 1139.

services . . . or . . . the extension of credit in connection with a commercial transaction . . . '. Neither is there anything akin to the requirement in the United States Model BIT (2004) that the alleged investment must have 'the characteristics of an investment'.[53] Indeed, nowhere in the principal part of the definition of 'Investment' (which in the English text is given its initial capital as a defined term, and should therefore take its meaning from the definition) does the word 'investment' actually appear.[54]

It is possible to argue from this that almost any right enjoyed by a foreign claimant against a person in a host state amounts to the defined term 'Investment', irrespective of whether it amounts to anything ordinarily denoted by the word 'investment'.

Such an argument is not without support in the cases. An example is the decision of the ad hoc Annulment Committee in *Malaysian Historical Salvors Sdn Bhd* v. *Malaysia*.[55] Here, the claimant contracted with the government of Malaysia to salvage a ship. The claimant's complaint, which it sought to advance before a sole arbitrator under the ICSID Convention, was of a breach of the guarantees contained in the United Kingdom–Malaysia BIT, namely an alleged denial of justice by the Malaysian courts in certain litigation concerning the contract.[56] The arbitrator declined jurisdiction on the ground that there had been no investment within the meaning of Article 25(1) of the ICSID Convention. The focus of the Annulment Committee's attention was thus on this issue.[57] But the Annulment Committee's decision as to whether there was an investment *within the terms of the BIT* is also notable. After reciting the relevant parts of the BIT, which were in similar terms to the provisions of the ECT set out above,[58] the Committee stated that:

> The Contract . . . is one of a *kind of asset*; what is precisely at issue between the Government and the [claimant] is a *claim to money and to performance under a contract having financial value*; the contract involves *intellectual property rights*; and the right granted to salvage may be treated as a *business*

53 United States Model BIT (2004), Article 1. See also Norway Model BIT (2007), Article 2. Moreover, Dolzer and Schreuer, *Principles of International Investment Law*, point out at p. 63, n. 108, that the draft Multilateral Agreement on Investments (MAI) would have been accompanied by 'an interpretative note . . . to indicate that, in order to qualify as an investment under the MAI, an asset must have had the characteristics of an investment . . . '

54 The technique of capitalising the first letter of defined terms, common in commercial contracts in the English language, is adopted only in the English text of the Treaty.

55 Decision on Annulment, 16 April 2009.

56 Sole Arbitrator's Award on Jurisdiction, 10 May 2007, paragraph 16.

57 See also below, p. 58.

58 United Kingdom–Malaysia BIT, Article 1(1)(a).

> *concession conferred under contract.* It follows that, by the terms of the [BIT], and for its purposes, the Contract is an investment. There is no room for another conclusion.[59]

There was no discussion in this context as to whether the claimant's contract with the Government had the characteristics of an investment, or as to what these characteristics might be: rather, the tribunal appears to have regarded it as clear that if the contract could be fitted into any of the sub-paragraphs of the BIT's definition of investment this was sufficient to make it an investment for the purposes of the BIT. The same holds true, it can be argued, for the ECT. As will be seen, reasoning similar to this prevailed in the ECT case of *Petrobart* v. *Kyrgyz Republic*,[60] discussed below.

However, other aspects of the drafting point the other way. 'Investment' may be a defined term for the purposes of the Treaty but it is surely unlikely that the draftsman intended thereby to divest the word of any sense of its more widely understood meaning.[61] As the tribunal in *Romak SA* v. *Uzbekistan* said of the Switzerland–Uzbekistan BIT, 'The term "investment" has a meaning in itself that cannot be ignored . . .'.[62] That this is so under the ECT is highlighted, at least in the English text, by the last two paragraphs of Article 1(6), which use the word 'Investment' (the initial capital denoting its status as a defined term) and the word 'investment' interchangeably. So does Article 10(12), which requires contracting parties to provide 'effective means for the assertion of claims and the enforcement of rights with respect to Investments, investment agreements, and investment authorizations'.[63]

That the meaning of 'Investment' ought to bear some relation to the ordinary meaning of that word is also apparent from Article 10(1), the Treaty's central provision on the protection of 'Investments'. For Article 10(1) requires parties (*inter alia*) to 'encourage and create stable, equitable, favourable and transparent conditions for Investors . . . to make Investments'. If 'Investment' literally *meant* 'asset' (as Article 1(6) says it does), this provision would make no sense as a matter of language.

59 Paragraphs 60–1 (emphasis added).
60 Award, 29 March 2005.
61 Though of course this would be theoretically possible. A treaty could provide that 'For the purposes of this treaty, "Black" means white' and, for the purposes of the treaty, it would. See, on the meanings of words, *Investors' Compensation Scheme Ltd* v. *West Bromwich Building Society* [1998] 1 WLR 896 per Lord Hoffmann at 914E.
62 Award, 26 November 2009, paragraph 180.
63 See also Article 14(6).

The third of the 'Understandings' with respect to the Treaty, discussed above,[64] also gives a strong clue as to what the Contracting Parties ought to be taken to have had in mind by 'Investment'. The notion of the 'management and operation of the Investment' and the ability to exercise 'influence over' the 'managing body' of the Investment is quite inconsistent with an Investment's consisting of no more than '... any right, property or interest in money or money's worth'.

One is thus driven to consider the broader meaning of 'investment'. In international investment arbitration generally, this question has most often arisen in the context of Article 25(1) of the ICSID Convention, which, it will be recalled, confers jurisdiction on the International Centre for Settlement of Investment Disputes to determine 'any legal dispute arising directly out of an investment' but leaves the term 'investment' undefined. The jurisprudence has largely settled on an understanding that the question whether a claimant has made an investment ought to be answered by reference to what are variously referred to as the '*Fedax* criteria'[65] and the '*Salini* test'.[66] However described, the broad effect of this understanding is that the claimant who has made an 'investment' will (or will usually) be able to demonstrate (i) a significant commitment of resources, in money, work, know-how or otherwise, to the relevant project, (ii) a 'certain duration' of that commitment (which in this context means commitment for a significant, rather than necessarily fixed or particularly long, period) and (iii) a sharing of the risk.[67] It is generally, though not exclusively, accepted that these features are not jurisdictional hurdles which must each be surmounted but, rather, typical characteristics of investments.[68]

64 P. 53.

65 McLachlan *et al.*, *International Investment Arbitration: Substantive Principles*, paragraph 6.16, after *Fedax NV* v. *Venezuela*, Decision on Jurisdiction, 11 July 1997.

66 Dolzer and Schreuer, *Principles of International Investment Law*, p. 68; Douglas, *The International Law of Investment Claims*, p. 198, after *Salini Costruttori and Italstrade* v. *Morocco*, Decision on Jurisdiction, 23 July 2001, paragraph 52.

67 Douglas, *The International Law of Investment Claims*, puts it more simply: his criteria are the commitment of resources to the economy of the host state entailing the assumption of risk in the expectation of a commercial return (p. 189 ff). This 'may well encapsulate an emerging synthesis': *Pantechniki SA Contractors & Engineers* v. *Albania*, Award, 28 July 2009, paragraph 36.

68 See, e.g., *Biwater Gauff (Tanzania) Ltd* v. *Tanzania*, Award, 24 July 2008; *Malaysian Historical Salvors Sdn Bhd* v. *Malaysia*, Decision on Annulment, 16 April 2009. For the contrary view see, e.g., *Kardassopoulos* v. *Georgia*, Decision on Jurisdiction, 6 July 2007, paragraph 119; *Mitchell* v. *Congo*, Decision on Annulment, 1 November 2006 (discussed below); and the Dissenting Opinion of Judge Shahabuddeen in *Malaysian Historical Salvors Sdn Bhd* v. *Malaysia*, Decision on Annulment.

A further feature (or, depending on one's view, hurdle) may be that the alleged investment contributes to the development of the host state. In *Mitchell* v. *Congo*,[69] an ICSID ad hoc Committee annulled the decision of an ICSID tribunal that the claimant had, by founding a law firm in the Congo, made an investment there, on the ground that the tribunal had made no finding of any contribution to the development of the Congo. On the other hand, in *LESI and ASTALDI* v. *Algeria*,[70] the tribunal expressly rejected the need to show a contribution to the host state's development, 'a condition . . . difficult to establish and implicitly covered by the three other elements'.[71] That the criterion might be difficult to establish was recognised by the ad hoc Committee in *Mitchell*, which suggested in consequence a markedly relaxed approach to the test:

> [the] contribution [need not] always be sizable or successful; and, of course, . . . tribunals do not have to evaluate the real contribution of the operation in question. It suffices for the operation to contribute in one way or another to the economic development of the host State, and this concept of economic development is, in any event, extremely broad but also variable depending on the case.[72]

It may be doubted whether a test of such vagueness is worth retaining at all.[73]

The suggestion that a putative investment will not qualify as such unless it can be shown to contribute to the development of the host state was also accepted by the sole arbitrator in *Malaysian Historical Salvors Sdn Bhd* v. *Malaysia*.[74] However, it was rejected (by a majority) by the ad hoc Annulment Committee.[75]

Schreuer has suggested that one of the objects stated in the Preamble to the ICSID Convention, namely 'the need for international co-operation for economic development and the role of private international investment therein', might 'indicate that there should be some positive impact on development [in order for an alleged investment to qualify as such under that Convention]'.[76] One could perhaps make a similar argument about the ECT. Development is not, in express terms, given as one of

69 Decision on Annulment, 1 November 2006. 70 Decision on Jurisdiction, 12 July 2006.

71 At paragraph 72(iv) (authors' translation from the French). 72 At paragraph 33.

73 Douglas, *The International Law of Investment Claims*, makes the same point at p. 202: 'Such an elastic concept is hardly conducive of legal certainty . . . '.

74 Award on Jurisdiction, 10 May 2007. 75 Decision on Annulment, 16 April 2009.

76 C. Schreuer, *The ICSID Convention: A Commentary* (Cambridge University Press, 2001), p. 125.

the Treaty's purposes, but the Preamble does refer to the parties' wish 'to catalyse economic growth by means of measures to liberalize investment and trade in energy',[77] from which it might be argued that a putative investment must be shown to promote (or, at least, to 'catalyse') economic growth. However, whether the reference is to development or to growth, it is submitted that the argument is logically unsound.[78] It simply does not follow from the fact that a treaty seeks, for a particular purpose, to protect a particular category of interest that it only protects interests which can be specifically proved to advance that purpose. It is no more logical than arguing that the right to move capital freely within the EU may only be exercised if in the particular case the movement can be proved to promote the 'constant improvements of the living and working conditions of [European] peoples' which the right was created in order to further.[79]

A further reason why the criterion of promotion of development ought to play no part in the definition of 'Investment' under the Energy Charter Treaty is that the Treaty is a multilateral one, many of whose contracting parties are states which already have a high level of economic development. Disputes which may fall to be determined under Article 26 will not necessarily conform to the pattern, familiar in international investment law generally, of developed-state investor versus developing state. While it may perhaps be meaningful to ask (say) whether an Italian-owned thermal energy project contributes to the development of Mongolia,[80] it is distinctly problematic to have to ask whether a Swedish-owned project to build a coal-fired power station contributes to the development of the Federal Republic of Germany.[81]

77 Preamble, fifth recital.

78 See *Saluka Investments BV* v. *Czech Republic*, Partial Award, 17 March 2006, paragraph 300, quoted above at p. 31.

79 See third recital and Article 63 of the Treaty on the Functioning of the European Union. It is notable that the second edition of *The ICSID Convention: A Commentary* (Cambridge University Press, 2009) does not repeat the suggestion that a positive impact on the host state's development might be a *sine qua non* of the existence of an investment. Rather, the authors state (at p. 134) that: 'The reference in the Convention's Preamble indicates that economic development is among the Convention's object and purpose [sic]. This would support the proposition that an international transaction that is designed to promote the host state's development enjoys the presumption of being an investment. But it does not follow that an activity does not obviously contribute to economic development must be excluded from the Convention's protection.'

80 See *Alstom Power Italia SpA, Alstom SpA* v. *Mongolia* (ICSID Case no. ARB/04/10) (settled 13 March 2003).

81 See *Vattenfall AB* v. *Germany* (ICSID Case No. ARB/09/6) (claim registered 17 April, 2009).

For these reasons, it is submitted that the better view, certainly so far as the ECT is concerned, is that there is no need to consider whether the alleged 'Investment' contributes to the economic development of the host state.[82]

In this context, the decision of the Stockholm Chamber of Commerce tribunal in *Petrobart* v. *Kyrgyz Republic*[83] is a striking one. The claimant, a British company,[84] had agreed to sell to a Kyrgyz state-owned company, KGM, a quantity of gas condensate in instalments over a period of a year. The claimant began delivering the condensate but KGM defaulted after paying only a few invoices. The claimant obtained judgment against KGM in the Kyrgyz courts. The Vice-Prime Minister personally intervened in the court process by writing a letter to the judge seeking a stay of the enforcement of the judgment. The government enacted a scheme by which KGM's assets became the property of a separate company. KGM was declared bankrupt during the stay of execution and the claimant was left with nothing. The merits were plainly on the claimant's side.

The claimant's first attempt to obtain redress was through UNCITRAL arbitration under the Law of the Kyrgyz Republic on Foreign Investments. However, the UNCITRAL tribunal rejected this claim, holding that the claimant had made no investment under the terms of that law. Notably, the UNCITRAL tribunal stated that:

> 'Foreign investment' is mostly defined as a transfer of tangible or intangible property from one country to another for the purpose of use in that country with a view to generating profit, or at least wealth, under the control of the owner of the property. Such transfers are to be distinguished from the much more frequent export transactions where goods are sold by manufacturers, or owners, in one State to traders or users in another State. Foreign investment involves a more permanent relationship between

82 C. Schreuer, 'Commentary on the ICSID Convention', (1996) 11 *ICSID Review – Foreign Investment Law Journal* 316 had suggested a further criterion, namely 'a certain regularity of profit and return', and this was identified by the tribunal in *Fedax NV* v. *Venezuela*, Decision on Jurisdiction, 11 July 1997 as another of the 'basic features of an investment'. However, this criterion did not appear in *Salini Costruttori and Italstrade* v. *Morocco*, Decision on Jurisdiction, 23 July 2001, and does not now appear to be advocated by Schreuer: see Dolzer and Schreuer, *Principles of International Investment Law*, p. 68. It is submitted that this criterion is not helpful: whilst regularity of returns might suggest the existence of an investment, the absence of such regularity is by no means decisive the other way.

83 Award, 29 March 2005.

84 In fact, a company incorporated in Gibraltar. This aspect of the case is discussed below at pp. 69–70.

> the foreign investor and the host State than is involved in the transitory international sales transaction. [The contract between the claimant and KGM] falls unquestionably into the latter category.[85]

The claimant next instituted arbitration under the ECT. The question was therefore whether the claimant had made an 'Investment' within the meaning of Article 1(6). The Stockholm Chamber of Commerce tribunal acknowledged that the contract 'did not involve any transfer of money or property as capital in a business in the Kyrgyz Republic but was a sales contract. It concerned the sale of goods at an agreed price.'[86] (There had been discussions about doing further business in the future but nothing had come of this.) The tribunal put the question in this way: 'whether [the claimant]'s right under the Contract to payment for goods delivered under the Contract was an asset and constituted an investment under the Treaty'.[87]

In its reasoning the tribunal made no mention of the *Salini/Fedax* criteria discussed above.[88] Rather, it focused on Article 1(6)(c) and Article 1(6)(f). Article 1(6)(c), it will be recalled, includes within the definition of Investment 'claims to money . . . associated with an Investment'.[89] The tribunal thought that it was:

> faced with the logical problem that the term 'Investment' is not only the term to be defined but is also used as one of the terms by which 'Investment' is defined. This means [the tribunal stated] that the definition is in reality a circular one which raises a logical problem and creates some doubt about the correct interpretation.

The tribunal therefore rested its decision on Article 1(6)(f): 'any right conferred by law or contract . . . to undertake any Economic Activity in the Energy Sector'. By Article 1(5), Economic Activity in the Energy Sector included an economic activity concerning the sale of Energy Materials and

85 Quoted at p. 5 of the Stockholm Chamber of Commerce tribunal's Award.

86 Award, p. 69. 87 Award, p. 71. 88 At pp. 57–60.

89 Article 1(6)(c), in full, refers to 'claims to money and claims to performance pursuant to contract having an economic value and associated with an Investment'. The tribunal, which appears only to have looked at the English text, was in some doubt as to what governed what in this sentence, and in particular as to whether a mere claim to money was free-standing or (as the tribunal assumed but did not decide) had to be associated with an Investment, or made pursuant to a contract having an economic value and associated with an Investment. The other (by Article 50, equally authentic) texts make clear that a mere claim to money is not free-standing; the draftsmen differ as a matter of grammar, however, as to whether it is the contract that must have economic value and be associated with an investment (as the French and Russian texts have it) or the claims themselves (as the German, Italian and Spanish texts have it).

Products. The gas condensate was such a Product. 'Thus', the tribunal concluded without further elucidation:

> a right conferred by contract to undertake an economic activity concerning the sale of gas condensate is an investment according to the Treaty. This must also include the right to be paid for such a sale. The Arbitral Tribunal thus concludes on this point that Petrobart was an investor having an investment in the Kyrgyz Republic . . . [90]

However, this reasoning is unconvincing for at least four reasons. First, it overlooks the fact that, for the reasons stated above,[91] the meaning of 'Investment' under the Treaty cannot be ascertained simply by reference to the list at Article 1(6)(a)–(f) without reference to the way in which the notion of investment has been understood in international investment arbitration more generally (and it is plain that a mere contract of sale would not be regarded as an investment in this wider context).

Second, even if one ignores the wider context, the tribunal's decision misreads Article 1(6)(f). The right referred to in Article 1(6)(f) is (if one reads into it Article 1(5)'s definition of 'Economic Activity in the Energy Sector') 'the right . . . to undertake an [economic activity concerning the exploration, extraction . . . [etc.], sale of Energy Materials and Products . . . ]'. The clear sense is of a right to at least some degree of continuous engagement in exploration, extraction, sale, etc. The debt which arose under the one-off sales contract between Petrobart and KGM was not, on any sensible construction, such a right.

Third, Article 1(6) contains two sub-paragraphs which deal with the status of mere claims to money much more specifically than subparagraph (f). Subparagraph (c), which was discussed by the tribunal but dismissed as circular, is in fact better read as a limiting provision: claims to money can amount to Investments only if they, or the contract under which they are made,[92] have an economic value and are associated with an Investment, which here must (to avoid circularity) mean an Investment as defined apart from this paragraph. Subparagraph (e), which was not mentioned by the tribunal, includes 'Returns' within the definition of Investment. By Article 1(9), 'Returns'

> means the amounts derived from or associated with an Investment, irrespective of the form in which they are paid, including profits, dividends, interest, capital gains, royalty payments, management, technical assistance or other fees and payments in kind.

90 At p. 72. 91 P. 56.

92 See n. 89 above as to the slight difference between the different language versions of the Treaty.

So again a claim to money is covered, provided that it derives from or is associated with an Investment, which again (to avoid circularity) must be understood as meaning Investment defined otherwise than by reference to this paragraph. It is submitted that on the conventional principle *generalia specialibus non derogant* the tribunal ought to have regarded these specific provisions as dealing with the position in preference to the more general provision in subparagraph (f).

Fourth, the tribunal failed to address the requirement of Article 26 that the putative Investment be one 'in the Area of' the Kyrgyz Republic. This aspect of the decision is dealt with below in the discussion of condition (4).

The Kyrgyz Republic appealed against the tribunal's decision to the Svea Court of Appeal on the ground (*inter alia*) that the award was not covered by a valid arbitration agreement because, contrary to the tribunal's finding, the claimant had not made an Investment. The Court heard evidence from Professor Adnan Amkhan, formerly Head of the Legal Affairs Department of the Energy Charter Secretariat, Brussels (2000–04), who had also given expert evidence in support of the claimant's case to the tribunal.[93] The Court of Appeal dismissed the appeal on this issue. Its reasoning, in full, was that:

> It follows from the investigation that the term investment can have different meanings in different international contexts. The meaning of the term as defined in the ECT has a wide scope of application. It is evident from the testimony given by Adnan Amkhan that when the ECT was negotiated it was an explicit intention to give investment a broad application. The Court of Appeal finds, as well as the Arbitral Tribunal, that the definitions in Article 1(6) and 1(5) in the ECT must be interpreted as including the investment made by Petrobart.[94]

It is unfortunate that the Court of Appeal did not take the opportunity to deliver a fully reasoned defence of its and the tribunal's view on this issue.[95]

93 See http://ita.law.uvic.ca/documents/Petrobart-AmkhanOpinionOctober2004.pdf (accessed July 2009).

94 Judgment of the Svea Court of Appeal, 19 January 2007; unofficial translation in (2007) 4/5 *Transnational Dispute Management*.

95 Douglas, *The International Law of Investment Claims*, strikingly describes the Svea Court of Appeal, in its decision in *Czech Republic* v. *CME Czech Republic BV* (15 May 2003), as standing 'as close as possible to the precipice of judicial abdication' (p. 69). Arguably in *Petrobart* the Court took a step forward.

### (iii) The Investment must be in the Area of the Contracting Party – Condition (3)

Article 1(10) defines what is meant in this context by 'Area':

> 'Area' means with respect to a state that is a Contracting Party:
>
> (a) the territory under its sovereignty, it being understood that territory includes land, internal waters and the territorial sea; and
> (b) subject to and in accordance with the international law of the sea: the sea, sea-bed and its subsoil with regard to which that Contracting Party exercises sovereign rights and jurisdiction.

It ought in most cases to be relatively easy to determine whether or not this condition for jurisdiction is met.[96]

Moreover, a tribunal which addresses this condition expressly is unlikely to confuse an Investment with some more transitory interaction which does not qualify as such: the notion of making an Investment 'in' a particular territory is consistent with the commitment of resources and sharing of risk for a certain duration (i.e., the *Salini/Fedax* criteria, discussed above).[97] As mentioned above, this is a further respect in which the decision of the tribunal (and of the Svea Court of Appeal which upheld the decision) in *Petrobart* v. *Kyrgyz Republic*[98] is questionable. Had the tribunal asked itself what exactly the claimant had invested 'in' the Kyrgyz Republic merely by agreeing to sell gas condensate to KGM, it might have reached a different conclusion. And as Douglas has pointed out, the second of the Treaty's Understandings, which fleshes out the meaning of Economic Activity in the Energy Sector,[99] is clearly predicated on the establishment by the Investor of some sort of presence in the host state.[100]

### (iv) The claimant must be an Investor of a Contracting Party – Condition (4)

Article 1(7) defines what is meant by an 'Investor of a Contracting Party'.

96 The only difficulties likely to arise are with regard to the extent of states' maritime jurisdiction, but even there states are unlikely to seek to resile from claims they have made elsewhere, e.g. in national legislation.

97 Pp. 57ff. 98 Award, 29 March 2005. 99 See above, p. 47.

100 Douglas, *The International Law of Investment Claims*, p. 194.

'Investor' means:

(a) with respect to a Contracting Party:
  (i) a natural person having the citizenship or nationality of or who is permanently residing in that Contracting Party in accordance with its applicable law;
  (ii) a company or other organization organized in accordance with the law applicable in that Contracting Party.

Whether or not this condition is met is a question of fact and of the law of the Contracting Party of which the claimant claims to be a national or in which he claims to reside, or in which (in the case of a company or other organisation) it is organised.

Issues can arise, however, when an alleged Investor holds two (or more) nationalities. This is most likely to arise with regard to individuals (natural persons), who form a small minority of claimants under investment treaties. Two situations are possible: (i) the Investor has the nationality of a Contracting Party to the ECT and of a state which is not a party to the Treaty; or (ii) the Investor has the nationality of the respondent state and of another ECT Contracting Party. The wording of Article 1(7) seems to cater for the first eventuality, as it permits a natural person who is merely permanently and lawfully resident in the territory of a Contracting Party (that is, whatever his or her nationality) to be treated, for the purposes of Article 26, as a national of that Contracting Party. Given this, applying the principle, it is difficult to see why a person holding the nationality of one Contracting Party should be disqualified from bringing a claim on the ground that he or she is a national of a state not party to the ECT. All that would appear to be required is that the Investor's Contracting Party nationality is valid and effective; it need not be his or her dominant nationality.[101] The ECT, however, says nothing about the second eventuality, so resort needs to be had to customary international law, which provides that it is the claimant's dominant nationality which is determinative.[102] It should be noted, however, that Article 25 of the ICSID Convention imposes its own criteria and prohibits claims by dual nationals against both of their states of nationality.[103]

101 See *Olguín* v. *Paraguay*, Award, 26 July 2001, paragraphs 61–2. The claimant had both Peruvian and US nationality and was domiciled in the US. Nevertheless, he was permitted to claim under the Peru–Paraguay BIT.

102 See Case No. A/18 (1984) 5 Iran–US Cl Trib Rep 251 (Full Tribunal, Iran–US Claims Tribunal).

103 Article 25(2)(a) of the ICSID Convention. See also *Champion Trading Company* v. *Egypt*, Decision on Jurisdiction, 21 October 2003, pp. 11–17.

### (v) The events with which the claim is concerned must have occurred at a date such as to give the tribunal jurisdiction – Condition (5)

The temporal limitations on the right to arbitration under Article 26 are contained within the definition of 'Investment' in Article 1(6), as follows:

> the term 'Investment' includes all investments, whether existing at or made after the later of the date of entry into force of this Treaty for the Contracting Party of the Investor making the investment and that for the Contracting Party in the Area of which the investment is made (hereinafter referred to as the 'Effective Date') provided that the Treaty shall only apply to matters affecting such investments after the Effective Date.

Entry into force is dealt with in Article 44:

> (1) This Treaty shall enter into force on the ninetieth day after the date of deposit of the thirtieth instrument of ratification, acceptance or approval thereof, or of accession thereto, by a state or Regional Economic Integration Organization which is a signatory to the Charter as of 16 June 1995.
>
> (2) For each state or Regional Economic Integration Organization which ratifies, accepts or approves this Treaty or accedes thereto after the deposit of the thirtieth instrument of ratification, acceptance or approval, it shall enter into force on the ninetieth day after the date of deposit by such state or Regional Economic Integration Organization of its instrument of ratification, acceptance, approval or accession.

The ninetieth day after the deposit of the thirtieth instrument of ratification fell on 16 April 1998 and the Treaty accordingly entered into force on that date for all the states and organisations which had ratified it up to that point.

For states which ratified the Treaty later, it entered into force ninety days after ratification in accordance with Article 44(2). As Article 1(6) makes clear, once in force the Treaty applies to conduct of states concerning Investments whenever made (although the tribunal's jurisdiction to determine a dispute concerning a particular Investment cannot, of course, extend to events which occurred before the claimant made the Investment[104]).

104 *AMTO* v. *Ukraine*, Award, 26 March 2008, paragraph 48.

### 3. Provisional application[105]

The application of conditions (4) and (5) is potentially complicated, however, by the Treaty's provisions on provisional application. These are found in Article 45:

> (1) Each signatory agrees to apply this Treaty provisionally pending its entry into force for such signatory in accordance with Article 44, to the extent that such provisional application is not inconsistent with its constitution, laws or regulations.
>
> (2)(a) Notwithstanding paragraph (1) any signatory may, when signing, deliver to the Depository a declaration that it is not able to accept provisional application. The obligation contained in paragraph (1) shall not apply to a signatory making such a declaration. Any such signatory may at any time withdraw that declaration by written notification to the Depository.
>
> (b) Neither a signatory which makes a declaration in accordance with subparagraph (a) nor Investors of that signatory may claim the benefits of provisional application under paragraph (1).
>
> ...
>
> (3)(a) Any signatory may terminate its provisional application of this Treaty by written notification to the Depository of its intention not to become a Contracting Party to the Treaty. Termination of provisional application for any signatory shall take effect upon the expiration of 60 days from the date on which such signatory's written notification is received by the Depository.
>
> (b) In the event that a signatory terminates provisional application under subparagraph (a), the obligation of the signatory under paragraph (1) to apply Parts III and V with respect to any Investments made in its Area during such provisional application by Investors

105 See A. Niebruegge, 'Provisional Application of the Energy Charter Treaty: The Yukos Arbitration and the Future Place of Provisional Application in International Law' (2007) 8 *Chicago Journal of International Law* 355; K. Hober and S. Nappert, 'Provisional Application and the Energy Charter Treaty: the Russian Doll Provision' (2007) 10 *International Arbitration Review* 53; G. Hafner, 'The "Provisional Application" of the Energy Charter Treaty' in C. Binder, U. Kriebaum, A. Reinisch and S. Wittisch (eds.), *International Investment Law for the 21st Century: Essays in Honour of Christoph Schreuer* (Oxford University Press, 2009), p. 593; W. Reisman, 'The Provisional Application of the Energy Charter Treaty' in G. Coop and C. Ribeiro (eds.), *Investment Protection and the Energy Charter Treaty* (New York: JurisNet, 2008), p. 47. See also A. Michie, 'The Provisional Application of Arms Control Treaties', (2005) 10 *Journal of Conflict and Security Law* 345.

> of other signatories shall nevertheless remain in effect with respect to those Investments for twenty years following the effective date of termination, except as otherwise provided in subparagraph (c).
>
> (c) ...[106]

The Energy Charter Treaty was signed on 17 December 1994. Australia, Iceland and Norway made declarations under Article 45(2) upon signature and have not yet deposited instruments of ratification, acceptance or approval, so the investment-protection aspects of the Treaty are of no effect as regards them or their Investors.[107] However, Belarus and Russia, which have not ratified the Treaty, signed it without indicating an inability to accept provisional application. Moreover, in the case of all states which *have* ratified the Treaty, there was a considerable period between signature and ratification. And on 20 August 2009 Russia gave notice under Article 45(3)(a) terminating its provisional application of the Treaty and of its intention not to become a Contracting Party.[108] The effect of provisional application is thus of great potential importance in practice.

The concept of the provisional application of a treaty is not new. The Vienna Convention on the Law of Treaties (1969) recognises the practice, though it says no more about it than that 'A treaty... is applied provisionally pending its entry into force if (a) the treaty itself so provides or (b) the negotiating states have in some other manner so agreed' (Article 25(1)) and that, subject to any more specific agreement on the subject, such provisional application is terminated in relation to a state if it notifies the other states parties of its intention not to become a party (Article 25(2)). The International Law Commission observed in 1966 that:

> Owing to the urgency of the matters dealt with in the treaty or for other reasons the States concerned may specify in a treaty... that it shall come into force provisionally. Whether in these cases the treaty is to be considered as entering into force in virtue [sic] of the treaty or of a

106 Subparagraph (c), which allowed states to apply the Treaty provisionally but at the same time declare themselves unwilling to accept the twenty years' obligation in subparagraph (b) if they terminated provisional application, is now academic because the only states which availed themselves of it have since ratified the Treaty.

107 Reisman, 'The Provisional Application of the Energy Charter Treaty,' p. 47, argues that such a declaration is of no effect unless it can be shown to be true, in the sense that the state actually is unable to accept provisional application because it is inconsistent with its constitution, laws or regulations. This is unsound for reasons discussed below.

108 See *Yukos Universal Ltd* v. *Russian Federation*, Interim Award on Jurisdiction and Admissibility, 30 November 2009, paragraph 34.

> subsidiary agreement may be a question. But there can be no doubt that such clauses have legal effect and bring the treaty into force on a provisional basis.[109]

Provisional application under the ECT has been considered in three cases.

In *Petrobart Ltd* v. *Kyrgyz Republic*,[110] the facts of which have already been mentioned,[111] the claimant was a company registered in Gibraltar, a territory for whose international relations the UK is responsible. When, on 17 December 1994, the UK signed the Treaty, it declared that the Treaty's provisional application should extend to the UK itself and to Gibraltar.[112] However, when the UK ratified the Treaty on 13 December 1996, it specified in its instrument of ratification that it was ratifying the Treaty in respect of the UK and two other territories for whose international relations the UK is responsible, namely Jersey and the Isle of Man. Gibraltar was not mentioned.[113] Since the events on which the claimant's complaint was based occurred after 13 December 1996, the question arose as to the effect as regards Gibraltar of this state of affairs. The tribunal dealt with the matter shortly:

> It could indeed be expected that the United Kingdom, if it wished the provisional application of the Treaty to Gibraltar to be terminated as a result of a ratification not including Gibraltar, should have made this clear by making a notification in line with Article 45(3)(a) or a declaration in some other form in connection with the ratification. In the Arbitral Tribunal's opinion, the fact that the ratification, for political or other reasons, did not include Gibraltar does not justify the conclusion that the United Kingdom intended to revoke the application of the Treaty to Gibraltar on a provisional basis.

Accordingly the tribunal held that it had jurisdiction to determine the claimant's claim.

109 International Law Commission, 'Draft Articles on the Law of Treaties with Commentaries' (1966) II *Yearbook of the International Law Commission*, 186, 210.

110 Award, 29 March 2005, VIII.7 *Stockholm Int. Arb. Rev.* 2005:3 111 P. 60.

112 The tribunal described this (at section VIII.2) as a declaration under Article 45(1) of the Treaty. It may perhaps also be described as a declaration under Article 40(1), which provides: 'Any state or Regional Economic Integration Organization may at the time of signature, ratification, acceptance, approval or accession, by a declaration deposited with the Depository, declare that the Treaty shall be binding upon it with respect to all the territories for the international relations of which it is responsible, or to one or more of them. Such declaration shall take effect at the time the Treaty enters into force for that Contracting Party.'

113 Award at section VIII.2.

It may be doubted whether the tribunal was right. Provisional application is a regime which applies 'pending [the Treaty's] entry into force'.[114] Once the Treaty entered into force for the UK, ninety days after 13 December 1996,[115] that regime ought to have been regarded as spent as far as the UK was concerned. The Treaty's provisional application to Gibraltar did not require express revocation; and the natural inference from the failure to mention Gibraltar in the instrument of ratification ought to have been that the UK did not intend the Treaty to apply to Gibraltar.

More detailed reviews of provisional application were undertaken in *Kardassopoulos* v. *Georgia*,[116] and in *Yukos Universal Ltd* v. *Russia*, *Hulley Enterprises Ltd* v. *Russia* and *Veteran Petroleum Ltd* v. *Russia*.[117]

Simplified somewhat, the facts in *Kardassopoulos* v. *Georgia* were that the claimant, a Greek national, had in the early 1990s entered into a joint venture with a Georgian state oil company to build a refinery and associated pipelines there. Georgia and Greece were both original signatories to the Treaty on 17 December 1994 and neither state elected to opt out of the effect of Article 45(1). Subsequently, over a period ending in 1996 or 1997, Georgia behaved in a way the effect of which was, on the claimant's case, to accomplish the unlawful expropriation, without compensation, of his investment. The Treaty entered into force (in the sense of being ratified) for both Greece and Georgia on 16 April 1998.[118] Thus the question directly raised was whether Georgia could be liable under the Treaty in respect of acts occurring between signature and ratification.

The tribunal in *Kardassopoulos* v. *Georgia* began its analysis of this question at Article 1(6). This, it will be recalled, provides that 'the Treaty shall only apply to matters affecting . . . investments after the Effective Date', 'Effective Date' being defined earlier in the sentence as 'the later of the date of *entry into force* of this Treaty for the Contracting Party of the Investor making the investment and that for the Contracting Party in the Area of which the investment is made' (emphasis added). The question boiled down to whether in this context 'entry into force' meant entry into force in the sense of what happens after deposit of instruments of ratification under Article 44, or the commencement of provisional

114 Article 45(1). 115 Article 44(2). 116 Decision on Jurisdiction, 6 July 2007.

117 Interim Awards on Jurisdiction and Admissibility, 30 November 2009. These three arbitrations were managed in parallel and three virtually identical Awards on Jurisdiction and Admissibility made. They are referred to here simply as the *Yukos* cases and references are to the Award on Jurisdiction and Admissibility in *Yukos Universal Ltd* v. *Russia*.

118 See p. 66 above.

application under Article 45(1).[119] Georgia argued that 'entry into force' must mean the former since otherwise 'the act of ratification and the entry into force of the ECT would have no purpose, because the obligation to perform would not then be dependent on ratification and/or the ECT's entry into force'.[120] One might add that the same question is raised by the very definition of Contracting Party in Article 1(2): '"Contracting Party" means a state or Regional Economic Integration Organization which has consented to be bound by this Treaty and for which the Treaty *is in force*' (emphasis added). And by Article 26 it is only disputes between a 'Contracting Party' and Investors of a 'Contracting Party' which are arbitrable at all.

Georgia submitted that provisional application 'must be aspirational in nature'. The tribunal dismissed this argument at once: provisional application is a course to which each signatory 'agrees' in Article 45(1): it is thus a matter of legal obligation, not 'aspiration'.[121] Nevertheless it had to be admitted that the ordinary meaning of Article 44 showed that 'entry into force' meant ratification, not signature. The tribunal considered whether there was a rule of customary international law as to the meaning of provisional application. It concluded not, but nevertheless found enough state practice

> to generate a generally accepted understanding of what is meant by [the] notion . . . Where what is in issue is, as in the present case, the provisional application of the whole treaty, then such provisional application imports the application of all of its provisions as if they were already in force, even though the treaty's proper or definitive entry into force has not occurred.[122]

The tribunal accepted that an 'inevitable consequence of a provisional application clause in a complex treaty is that some of the treaty's language . . . may not fit precisely with the situation created by its provisional application'. But since Article 45(1) is clear that it is 'this Treaty', as a whole, which must be provisionally applied, the solution was 'to rely on an implicit acceptance of the need to apply [the Treaty] (provisionally) on a mutatis mutandis basis'.[123] This conclusion was reinforced, in the tribunal's view, by the object and purpose of the Treaty.[124] Accordingly (and subject to the qualification next discussed),

119 Decision on Jurisdiction, 6 July 2007, paragraph 203. 120 Paragraph 76.
121 Paragraph 209. 122 Paragraph 219. 123 Paragraph 220.
124 Paragraph 214.

> the language used in Article 45(1) is to be interpreted as meaning that each signatory State is obliged, even before the ECT has formally entered into force, to apply the whole ECT as if it had already done so, and [Effective Date] . . . is to be interpreted as meaning the date on which the ECT became provisionally applicable for Georgia and Greece.[125]

It is submitted that the tribunal was plainly right to reach this conclusion. To hold otherwise would have been to strip Article 45(1) of all real effect.

The concluding words of Article 45(1) contain, however, an important qualification to the obligation to apply the Treaty provisionally: a signatory only agrees to do so 'to the extent that such provisional application is not inconsistent with its constitution, laws or regulations'. Were it not for this qualification, any such inconsistency would be no excuse for a failure to apply the Treaty provisionally since, by Article 27 of the Vienna Convention on the Law of Treaties (1969), a state 'may not invoke the provisions of its internal law as justification for its failure to perform a treaty' and, by Article 46(1), 'may not invoke the fact that its consent to be bound by a treaty has been expressed in violation of a provision of its internal law regarding competence to conclude treaties as invalidating its consent . . . '.[126]

But to what sort of inconsistency does the qualification in Article 45(1) of the Treaty refer? In using the words 'to the extent that such provisional application is not inconsistent . . . ', rather than spelling out exactly what must be inconsistent with the constitution etc. in order for provisional application not to be required of a state, the draftsman has perhaps sacrificed clarity for concision.[127] The qualification might mean (i) that provisional application does not apply where the constitution etc. of the state in question do not empower the executive to bind the state by treaty, even provisionally, without some as-yet-unobtained authorisation from some other organ of government. Or it might mean (ii) that provisional application does not apply where, although the executive may in principle bind the state in this way without any such authorisation, it may not do so so as to impose, before ratification, the particular obligations imposed by the ECT on which the claimant seeks to rely. Or it might mean that a state may escape provisional application in either case.

125 Paragraph 223.

126 Unless 'the violation was manifest and concerned a rule of its internal law of fundamental importance': Article 46(1), concluding words. These Articles may be regarded as aspects of the basic principle, *pacta sunt servanda*.

127 The texts in other languages are no clearer.

Certainly, the words 'to the extent that' suggest that the drafters did not have in mind solely the case where provisional application, in principle, either is or is not consistent with a state's constitution etc. For if they did, why not write: 'Each signatory agrees to apply this Treaty provisionally... *if* such provisional application is not inconsistent... '?[128] Rather, the drafting suggests an intention to accommodate the possibility that different Contracting Parties may vary in the 'extent' to which their domestic arrangements permit provisional application of the Treaty.

It is therefore arguable that the exception to provisional application applies where either or both of cases (i) and (ii) mentioned above apply[129] (though, as will be seen, there is authority suggesting that only case (i) will do[130]). However, since the basic rule enacted in Article 45(1) is one of provisional application, it ought to be for the state which seeks to bring itself within the qualification to do so by showing plainly how its constitution, laws or regulations entitle it not to be subject to provisional application, either generally or (if this argument is open) in relation to the specific obligation relied on by the claimant.[131]

The qualification in Article 45(1) was considered in *Kardassopoulos* v. *Georgia*. The tribunal considered, but rejected on the evidence provided to it, Georgia's argument that provisional application was inconsistent, in principle, not only with its own constitution but also with that of the claimant's home state, Greece.[132]

It may be noted that the tribunal in *Kardassopoulos* v. *Georgia* approached the qualification in Article 45(1) on the footing that all that was required, in order for it to have effect, was that provisional application in fact be inconsistent with the constitution, laws or regulations of either of the two relevant Contracting Parties. It has been argued, however, that a signatory may only avail itself of the qualification in Article

128 As discussed below, this argument was put in the *Yukos* cases.

129 It is clear, however, from the *travaux préparatoires* that what the parties had in mind was case (i): Y. Banifatemi, Conference paper delivered at 'Energy Dispute Resolution: Investment Protection, Transit and the Energy Charter Treaty', Brussels, 23 October 2009 (see www.encharter.org/index.php?id=472).

130 See the discussion of the *Yukos* cases, below, pp. 74ff.

131 *Kardassopoulos* v. *Georgia*, Decision on Jurisdiction, 6 July 2007, paragraph 229. Of course, if the executive was manifestly incompetent to give the state's consent to be bound by the Treaty (in the sense that this would have been objectively evident to any state conducting itself in accordance with normal practice and in good faith) by virtue of a rule of its internal law of fundamental importance, the state would not be bound by the Treaty anyway: see Article 46(1) and (2) of the Vienna Convention on the Law of Treaties (1969).

132 At paragraphs 230–46.

45(1) if two conditions are satisfied: (i) at the time of signing the Treaty, it made a declaration under Article 45(2)(a) that it was 'not able to accept provisional application'; and (ii) this declaration was true in the sense that, at the time of making the declaration, provisional application really was inconsistent with the signatory's constitution, laws or regulations.[133] This argument is not well founded. The first supposed condition disregards the plain terms of Article 45(1) by which 'Each signatory agrees to apply this Treaty provisionally . . . to the extent that such provisional application is not inconsistent with its constitution, laws or regulations': this contains no hint that the qualification is only available to signatories which have made a declaration under Article 45(2)(a). The second supposed condition is inconsistent with the express provision in Article 45(2)(a) that 'The obligation contained in paragraph (1) shall not apply to a signatory making such a declaration.'[134] It is notable in this context that, of the three states which have signed the Treaty but lodged an express declaration under Article 45(2)(a), only one (Iceland) followed its strict wording by declaring that it was 'not able' to accept provisional application; Australia and Norway merely stated that they '[did] not accept' provisional application.[135]

The tribunal in the *Yukos* cases[136] had to consider allegations of breaches of Part III of the ECT by Russia, a state which, as noted above, signed but never ratified the ECT. Russia accepted that the *principle* of provisional applicability was not 'inconsistent with its constitution, laws or regulations'.[137] But it argued that the tribunal lacked jurisdiction to hear the claimants' claims because provisional application of the particular substantive provisions of the ECT on which the claims were based would be 'inconsistent with its constitution, laws or regulations'.[138] The claimants argued that what matters is not inconsistency of the relevant substantive obligations but of the *principle* of provisional application.[139]

133 Reisman, 'The Provisional Application of the Energy Charter Treaty', p. 47.

134 The point is perhaps brought out even more clearly in the French text, which refers to '*une déclaration* selon laquelle *il n'est pas en mesure d'accepter l'application provisoire*', and the Italian text, which has '*una dichiarazione* secondo cui *non può accettare l'applicazione provvisoria*' (emphases added): what matters is not the 'true' position but the position 'according to' the declaration.

135 M. Polkinghorne and L. Gouiffès, 'Provisional Application of the Energy Charter Treaty: the Conundrum', Conference paper delivered at 'Energy Dispute Resolution: Investment Protection, Transit and the Energy Charter Treaty', Brussels, 23 October 2009 (see www.encharter.org/index.php?id=472).

136 See n. 117 above. 137 Paragraph 330. 138 Paragraph 293.

139 Paragraph 292.

The claimants argued in addition that the qualification in Article 45(1) ('to the extent that such provisional application is not inconsistent') could only be relied on by a host state if either it had made a declaration under Article 45(2)(a) ('that it is not able to accept provisional application') or it had made some other form of prior declaration to similar effect.[140] Russia had done neither.

The tribunal had 'little difficulty' in rejecting these last contentions. 'Nothing in the language of Article 45 suggests that the Limitation Clause[141] in Article 45(1) is dependent on the mandatory making of a declaration under Article 45(2)';[142] and 'the tribunal cannot read into Article 45(1) of the ECT a notification requirement which the text does not disclose and which no recognized legal principle dictates'.[143]

As to whether the qualification in Article 45(1) applies only where provisional application is *in principle* inconsistent with a host state's constitution, laws or regulations, or whether it also applies where the provisional application of particular provisions of the Treaty would be so inconsistent, the tribunal in the *Yukos* cases came down firmly in favour of the former: 'by signing the ECT the Russian Federation agreed that the Treaty *as a whole* would be applied provisionally pending its entry into force unless *the principle* of provisional application itself were inconsistent "with its constitution, law or regulations"'.[144]

For the tribunal in the *Yukos* cases, the 'key' to the interpretation of the qualification in Article 45(1) was 'the use of the adjective "*such*" in the phrase "*such provisional application*"'.[145] Article 45(1), the tribunal observed, may be rewritten as: 'Each signatory agrees to apply this Treaty provisionally . . . to the extent that *the provisional application of this Treaty* is not inconsistent with its constitution, laws and regulations.'[146] This much is plainly right; indeed, self-evident. However, the logic of the tribunal's next assertion is less obvious:

> In order to interpret the meaning of the Limitation Clause in Article 45(1), and thereby determine the scope of Respondent's obligation under Article 45(1), the Tribunal must therefore determine what is meant by 'the provisional application of this Treaty,' for it is the inconsistency of 'such provisional application' which determines the scope of Respondent's obligation under Article 45(1). There are two possible interpretations of the

140 Paragraph 248(a) and (b).

141 As the tribunal, perhaps confusingly to a common lawyer, called the qualification in Article 45(1).

142 Paragraph 262.

143 Paragraph 283.

144 Paragraph 301, emphasis in original.

145 Paragraph 304, emphasis in original.

146 Paragraph 305.

> phrase 'the provisional application of this Treaty': it can mean either 'the provisional application of the entire Treaty' or 'the provisional application of some parts of the Treaty'.[147]

Put this way, the question admits of only one answer, and the tribunal unsurprisingly chose the former – 'the provisional application of the entire Treaty' – as better according with the ordinary meaning of the phrase 'the provisional application of this Treaty'.[148] But it may respectfully be doubted if the question *ought* to be put this way. To do so is to ignore the words which precede 'such provisional application', namely 'to the extent that'. The real question is not the meaning in isolation of the words, 'provisional application of this Treaty', but the meaning of the whole phrase, 'to the extent that [the provisional application of this Treaty] is not inconsistent with . . . '. Even if 'the provisional application of the Treaty' means 'the provisional application of the entire Treaty' (as it probably does), it is not at all obvious why a state which agrees to apply 'the entire Treaty' provisionally, but only '*to the extent that* such provisional application [of the entire Treaty] is not inconsistent with its constitution, laws or regulations' must thereby be taken to have agreed to apply the entire Treaty provisionally unless provisional application of the entire Treaty is impermissible in principle under its constitution, or under a law or (improbably, as Russia pointed out[149]) a regulation. As Russia had argued before the tribunal, '"[t]o the extent that" is precisely the language used when drafters of a clause in a treaty or statute wish to make clear that a provision is to be applied only insofar as what then follows is the case'.[150] The Tribunal agreed with this proposition but gave it little weight: 'Far from being determinative of the meaning of the Limitation Clause, however, the use of the introductory words "to the extent that" requires the Tribunal to examine carefully the words that follow . . . '.[151]

There is perhaps an analogy with a well-known provision of UK legislation, namely Section 3(1) of the Human Rights Act 1998. This provides that: 'So far as it is possible to do so, . . . legislation must be read and given effect [by the courts] in a way which is compatible with the [European] Convention rights.' No-one doubts that 'the Convention rights' means all of them. But no-one suggests that (as the tribunal's logic implies) it follows from this fact that 'so far as it is possible to do so' imports a once-and-for-all test of principle, rather than a requirement to analyse in

147 Paragraphs 307–8. 148 Paragraph 308. 149 Paragraph 303.
150 Paragraph 294. 151 Paragraph 303.

each case the particular right in question and how far it is possible to read the relevant legislation compatibly with it.

The tribunal in the *Yukos* cases sought to bolster its view on the ordinary meaning of the qualification in Article 45(1) with arguments of legal policy. A reading which allowed a state to modulate the effect of provisional application depending on the consistency of its internal law with provisional application of the particular obligation relied upon by the claimant 'would undermine the principle that provisional application of a treaty creates binding obligations' and 'create unacceptable uncertainty in international affairs'.[152] It would be inconsistent with international law's 'underlying value against self-judgement and strong presumption of the separation of international from national law'.[153] As arguments *de lege ferenda*, these are powerful considerations. What may be more open to argument is whether or not they are sufficient to outweigh what (on one view at least) Article 45(1) clearly provides.

## 4. Article 17 – denial of advantages

As has been noted, the substantive obligations assumed by Contracting Parties towards Investors and their Investments are contained in Part III. The last article in Part III is Article 17. This provides that:

> Each Contracting Party reserves the right to deny the advantages of this Part to:
>
> (1) a legal entity if citizens or nationals of a third state own or control such entity and if that entity has no substantial business activities in the Area of the Contracting Party in which it is organized; or
> (2) an Investment, if the denying Contracting Party establishes that such Investment is an Investment of an Investor of a third state with or as to which the denying Contracting Party:
> (a) does not maintain a diplomatic relationship; or
> (b) adopts or maintains measures that:
> (i) prohibit transactions with Investors of that state; or
> (ii) would be violated or circumvented if the benefits of this Part were accorded to Investors of that state or to their Investments.[154]

152 Paragraphs 314–15.

153 Paragraph 316, quoting expert evidence of Professor Crawford.

154 Similarly-worded provisions appear in many BITs – see, e.g., US Model BIT (1994), Article XII; US Model BIT (2004), Article 17; Canada Model BIT (2004), Article 18; Austria Model BIT, Article 10 – and in the NAFTA, Article 1113 – though it appears that most BITs do not contain such provision (S. Jagusch and A. Sinclair, 'Denial of

The arbitral tribunal in *AMTO* v. *Ukraine* observed that:

> As the purpose of the ECT is to establish a legal framework 'in order to promote long-term cooperation in the energy field, based on complementarities and mutual benefits . . . ' [(Article 2)] then the potential exclusion of foreign owned entities from ECT investment protection under Article 17 is readily comprehensible. 'Long term economic cooperation', 'complementarities' or 'mutual benefits' are unlikely to materialise for the host State with a State that serves as a nationality of convenience devoid of economic substance for an investment vehicle, or a State with which it does not enjoy normal diplomatic or economic relations.[155]

The meaning of 'substantial business activities' in Article 17(1), deduced in the light of this purpose, was shortly (and, it is submitted, correctly) summarised in the same case:

> 'substantial' in this context means 'of substance, and not merely of form'. It does not mean 'large', and the materiality not the magnitude of the business activity is the decisive question.[156]

'Business activities', it is submitted, are activities such as buying, selling, contracting etc., not activities such as filing returns and holding meetings which are required merely because of the legal entity's existence.[157] A company with substantial business activities may be contrasted with one which is a 'mere shell'.[158]

It will be recalled that Article 1(7)(a) defines an 'Investor' 'with respect to a Contracting Party' as:

> (i) a natural person having the citizenship or nationality of or who is permanently residing in that Contracting Party in accordance with its applicable law;
> (ii) a company or other organization organized in accordance with the law applicable in that Contracting Party;

Conversely, Article 1(7)(b) defines an 'Investor' 'with respect to a "third state"' as

Advantages under Article 17(1)' in G. Coop and C. Ribeiro (eds.), *Investment Protection and the Energy Charter Treaty* (New York: JurisNet, 2008), p. 17 at p. 23).

155 Award, 26 March 2008, paragraph 61. 156 Paragraph 69.

157 Jagusch and Sinclair, 'Denial of Advantages under Article 17(1)' p. 17 at p. 19.

158 See *Generation Ukraine Inc* v. *Ukraine*, Award, 13 September 2003, paragraph 15.5 (quoting the US State Department's interpretation of the equivalent provision in the United States–Ukraine BIT). D. D'Allaire, 'The Nationality Rules under the Energy Charter Treaty: Practical Considerations', (2009) 10 *Journal of World Investment and Trade* 39 at 57 suggests that 'substantial' means large.

a natural person, company or other organization 'which fulfils, mutatis mutandis, the conditions specified in subparagraph (a) for a [person who is an Investor with respect to a] Contracting Party'.

Although this is not spelled out in Article 17(2), it is submitted that an Investment will be an Investment 'of' an Investor of a third state for its purposes when it is, in substance even if not formally, owned or controlled by an Investor 'with respect to a "third state"'.[159]

A 'third state', it is submitted, means a state which is not a Contracting Party: this is apparent from the way '"Investor"... with respect to a Contracting Party' and '"Investor" with respect to a "third state"' are presented in Article 1(7) as opposites.[160] In the *Yukos* cases[161] it was argued by Russia at one stage that the claimants, which were Manx and Cypriot companies (both jurisdictions being Contracting Parties), had no substantial business activities in the Isle of Man or Cyprus and were owned and controlled by Russian nationals; and that these Russian nationals were to be regarded for the purposes of Article 17(1) as 'nationals of a third state'. The tribunal dismissed this argument shortly: 'The Treaty clearly distinguishes between a Contracting Party (and a signatory), on the one hand, and a third state, which is a non-Contracting Party, on the other.' Russian nationals were not 'nationals of a third state'.[162] The tribunal in *AMTO* v. *Ukraine*[163] observed that it was a 'difficult interpretative issue' (albeit one that did not fall for determination in the case) whether, in an arbitration between a Latvian company and Ukraine, Russia was to be regarded as a third state. However, it is submitted that the better view is that in any dispute between an Investor of a Contracting Party and a Contracting Party, the relevant ownership or control for the purposes of Article 17(1) is that of a national of a third state only if such person is a national of a state which is not a Contracting Party: it would not be sufficient if he were a national of a Contracting Party which was neither the Investor's state nor the host state. This conclusion may be supported both as a matter of ordinary wording – because of the antithesis drawn in

159 See, by analogy, the third Understanding (as to ownership or control by an Investor of a Contracting State) (above, p. 53). The equivalent provisions of the BITs mentioned above, n. 154, and of the NAFTA, all expressly use the words 'own or control', as does the ECT itself in Article 17(1). It is not clear why the draftsman of the ECT did not adopt this language but there seems little reason to think that any different meaning was intended.

160 And see *Plama Corporation* v. *Bulgaria*, Decision on Jurisdiction, 8 February 2005, paragraph 170.

161 *Yukos Universal Ltd* v. *Russia*, *Hulley Enterprises Ltd* v. *Russia* and *Veteran Petroleum Ltd* v. *Russia*, Interim Awards on Jurisdiction and Admissibility, 30 November 2009.

162 Paragraph 544. 163 Award, 26 March 2008, paragraph 67.

Article 1(7) – and in the light of the ECT's object and purpose – because the mischief which Article 17 permits a state to avoid is that of conferring benefits on nationals of states which are not themselves prepared to submit to the burden of being a Contracting Party.

A number of further questions arise concerning Article 17. First, whether it presents a jurisdictional hurdle for a claimant or raises a question of admissibility.[164] Second, where the burden of proof lies under Article 17(1). Third, how a Contracting State may go about denying an Investor or Investment the advantages of Part III and with what consequence.

### *(a) Jurisdiction or admissibility*

Whether the successful invocation of Article 17 by a respondent operates (i) to deprive the tribunal of jurisdiction to determine the dispute or (ii) to compel the tribunal, in the exercise of its jurisdiction, to dismiss the claim as inadmissible is not altogether clear. It was extensively discussed in *Plama Consortium* v. *Bulgaria*.[165] The claimant was a company registered in Cyprus (a Contracting Party), but the respondent contended that the claimant had no substantial business activities there and that the claimant had not established that it was owned or controlled by a national of a Contracting Party.[166] In these circumstances the respondent argued that the tribunal lacked jurisdiction to determine the substance of the parties' dispute. As the tribunal summarised the argument:

> To establish [the Claimant's] consent to ICSID arbitration, there must be a dispute that concerns an alleged breach of an ECT Part III obligation. If the Arbitral Tribunal were to decide that the circumstances are present to satisfy an Article 17(1) denial, then the facts alleged by the Claimant necessarily would be incapable of forming the basis of a claim that ECT Part III has been breached.[167]

There is a good deal to be said for this argument. As has been discussed above,[168] a condition which must be satisfied in order for the tribunal to have jurisdiction to determine the substance of the dispute is that the dispute 'concern an alleged breach of an obligation of the [host Contracting

164 See above, pp. 39–40, as to the distinction and its significance.

165 Decision on Jurisdiction, 8 February 2005.

166 Paragraph 31. Whether this was anyway a sufficient averment under Article 17(1) may be doubted since the burden was on the respondent to show that the claimant was caught by the provision, not on the claimant to show that it was not: see below.

167 Paragraph 85. 168 See pp. 45–6.

Party] under Part III' (Article 26(1)). The test, at the jurisdictional stage, is whether the claimant's allegations of fact, if true, might amount to a breach of one or more of the relevant obligations: if not, the tribunal lacks jurisdiction. The obligations are the correlative of the 'advantages of this Part [i.e. Part III]', which Article 17 permits the host Contracting Party to deny where the conditions described in either paragraph are met. It follows that a claimant caught by Article 17 is not owed any obligations under Part III. Such a claimant's allegations of fact, even if true, will never be capable of amounting to a breach of obligation under Part III. There is therefore no dispute concerning an alleged breach of such an obligation and no jurisdiction to determine the claim.

Curiously, however, in its decision the tribunal addressed a somewhat different argument: 'that the denial [in Article 17] of such "advantages" are [sic] not limited to those conferred by Part III of the ECT but include also all advantages relating to Part III, including the right to invoke international arbitration under Article 26 of Part V of the ECT alleging any breach of Part III'.[169] This was readily (and rightly) dismissed in the light of the clear language of Article 17, which expressly applies the denial only to 'the advantages of this Part [III]'. The right to invoke arbitration is not an advantage of Part III because it is found in Article 26, which is located in Part V. To suggest otherwise 'would require a gross manipulation of language'.[170] The tribunal considered whether such manipulation was permissible and, predictably, decided not.[171]

Thus the tribunal in *Plama Consortium* v. *Bulgaria* did not deal squarely with the argument that, where it applies on the facts, Article 17, by relieving a host state of its Part III obligations, deprives a dispute of the character which it must have for it to be arbitrable under Article 26, namely

169 Paragraph 146. 170 Paragraph 147.

171 More curiously still, the tribunal sought to bolster its conclusion by suggesting (at paragraph 149) that if Article 17 was construed as a jurisdictional provision, this would prevent a tribunal from determining whether it was applicable at all. This is, of course, to overlook the fact that the tribunal has jurisdiction to determine its jurisdiction (see above, p. 42). A respondent which relies on Article 17 as depriving the tribunal of jurisdiction no more deprives the claimant of a *hearing* than a respondent which contends that some other jurisdictional condition has not been met (e.g., that the claimant has not made an 'Investment'). In either case it will be for the tribunal to hear and determine the jurisdictional objection, whether separately or alongside the merits. See also Douglas, *The International Law of Investment Claims*, p. 470. (Douglas also criticises the tribunal in *Plama Corporation* v. *Bulgaria* for describing Article 17(1) as going to the merits rather than as being a matter of admissibility, but it is clear that the tribunal was simply using 'merits' rather loosely to mean 'as opposed to jurisdiction'.)

that it 'concern an alleged breach of an obligation . . . under Part III'. It has been suggested that the argument is flawed because 'the investors having standing to bring claims under the ECT are defined in Article 1(7), not Article 17(1)'.[172] But this is no answer because Article 1(7), by defining 'Investor', merely supplies one of the elements which must be fed in to Article 26(1) to determine whether the dispute is one over which the tribunal has jurisdiction. The tribunal in *Generation Ukraine Inc* v. *Ukraine* asserted that the denial of benefits provision in the United States–Ukraine BIT 'is not . . . a jurisdictional hurdle . . . ; instead it is a potential filter on the admissibility of claims which can be invoked by the Respondent state'.[173] But no reasons were given in circumstances where the respondent's denial of benefits failed on the facts.

The tribunal in the *Yukos* cases also held, rightly, that a valid denial, under Article 17, of the advantages of Part III of the Treaty could not in itself deprive the tribunal of the jurisdiction conferred on it by Part V of the Treaty; and in these circumstances held that Article 17 could not go to jurisdiction.[174] But the tribunal does not appear to have addressed the somewhat different argument discussed above; and indeed it appears to have been common ground that the objection under Article 17 was to the admissibility of the claims, not to the jurisdiction of the tribunal to determine them.[175]

In these circumstances the law is not necessarily settled. It would still in the authors' submission be open to a tribunal to hold that Article 17 goes to its jurisdiction.[176] It should be borne in mind, however, that what really matters is not the view of the point taken by arbitral tribunals themselves – after all, a refusal to consider a claim on its merits has the same effect whether it is motivated by a belief that the tribunal lacks jurisdiction to do so or a belief that the claim is inadmissible – but the view taken by *ad hoc* Committees or courts to whom complaint is made by parties

172 A. Sinclair, 'The Substance of Nationality Requirements in Investment Treaty Arbitration', (2005) 20 *ICSID Review – Foreign Investment Law Journal* 357 at 382. See also Douglas, *The International Law of Investment Claims*, p. 468.

173 Award, 13 September 2003, paragraph 15.7. The United States–Ukraine BIT, in contrast with the ECT but in common with many other BITs, refers to the denial of the advantages 'of this Treaty' and not merely of the part containing the host state's substantive obligations, so one might have thought that the argument that the denial of benefits went to jurisdiction was a stronger one.

174 Paragraph 441.

175 Paragraph 443. If this is correct, this was a surprising concession by Russia given its potential consequences in terms of the enforceability of any subsequent substantive Award.

176 See Shore, 'The Jurisdiction Problem in Energy Charter Treaty Claims', 63.

aggrieved at the determination of a 'denial of benefits' objection. Only at that stage does it become crucial to know whether the determination was a jurisdictional one, which there may be power to review, or one made within jurisdiction, which there will not.

### *(b) Burden of proof*

Article 17(2) (no diplomatic relationship, etc.) expressly provides that it is for the respondent to establish the facts relied on in support of the denial of advantages. In Article 17(1) (no substantial business activities, etc.), by contrast, there is no reference to the question of who must prove what. There is no obvious reason for the difference. On ordinary principles, the burden of proof lies on the person advancing a particular allegation.[177] Thus it is for a claimant to prove that it is an Investor of a Contracting Party and owns or controls an Investment.[178] However, where a respondent seeks to take advantage of Article 17(1) to defeat the claim (or the right to bring a claim) which the claimant would otherwise have, it ought to be for the respondent to prove the facts on which it relies.[179] Of course, the claimant is probably in a much better position than the respondent to know who owns or controls it and what business activities it carries on in the Area of the Contracting Party in which it is organised, and for this reason the tribunal will be ready to draw inferences against a claimant which is unforthcoming in giving disclosure or answers to reasonable questions on this subject.[180] But this does not alter the incidence of the burden of proof, which remains on the respondent. No significance ought to be read into the draftsman's omission to provide for this expressly in Article 17(1).

### *(c) How the advantages of Part III are denied*

Article 17 does not provide that, in the cases mentioned in its paragraphs (1) and (2), the advantages of Part III do not accrue to the claimant but, rather, that each Contracting Party 'reserves the right to deny' them. This wording led the tribunal in *Plama Consortium* v. *Bulgaria*,[181] which was

177 See, e.g., D'Allaire, 'The Nationality Rules under the Energy Charter Treaty: Practical Considerations', 57 and the authorities there cited.

178 Article 1(6), (7); third Understanding.

179 *AMTO* v. *Ukraine*, Award, 26 March 2008, paragraph 65; *Generation Ukraine Inc* v. *Ukraine*, Award, 13 September 2003, paragraph 15.7.

180 *AMTO* v. *Ukraine*, Award, 26 March 2008, paragraph 65. D'Allaire, 'The Nationality Rules under the Energy Charter Treaty: Practical Considerations', 58.

181 Decision on Jurisdiction, 8 February 2005.

considering Article 17(1), to conclude that 'the existence of a "right" is distinct from the exercise of that right' and that 'a Contracting State must exercise its right before applying it to an investor and be seen to have done so'.[182] As to how this right ought to be exercised:

> The exercise would necessarily be associated with publicity or other notice so as to become reasonably available to investors and their advisers. To this end, a general declaration in a Contracting State's official gazette could suffice; or a statutory provision in a Contracting State's investment or other laws; or even an exchange of letters with a particular investor or class of investors.[183]

The tribunal further held that, given the purposes of the ECT, such exercise of the right under Article 17(1) ought to have only prospective effect:

> The covered investor enjoys the advantages of Part III unless the host state exercises its right under Article 17(1) ECT; and a putative covered investor has legitimate expectations of such advantages until that right's exercise. A putative investor therefore requires reasonable notice before making any investment in the host state whether or not that host state has exercised its right under Article 17(1) ECT. At that stage, the putative investor can so plan its business affairs to come within or without the criteria there specified, as it chooses. It can also plan not to make any investment at all or to make it elsewhere. After an investment is made in the host state, the 'hostage-factor' is introduced; the covered investor's choices are accordingly more limited; and the investor is correspondingly more vulnerable to the host state's exercise of its right under Article 17(1) ECT. At this time, therefore, the covered investor needs at least the same protection as it enjoyed as a putative investor able to plan its investment. The ECT's express 'purpose' under Article 2 ECT is the establishment of '... a legal framework in order to promote long-term co-operation in the energy field ... in accordance with the objectives and principles of the Charter' (emphasis supplied). It is not easy to see how any retrospective effect is consistent with this 'long-term' purpose.[184]

Essentially the same approach was adopted by the tribunal in the *Yukos* cases,[185] which endorsed the reasoning of the tribunal in *Plama Consortium* v. *Bulgaria*.

It may be doubted whether this reasoning is altogether sound.[186] It rests heavily on the distinction supposedly drawn by the Treaty's framers

182 Paragraphs 155, 157. 183 Paragraph 157. 184 Paragraph 161.

185 *Yukos*, Interim Awards on Jurisdiction and Admissibility, 30 November 2009, paragraph 456.

186 L. Mistelis and C. M. Baltag, 'Denial of Benefits and Article 17 of the Energy Charter Treaty', (2009) *Penn State Law Review* 1301 at 1319 assert without giving reasons that:

between the right to deny a party the advantages of Part III and the exercise of that right. From this distinction the tribunals read into Article 17 a mechanism for exercising the right, which the framers themselves omitted to provide for, and a rule, again unstated, that such exercise should only be prospective in nature. Yet the ordinary meaning of 'Each Contracting Party reserves the right to deny the advantages of this Part to . . . ' is surely simpler: it is that a Contracting Party need not, in favour of an entity or Investment of a type mentioned in paragraphs (1) or (2), afford fair and equitable treatment, most constant protection and security, most-favoured nation status or any of the other advantages otherwise conferred on Investors and their Investments by Part III. Accordingly, if it takes the point, a Contracting Party has an answer to any claim by an entity or Investment mentioned in paragraphs (1) or (2). 'Reserves the right to deny' is merely a more elaborate way of saying 'may deny'. It is notable that the United States Model BIT (1994) used 'reserves the right to deny',[187] but the NAFTA, the draft Multilateral Agreement on Investments (MAI), the United States Model BIT (2004) and many other BITs simply use 'may deny' in the course of otherwise very similar provision for the denial of advantages.[188] Since there is no reason to think that any shift in policy in this respect was intended as between the United States Model BIT (1994) and the other instruments mentioned, it is reasonable to conclude that no-one attributed to the formulation 'reserves the right to deny' the significance which it had for the *Plama* and *Yukos* tribunals.

The *Plama* tribunal drew support for its conclusion from a comparison of Article 17 with the ASEAN Framework Agreement on Services (1995) which provides, in its Article VI: 'The benefits of this Framework Agreement shall be denied to' certain categories of person.[189] But this is a different provision, positively excluding certain persons from benefit under the treaty rather than permitting states not to extend that benefit to them. To say, as the tribunal did, that the draftsman of the ECT could have used different language is to say no more than that the parties to the

'There is no doubt that that the "denial of benefits" right must be exercised by the denying state.'

187 Article XII.

188 Article 1113 of the NAFTA; draft Multilateral Agreement on Investments (see 'Consolidated Texts and Commentary', 13 May 1997 (OECD reference: DAFFE/MAI(97)1/REV2) at p. 96); Article 18 of the Canada Model BIT (2004); Article 10 of the Austria Model BIT; see also OECD, *International Investment Law: Understanding Concepts and Tracking Innovations* (Paris: OECD, 2008) at p. 28.

189 Paragraph 156.

ECT could have made different provision: it casts no light on the meaning of the provision which actually was made. Other comparisons might arguably have been more useful. NAFTA Article 1113 expressly makes the denial of benefits to enterprises owned by non-Parties without substantial business activities at the place of organisation, though not the denial of benefits to enterprises controlled by non-Parties with whom there are no diplomatic relations etc., subject to detailed requirements of prior notification and consultation.[190] The MAI, too, included detailed prior notification and consultation requirements, though these appeared in the draft in square brackets, suggesting that, at the point the negotiations were called off, the negotiating parties had not yet agreed whether such prior notification and consultation ought to be required – in which case there needed to be provision for it – or was unnecessary. The *Plama* tribunal looked at NAFTA Article 1113(2), which in its view did 'suggest that the Tribunal's interpretation [as to the need to give notice in the gazette, etc.] is not unreasonable as a practical matter'.[191] However, a more persuasive deduction from Article 1113 (and from the MAI) might have been that if the parties to the ECT had intended the denial of advantages to be subject to a requirement of prior notification, they would have said so and explained how such notification should be given.[192]

The decision of the *Plama* tribunal and the *Yukos* tribunal on Article 17(1), if it is right, not only strips Article 17(1) of much of its effect in practice, but has the same consequence for Article 17(2). For paragraph (2) is also governed by the crucial wording, 'reserves the right to deny'. It follows that a Contracting Party's rights under paragraph (2) – to deny the advantages of Part III of the Treaty to an Investment of a state with which it does not maintain diplomatic relations or against which it maintains measures which would be violated if those advantages were granted – must also be dependent on notice and prospective only.[193] It is not impossible that the Contracting Parties intended this significant constraint on the effectiveness of diplomatic and sanctions-based steps which they might wish to take against non-Parties, but it must surely be open to question.

In spite of the considerable weight of authority supporting the contrary view, the better view, it is submitted, is that Article 17 itself constitutes notice to any would-be Investor that, if matters are structured so as to fall

190 Article 18 of the Canada Model BIT (2004) is to the same effect.

191 Paragraph 157.

192 As, indeed, they did in Article 45(2)(a) with regard to the election not to accept provisional application of the Treaty: see above, p. 67.

193 Compare Article 1113 of the NAFTA and Article 18 of the Canada Model BIT, both of which exclude this ground from the requirement to give notice.

within paragraphs (1) or (2), it cannot count on enjoying the advantages of Part III. A claimant caught by paragraphs (1) or (2) cannot complain if, when a dispute is sought to be arbitrated under Article 26, it is met by reliance on Article 17.[194]

### 5. Misconduct on the part of the Investor

Many BITs contain, as part of the definition of 'investment', a requirement that it be made in accordance with the laws of the host state.[195] A would-be investment made by a claimant otherwise than in accordance with such laws does not qualify for protection under the treaty, such a claimant does not qualify as an investor and a tribunal has no jurisdiction to hear the claimant's claim.[196]

No such provision is made in the ECT. However, in *Plama Consortium* v. *Bulgaria*,[197] the question arose as to the effect of what the tribunal found to have been the 'deliberate concealment amounting to fraud'[198] by which the claimant had obtained from the host state its shareholding in the investment whose treatment by the host state formed the basis of the claim. The effect of the claimant's behaviour was to render its agreement to obtain the shareholding unlawful under Bulgarian law.[199] The tribunal had little hesitation in holding that, despite the absence of express provision to this effect, 'the substantive protections of the ECT cannot apply to investments that are made contrary to law'.[200]

A more problematic question is whether the implicit obligation to comply with the host Contracting Party's law in making an Investment amounts to a question of jurisdiction or admissibility. In *Plama*, the tribunal held at the jurisdictional stage that the respondent's complaints about the claimant's conduct in acquiring the investment did not go to its jurisdiction. The relevant part of the definition of Investment in Article

194 Of course, if the host Contracting Party had encouraged the investment with full knowledge of the matters later relied on as bringing the case within Article 17, the claimant would have a good argument that the Contracting Party was estopped from reliance on the provision. For estoppel in international law, see Brownlie, *Principles of Public International Law*, p. 643.

195 See Dolzer and Schreuer, *Principles of International Investment Law*, pp. 84–8; McLachlan *et al.*, *International Investment Arbitration: Substantive Principles*, pp. 181–2.

196 *Fraport* v. *Philippines*, Award, 16 August 2007; see also *Inceysa Vallisoletana* v. *El Salvador*, Award, 2 August 2006. Such provision does not disqualify a claimant on the basis of 'minor errors': *Salini Costruttori and Italstrade* v. *Morocco*, Decision on Jurisdiction, 23 July 2001, paragraph 86.

197 Award, 27 August 2008. 198 Paragraph 135. 199 Paragraph 137.

200 Paragraph 139. The claimant's claim was also dismissed on the merits.

1(6) was 'any right conferred by law or contract [etc.]'. 'That definition', the tribunal held, 'would be satisfied by a contractual or property right even if it were defeasible'.[201] This statement is clearly right. Moreover, the tribunal's decision that it had jurisdiction was correct as the case turned out, for at the substantive stage the tribunal rejected an argument that as a matter of Bulgarian law the relevant agreement was void *ab initio* in favour of an argument that it was 'subject to invalidation', i.e. defeasible.[202] If, however, the finding had been that the agreement was not merely defeasible but void *ab initio*, it is difficult to see on what basis the tribunal could have been said to have had jurisdiction to determine the admissibility or merits of the dispute. For, in short, a claimant whose putative investment is in fact of no legal effect under the law of the host Contracting Party is not an Investor, does not have an Investment and is owed no obligations under Part III.

201 Decision on Jurisdiction, 8 February 2005, at paragraph 128.
202 Paragraphs 102, 130–7.

# 4

# European Union law and the Energy Charter Treaty

## 1. Introduction

The European Union (as successor to the European Communities) and all of the EU member states are parties to the Energy Charter Treaty. From the EU law perspective, the ECT is a 'mixed agreement'; that is, an agreement parts of which fall within the EU's competence and parts of which fall within the competences of the member states.[1] In particular, at the time of its adoption foreign investment fell within the competences of the member states (although this has now changed, at least as regards foreign direct investment, which the Lisbon Treaty has brought within the Common Commercial Policy).[2]

The fact that the ECT is a treaty to which the EU and its member states are parties distinguishes it from the numerous BITs entered into by individual member states. It has been argued (albeit, it is submitted, plainly wrongly) that intra-EU BITs (BITs entered into between two EU member states before either or both were EU member states) automatically terminate on both parties becoming EU members.[3] However, given the ECT's status as a mixed agreement to which the EU is itself a party, participation in it cannot be per se incompatible with member states' obligations. Several member states' extra-EU BITs (BITs entered into between a

1 See, generally, D. O'Keefe and H. Schermers (eds.), *Mixed Agreements* (Deventer: Kluwer Law & Taxation Publishers and Leiden: the Europa Instituut, 1983); C. Hillion and P. Koutrakos (eds.), *Mixed Agreements Revisited* (Oxford: Hart Publishing, 2010). The question of state responsibility for the acts of the EU, and vice versa, is discussed in Chapter 7.

2 Treaty on the Functioning of the European Union (Consolidated Version), OJ C 115/47, 9.5.2008 (TFEU), Article 207.

3 In *Eastern Sugar BV* v. *Czech Republic*, Partial Award, 27 March 2007, a claim under the Netherlands–Czech Republic BIT, this was the submission of the Czech Republic. It was roundly rejected, principally on the ground of the lack of such provision in the treaty of accession (at paragraphs 142–87). The European Commission wrote to the tribunal expressing the view that the BIT ought to be terminated by agreement between the Contracting States.

member state and a non-member state) have been held to contain provisions which violate EU law on the ground that they have the potential to impede possible restrictions on capital movements[4] (although this does not mean that the BITs are themselves invalid, only that the member states party to them are under an obligation to remove the incompatibilities). Again, however, although Article 14 of the ECT on capital transfers is similar to the BIT provisions held to be inconsistent with EU law in these cases, as the EU, as well as its member states, has entered into the ECT, it can be seen as having limited its own competence to restrict capital movements in the Energy Sector.[5]

To say all of this, however, does not answer the question of the extent to which the provisions of Part III of the ECT apply in the intra-EU context nor, more generally, of the relevance of EU law to Investor–state disputes – both intra- and extra-EU – brought under Article 26. This is an issue that has already arisen. The first case brought under Article 26 of the ECT – *AES* v. *Hungary*[6] – was brought by a UK investor in the Hungarian electricity industry in 2001. The claim was settled and arbitral proceedings discontinued in 2002. However, in 2007 AES brought a new claim against Hungary ('*AES* v. *Hungary (No. 2)*'),[7] as did Electrabel, another investor in the Hungarian electricity industry.[8] Both claims involved acts of the Hungarian government, after Hungary's entry into the EU in 2004, allegedly taken to ensure its compliance with EU rules on state aid following an investigation by the European Commission. In both cases, the Commission made a request to the tribunal under Rule 37(2) of the ICSID Arbitration Rules to file submissions as a non-disputing party. Both requests were granted, at least in part, and the Commission filed written submissions with the two tribunals. Reports indicate that, in *AES* v. *Hungary (No. 2)*, the tribunal limited the Commission's submission to thirty pages and restricted it to general discussion of the relationship between the ECT and EU law. The Commission was not permitted to raise

4 Case C-205/06 *Commission of the European Communities* v. *Austria* [2009] 2 CMLR 50; Case C-249/06 *Commission of the European Communities* v. *Sweden* [2009] 2 CMLR 49; Case C-118/07 *Commission of the European Communities* v. *Finland* [2010] All ER (EC) 558.

5 Articles 64(2), 66 and 75 TFEU permit, but do not require, the EU to enact restrictions on capital movements: see T. Eilmansberger, 'Bilateral Investment Treaties and EU Law' (2009) 48 *Common Market Law Review* 383 at 411–12.

6 *AES Summit Generation Ltd* v. *Republic of Hungary* (ICSID Case No. ARB/01/04).

7 *AES Summit Generation Ltd and AES-Tisza Erőmű Kft.* v. *Republic of Hungary* (ICSID Case No. ARB/07/22).

8 *Electrabel SA* v. *Republic of Hungary* (ICSID Case No.ARB/07/19).

objections to the tribunal's jurisdiction, as no such challenge had been made by Hungary.[9] Unfortunately, the Commission has not been willing to publish its submissions. Moreover, although the tribunal's Award in *AES* v. *Hungary (No. 2)* 'acknowledge[d] the efforts made by the European Commission to explain its own position to the Tribunal',[10] it made no reference to their content. Whatever arguments were included in the Commission's submissions have to be deduced from the comments of its representatives in other forums.

## 2. Investment disputes within the EU[11]

At first sight, it would appear that the ECT should apply to intra-EU disputes, as there is nothing in the Treaty itself to indicate otherwise. In particular, there is no 'disconnection clause', as has been included in other treaties to which the EU and member states are party, providing that the ECT does not apply in their relations *inter se* which they have agreed will be governed by EU law.[12] Moreover, in a number of other places in the Final Act of the European Energy Charter Conference similar provisions do appear with respect to treaties other than the EU treaties. Thus, in Annex 2, a Decision of the Energy Charter Conference provides that, in the event of a conflict between the Svalbard Treaty and the ECT, the Svalbard Treaty shall prevail to the extent of the conflict. In addition, the European Communities and their member states, on the one hand, and Russia, Ukraine, Kazakhstan, Kyrgyzstan, Tajikistan and Uzbekistan, on the other, each made Declarations that trade between them in nuclear materials would be exclusively governed by a specific agreement, to be concluded, and, until then, by the 1989 EC–USSR Agreement on Trade and Economic and Commercial Cooperation.[13]

However, in spite of these indications, it needs to be considered (i) whether an arbitral tribunal has jurisdiction to entertain a claim by an

9 L. Peterson, 'ICSID Tribunal will Permit European Commission to File Legal Brief in Energy Charter Treaty Arbitration', (2008) 16(1) *Investment Arbitration Reporter*, 11 December 2008.

10 *AES* v. *Hungary (No. 2)*, Award, 23 September 2010, paragraph 8.2.

11 See H. Wehland, 'Intra-EU Investment Agreements and Arbitration: Is European Community Law an Obstacle?' (2009) 58 *International and Comparative Law Quarterly* 297.

12 See C. Tietje, 'The Applicability of the Energy Charter Treaty in ICSID Arbitration of EU Nationals vs. EU Member States', (2008) *Institut für Wirtschaftsrecht, Martin Luther Universität Halle-Wittenberg Essays on Transnational Economic Law*, 10–11 and (2009) 6 *Transnational Dispute Management* 5.

13 The EC and their member states also made a Declaration clarifying the relevance of what is now Article 54 of the TFEU with respect to Article 25 of the ECT. See p. 99 below.

Investor of one EU member state against another EU member state; (ii) whether such a tribunal ought to entertain such a claim as a matter of admissibility;[14] and (iii) what (if any) impact the respective parties' membership of the EU ought to have on the merits.

### *(a) Jurisdiction*

It has been argued by the European Commission that the terms 'Contracting Party' and 'Investor of another Contracting Party' in Article 26(1) of the ECT ought to be read so as to preclude arbitration in such circumstances.[15] For 'Contracting Party' means not only a state but also a 'Regional Economic Integration Organization which has consented to be bound by this Treaty and for which this Treaty is in force'[16] and the EU is such an organisation. Thus, it is said, where the claim is brought by an Investor based in one member state against another member state, it is not a claim against 'another' Contracting Party within the terms of Article 26(1) and the tribunal therefore lacks jurisdiction.

Only '[d]isputes between a Contracting Party and an Investor of another Contracting Party relating to an Investment of the latter in the Area of the former' may be brought under Article 26. 'Area' is defined in Article 1(10) of the Treaty,[17] which provides that:

> With respect to a Regional Economic Integration Organization which is a Contracting Party, Area means the Areas of the member states of such Organization, under the provisions contained in the agreement establishing that Organization.

Any claim brought by a national of one EU member state against another member state or the EU would be a dispute relating to an Investment in the EU's Area. Moreover, nationals of any EU member states are also EU citizens under Community law.[18] Consequently, it may be said, in such circumstances the claimant would be seeking to claim in relation to an Investment in the Area of a Contracting Party of which it is a national.

This argument is, however, unsound. It depends upon a reading of the ECT under which any Investor based in an EU member state must be

14 See Chapter 3 as to the distinction between jurisdiction and admissibility.

15 E. Paasivirta (Legal Service, European Commission), Conference paper delivered at 'Energy Dispute Resolution: Investment Protection, Transit and the Energy Charter Treaty', Brussels, 23 October 2009 (www.encharter.org/index.php.id=47e)

16 Article 1(2).

17 But see also Article 40 of the ECT.

18 Article 20(1) of the TFEU, first sentence, provides that 'Citizenship of the Union is hereby established. Every person holding the nationality of a member state shall be a citizen of the Union.'

regarded as being, and as being only, an Investor of the EU; a reading for which there is no warrant in the text or elsewhere. In the first place, as a matter of EU law, 'Citizenship of the Union shall complement and not replace national citizenship.'[19] This is relevant because a person's nationality under international law is determined primarily by application of the national law of the state whose nationality is claimed.[20] Indeed, the definition of 'Investor' in Article 1(7) makes no mention of REIOs.[21]

European citizenship applies to individuals, not corporations. It is possible to establish a European limited liability company (a European Company or *Societas Europaea*).[22] However, the purpose of this is a limited one: to enable companies incorporated in different member states to merge or form holding companies or joint subsidiaries while avoiding the legal and practical difficulties arising from the existence of the member states' different legal systems, and as of October 2009 fewer than 500 such companies had been established.[23] One can, of course, argue that any company established under the laws of any EU member state is an Investor of the EU because the law in accordance with which it was organised is a law 'applicable in' the EU, but this seems a rather strained reading of the text of Article 1(7). In any case, it is difficult to see why an Investor cannot be both an EU national and a national of an EU member state, meaning that in bringing a claim against another member state, as opposed to the EU, it is not bringing a claim against its state of nationality. At worst, the claim would throw up an issue of dual nationality, which does not prevent claims under the ECT, and which would only arise if the respondent were the EU, rather than another member state.[24]

### *(b) Admissibility*

A further argument advanced by the European Commission (presumably in case its argument as to the lack of jurisdiction fails) is that a tribunal constituted under Article 26 ought, as a matter of admissibility, to decline to arbitrate disputes between member states and Investors of member

19 Article 20(1) of the TFEU, second sentence.

20 See *Soufraki* v. *United Arab Emirates*, Award, 7 July 2004, paragraph 55.

21 For further analysis of Article 1(7), see pp. 64–5 above.

22 See Council Regulation 2001/2157/EC, OJ L 294, 10.11.2001.

23 See ETUI (2009), European Company (SE) Factsheets, http://ecdb.worker-participation.eu

24 At the most, all that would be required would be to show that the claimant's member state nationality was his dominant nationality: see Case No. A/18 (1984) 5 Iran–US Cl Trib Rep 251 (Full Tribunal, Iran–US Claims Tribunal). Given the expressly complementary nature of EU citizenship, however, in most cases this should not be difficult.

states on the ground that to do so would be contrary to the 'applicable rules and principles of international law' which it is bound by Article 26(6) to apply.[25] It is submitted that this argument, too, is unsound. There may perhaps emerge a principle of EU law that claims dealing with the subject-matter of Part III of the ECT ought to be dealt with otherwise than by international arbitration.[26] But, although EU law arises ultimately under international treaty,[27] any such principle would not constitute a 'rule' or 'principle' of international law: the reference in Article 26(6) is surely to customary international law rules and principles. And, in any event, the Commission's argument overlooks the tribunal's primary duty under Article 26(6), which is to 'decide the issues in dispute in accordance with this Treaty': the Treaty contains no words which might sensibly be thought to compel a tribunal not to entertain disputes between an EU member state and Investors of another member state.[28]

A further reason for doubting the correctness of the European Commission's views in this area derives, it is submitted, from the very nature of international investment arbitration. For it is widely argued that an investment protection treaty should be 'regarded as conferring or creating direct rights in international law in favour of investors either from the outset, or at least (and in this event retrospectively) as and when they pursue claims'.[29]

If this analysis is correct, it is counterintuitive to accept that such directly-conferred rights might be diminished or removed by reference to international instruments – here, the TEU and TFEU – to which the Investor's state happens to be party.

This is not to say that issues covered by Part III ECT are not regulated by EU law. The effects of EU law, however, go (if at all) to the merits of the claim, not to whether a tribunal constituted under Article 26 has jurisdiction to hear it or whether it is admissible.

25 Paasivirta, Conference paper, 23 October 2009.

26 See Case C-459/03 *Commission of the European Communities* v. *Republic of Ireland* [2006] ECR I-4635.

27 The Treaty on European Union (TEU) and the Treaty on the Functioning of the European Union (TFEU).

28 In *Eastern Sugar BV* v. *Czech Republic*, Partial Award, 27 March 2007, a claim under the Netherlands–Czech Republic BIT, the European Commission wrote to the tribunal expressing the view that the BIT ought to be terminated by agreement between the Contracting States. The Czech Republic argued that EU accession brought about, by itself, the termination both of the jurisdiction of the tribunal and of the claim's admissibility. These contentions were both rejected (see paragraphs 142–87).

29 *Ecuador* v. *Occidental Exploration and Production Co* [2005] EWCA Civ 1116, [2006] QB 432 [18]; and see the sources there quoted.

### *(c) Merits*

In this regard, the Commission's view appears to be that EU law applies on the basis of, first, the applicable law provisions in Article 26(6) of the ECT and, second, the principle set out in Article 31(3)(c) of the VCLT.

Article 26(6) of the ECT, it will be recalled, provides that: 'A tribunal... shall decide the issues in dispute in accordance with this Treaty and applicable rules and principles of international law.' According to the Commission, in any intra-EU ECT case the applicable rules of international law include EU law and there exists a (rebuttable) presumption that compliance with EU law satisfies the requirements of the ECT. The argument is, in substance, that an arbitral tribunal constituted under Article 26 of the ECT should approach the issue in the same manner as did the Grand Chamber of the European Court of Human Rights in *Bosphorus* v. *Ireland*, where it stated that:

> In the Court's view, State action taken in compliance with such legal obligations [i.e. under EU law] is justified as long as the relevant [international] organisation is considered to protect fundamental rights, as regards both the substantive guarantees offered and the mechanisms controlling their observance, in a manner which can be considered at least equivalent to that for which the Convention provides... By 'equivalent' the Court means 'comparable'; any requirement that the organisation's protection be 'identical' could run counter to the interest of international cooperation pursued... However, any such finding of equivalence could not be final and would be susceptible to review in the light of any relevant change in fundamental rights protection.
>
> If such equivalent protection is considered to be provided by the organisation, the presumption will be that a state has not departed from the requirements of the Convention when it does no more than implement legal obligations flowing from its membership of the organisation.[30]

Thus it should be presumed that EU law provides protection to member states' Investors and their Investments in the Energy Sector within the Area of the EU equivalent to that provided by Part III of the ECT, so that compliance with EU law, in and of itself, satisfies the requirements of Part III.

Article 31(3) of the VCLT, it will be recalled, provides that, when interpreting a treaty: 'There shall be taken into account... (c) any relevant rules of international law applicable to the parties.' In the Commission's

30 *Bosphorus Hava Yolları Turizm ve Ticaret Anonim Şirketi* v. *Republic of Ireland* (2006) 42 EHRR 1, paragraphs 154–5.

view, in intra-EU ECT cases, the relevant rules of international law to be taken into account when interpreting the ECT include EU law. The argument here is that the two regimes should, if possible, be read compatibly, so as to ensure simultaneous compliance with both.

Both arguments seem to start from the same premise (the principle of systemic integration[31]) and come to the same conclusion. Two critiques of this approach have, however, been advanced.

The first argues that EU law is irrelevant under both Article 26(6) of the ECT and the principle of systemic integration enunciated in Article 31(3)(c) of the VCLT because it is not part of international law. The EC Treaty (now the TFEU), it has been claimed, is the 'basic constitutional charter' of the EU.[32] As such, it is no more relevant than the constituting order of any state party to the ECT. Just as a state cannot plead its own national law in order to justify or excuse a breach of its international legal obligations, so neither can the EU or its member states plead the dictates of EU law to justify non-compliance with their obligations under the ECT. One might, however, think that this view ignores the fact that the TEU and the TFEU are treaties and treaties are the quintessential international law instrument. It will be recalled that in its judgment in *van Gend en Loos* the European Court of Justice stated that:

> The Community constitutes a new legal order of *international law* for the benefit of which the states have limited their sovereign rights, albeit within limited fields and the subjects of which comprise not only member states but also their nationals. Independently of the legislation of member states, community law therefore not only imposes obligations on individuals but is also intended to confer upon them rights which become part of their legal heritage. These rights arise not only where they are *expressly granted by the treaty*, but also by reason of obligations *which the treaty imposes* in a clearly defined way upon individuals as well as upon the member states and upon the institutions of the community.[33]

This might be thought to be the correct view, at least from the international law perspective.[34] In subsequent judgments, however, the ECJ has spoken

31 See C. McLachlan, 'The Principle of Systemic Integration and Article 31(3)(c) of the Vienna Convention' (2005) 54 *International and Commercial Law Quarterly* 279.

32 Case 294/83 *Parti ecologiste 'Les Verts'* v. *Parliament* [1986] ECR 1339, paragraph 23.

33 Case 26–62 *NV Algemene Transport-en Expeditie Onderneming van Gend en Loos* v. *Netherlands Administratie der Belastingen* [1963] ECR 1 at 12 (emphasis added).

34 For discussion, see O. Spiermann, 'The Other Side of the Story: An Unpopular Essay on the Making of the European Community Legal Order' (1999) *European Journal of International Law* 763.

simply of a 'new legal order'.[35] This approach, viewing EU law as a self-contained legal order, perhaps reached its apogee in *Kadi*, where Advocate General Maduro considered 'how the relationship between the international legal order and the Community legal order must be described':

> The logical starting point of our discussion should, of course, be the landmark ruling in *Van Gend en Loos*, in which the Court affirmed the autonomy of the Community legal order. The Court held that the Treaty is not merely an agreement between states, but an agreement between the *peoples* of Europe. It considered that the Treaty had established a 'new legal order', beholden to, but distinct from the existing legal order of public international law. In other words, the Treaty has created *a municipal legal order* of trans-national dimensions, of which it forms the 'basic constitutional charter'.[36]

Although the European Court of Justice did not, in terms, adopt all of the elements of the Advocate General's reasoning, its judgment in *Kadi* does appear to be based on similar premises, with the Court holding that obligations imposed on the member states by the United Nations Charter cannot prevail over principles that 'form part of the very foundations' of the Community legal order,[37] despite Article 103 of the Charter providing that obligations under the Charter override all other treaty obligations. It might thus be thought that the issue whether the EU legal order is part of international law or should be viewed as a municipal legal order is quite finely balanced.

The second critique simply questions the practical effect of the Commission's desired approach. It asks: to what extent does presuming an act done in conformity with EU law to be in compliance with the ECT differ from placing the burden of proof on applicants to show that a respondent state's conduct breached the ECT? Looked at from this perspective, the problem becomes one of legal argument. A claimant must show not only that the impugned conduct was in breach of the respondent's obligations

35 See, e.g., Opinion 1/91 (Draft Treaty on a European Economic Area) [1991] ECR I-1061, where the ECJ stated that 'the EEC Treaty, albeit concluded in the form of an international agreement, none the less constitutes the constitutional charter of a Community based on law. As the Court of Justice has consistently held, the Community treaties established a new legal order for the benefit of which the States have limited their sovereign rights, in ever wider fields, and the subjects of which comprise not only Member States but also their nationals.'

36 Case C-402/05P *Kadi* v. *Council of the European Union and Commission of the European Communities*, Opinion of Advocate General Maduro, 16 January 2008, [2008] ECR I-6351, [2009] 1 AC 1225, paragraph 21 (citations omitted and emphasis added).

37 Paragraph 304.

under Part III of the ECT but, if the respondent argues that it was justified in so acting under EU law, that EU law fails to provide protections for Investors equivalent (that is, comparable, but not necessarily identical) to those embodied in Part III of the ECT. However, as Part III ECT contains obligations of results rather than of conduct or means, there would seem to be no practical difference between protections which are equivalent and protections which are identical.[38]

In these circumstances, the position was, in the authors' view, correctly stated by the arbitral tribunal in *AES* v. *Hungary (No. 2)*:

> [T]he dispute is about the conformity or non-conformity of Hungary's acts and measures with the ECT. Therefore, it is the behaviour of the state ... which must be analyzed in light of the ECT, to determine whether the measures, or the manner in which they were introduced, [complained of by the claimant investor] violated [the obligations contained in Part III of] the Treaty. The question of whether Hungary was, may have been, or may have felt obliged under EC law to act as it did, is only an element to be considered by this Tribunal when determining [under Part III] the 'rationality', 'reasonableness', 'arbitrariness' and 'transparency' of [what Hungary did].[39]

### 3. Investment disputes between member states and Investors of non-member states

As regards nationals of non-EU member state parties to the ECT, EU law is *res inter alios acta.* Article 31(3)(c) of the VCLT does not apply, because the provisions of EU law are not 'relevant rules of international law applicable to the parties'. Questions of EU law, in this context, are questions of fact, relevant to the same extent as questions of Contracting Parties' domestic law.

This is not to say that EU law is wholly irrelevant to the determination of breaches of the provisions of Part III of the ECT. Article 25(1) of the ECT provides that:

> The provisions of this Treaty shall not be so construed as to oblige a Contracting Party which is party to an Economic Integration Agreement (hereinafter referred to as 'EIA') to extend, by means of most favoured nation treatment, to another Contracting Party which is not a party to that EIA any preferential treatment applicable between the parties to that EIA as a result of their being parties thereto.

38 It might also be thought that such an argument is contrary to the tenor of Article 16 ECT: see p. 34 above.

39 *AES* v. *Hungary (No. 2)*, Award, 23 September 2010, paragraph 7.6.9.

Article 25(1) follows on from Article 24(4)(a), which establishes an MFN exception for members of free-trade areas and customs unions. However, Article 25(1) applies across the ECT, not just to the treatment of Investors, as does Article 24(4)(a). Article 25(2) defines an EIA as:

> an agreement substantially liberalizing, inter alia, trade and investment, by providing for the absence or elimination of substantially all discrimination between or among parties thereto through the elimination of existing discriminatory measures, either at the entry into force of that agreement or on the basis of a reasonable time frame.

It is clear that the EU falls within this definition, as is confirmed by the Declaration made by the Communities and their member states with respect to Article 25.

In addition the Energy Charter Conference adopted a Decision with respect to Articles 24(4)(a) and 25. The Decision provides that:

> An Investment of an Investor referred to in Article 1(7)(a)(ii), of a Contracting Party which is not party to an EIA . . . shall be entitled to treatment accorded under such EIA . . . provided that the Investment:
>
> (a) has its registered office, central administration or principal place of business in the Area of a party to that EIA . . . or
> (b) in case it only has its registered office in that Area, has an effective and continuous link with the economy of one of the parties to that EIA . . .

The European Communities and their member states' Declaration, in turn, states that:

> The European Communities and their Member States recall that, in accordance with article 58 of the Treaty establishing the European Community:
>
> (a) companies or firms formed in accordance with the law of a Member State and having their registered office, central administration or principal place of business within the Community shall, for the right of establishment pursuant to Part Three, Title III, Chapter 2 of the Treaty establishing the European Community, be treated in the same way as natural persons who are nationals of Member States; companies or firms which only have their registered office within the Community must, for this purpose, have an effective and continuous link with the economy of one of the Member States;
> (b) 'companies and firms' means companies or firms constituted under civil or commercial law, including co-operative societies, and other legal persons governed by public or private law, save for those which are non-profitmaking.

> The European Communities and their Member States further recall that:
>
> Community law provides for the possibility to extend the treatment described above to branches and agencies of companies or firms not established in one of the Member States; and that, the application of Article 25 of the Energy Charter Treaty will allow only those derogations necessary to safeguard the preferential treatment resulting from the wider process of economic integration resulting from the Treaties establishing the European Communities.

As it relates to Part III of the ECT, Article 25 allows derogation from the MFN obligation contained in Article 10(3) insofar as the relevant preferential treatment is accorded to nationals of other EU member states by virtue of those states' membership of the EU. However, it should also be recalled that Article 10(7) requires ECT Contracting Parties to accord MFN *or national* treatment, whichever is most favourable. If other EU nationals are merely treated as well as an EU member state's own nationals, then what is denied under Article 25(1) (MFN) is required under Article 10(3) (national treatment). Indeed, even if an Investor is not entitled to MFN, its Investment may well be, as both the Energy Charter Conference's Decision and the European Communities and their member states' Declaration make clear. If the Investment is a company or firm whose central administration or principal place of business is within the Community, or whose registered office is within the Community and the company or firm has an effective and continuous link with the economy of one of the member states, it will itself benefit from such preferential treatment. This would seem to leave little scope for Article 25 effectively to apply.

## 4. Dispute settlement under Article 26 and the European Union

Following their signing of the ECT, the European Communities submitted a statement to the Energy Charter Secretariat pursuant to Article 26(3)(b)(iii) of the Treaty. In Article 26(3), Contracting Parties give unconditional consent to the submission of Investor–State disputes to international arbitration or conciliation in accordance with the provisions of Article 26. However, Contracting Parties listed in Annex ID to the Treaty do not consent to arbitration or conciliation when the Investor has previously submitted the dispute to the Contracting Party's own courts or administrative tribunals, or in accordance with any applicable previously agreed dispute settlement procedure. The European

Communities are listed in Annex ID and therefore had to provide a written statement pursuant to Article 26(3)(b)(ii) of their relevant policies, practices and conditions.

The statement itself, in relevant part, reads as follows.

> The European Communities are a regional economic integration organisation within the meaning of the Energy Charter Treaty. The Communities exercise the competences conferred on them by their Member States through autonomous decision-making and judicial institutions.
>
> The European Communities and their Member States have both concluded the Energy Charter Treaty and are thus internationally responsible for the fulfilment of the obligations contained therein, in accordance with their respective competences.
>
> The Communities and the Member States will, if necessary, determine among them who is the respondent party to arbitration proceedings initiated by an Investor of another Contracting Party. In such case, upon the request of the Investor, the Communities and the Member States concerned will make such determination within a period of 30 days.
>
> The Court of Justice of the European Communities, as the judicial institution of the Communities, is competent to examine any question relating to the application and interpretation of the constituent treaties and acts adopted thereunder, including international agreements concluded by the Communities, which under certain conditions may be invoked before the Court of Justice.
>
> Any case brought before the Court of Justice of the European Communities by an investor of another Contracting Party in application of the forms of action provided by the constituent treaties of the Communities falls under Article 26(2)(a) of the Energy Charter Treaty. Given that the Communities' legal system provides for means of such action, the European Communities have not given their unconditional consent to the submission of a dispute to international arbitration or conciliation.
>
> As far as international arbitration is concerned, it should be stated that the provisions of the ICSID Convention do not allow the European Communities to become parties to it. The provisions of the ICSID Additional Facility also do not allow the Communities to make use of them. Any arbitral award against the European Communities will be implemented by the Communities' institutions, in accordance with their obligation under Article 26(8) of the Energy Charter Treaty.[40]

40 Statement submitted by the European Communities to the Secretariat of the Energy Charter Treaty pursuant to Article 26(3)(b)(ii) of the Energy Charter Treaty, OJ L 336, 23.12.1994, p. 115 (footnotes omitted).

The Statement will be analysed in greater depth later.[41] However, in the current instance, it is helpful in that it identifies the relevant domestic tribunals – the European Court of Justice and the Court of First Instance – for bringing a claim under Part III of the ECT against the EU. A footnote to the statement also provides that:

> Article 26(2)(a) is also applicable in the case where the Court of Justice of the European Communities may be called upon to examine the application or interpretation of the Energy Charter Treaty on the basis of a request for a preliminary ruling submitted by a court or tribunal of a member state in accordance with Article 177 of the EC Treaty.

The ECT, of course, has effect as a treaty in EU law, so an alternative to bringing arbitration proceedings under Article 26 would be to bring judicial proceedings against the EU or the relevant member state.[42] Treaties entered into by the EU form part of the Community legal order and it might be thought that the provisions of Part III, at least, of the ECT, have direct effect so that they can be relied upon before (now) the General Court and the ECJ and in the national courts of the member states.[43] This might, however, from the perspective of the Investor be seen as a less attractive alternative, not least because the view of such a court on the relationship between EU law and the ECT may not coincide with that of an arbitral tribunal.

The Statement also recalls that the European Communities cannot be parties to the ICSID Convention, which is only open to signature and ratification by states,[44] nor can they make use of the ICSID Additional Facility Rules, which require that the respondent party to arbitration proceedings brought under them be a state.[45] This means that arbitration proceedings under Article 26 of the ECT can only be submitted to a sole arbitrator or an *ad hoc* arbitral tribunal established under the UNCITRAL Arbitration Rules, or to arbitral proceedings under the Arbitration Institute of the Stockholm Chamber of Commerce. This, of course, has the disadvantage that any award may be challenged in the national courts of the seat of the arbitration.

41 See pp. 174ff. below.

42 Under Article 26(2)(a) of the ECT. See the discussion in Chapter 6.

43 See, as to the principle of direct effect in EU law, Case 26/62, *NV Algemene Transport-en Expeditie Onderneming van Gend en Loos* v. *Nederlandse Administratie der Belastingen* [1963] ECR 1, [1963] CMLR 105.

44 See Articles 67 and 68 of the ICSID Convention.

45 Article 2, ICSID Additional Facility Rules.

The Statement does, however, provide that any award against the Communities will be implemented by the Communities' institutions, in accordance with their obligation under Article 26(8) of the ECT, which provides that:

> The awards of arbitration . . . shall be final and binding upon the parties to the dispute . . . . Each Contracting Party shall carry out without delay any such award . . .

One might perhaps think that the EU has thus committed not to challenge any award made against it. However, this would probably be a mistake. At least in some national legal systems, the fact that an award is said to be 'final and binding' does not mean that it cannot be challenged in the courts. It simply means that an award is final, conclusive and binding in that it creates a *res judicata* and an issue estoppel.[46]

This leads to one final point. The ECJ has held that the national courts of EU member states must, if asked to do so, annul or refuse to enforce an arbitral award which has been obtained contrary to the EU law on concerted trade practices etc.; and that such law amounts to public policy under Article V(2)(b) of the New York Convention (which permits a court to refuse enforcement on the ground of public policy).[47] It is not hard to envisage a similar argument appealing to the ECJ in connection with proceedings in the courts of a member state concerned with a challenge to, or a disputed attempt to enforce, an ECT award obtained in arbitral proceedings instigated by an Investor of one EU member state against another member state. This could, however, apply only with regard to SCC, UNCITRAL and Additional Facility awards, so claimants might for this reason prefer to arbitrate their disputes (against respondents other than the EU) under the ICSID Convention.

46 See, e.g., *Essex County Council* v. *Premier Recycling Ltd* [2006] EWHC 3594 (TCC), [2007] BLR 233 and *Shell Egypt West Manzala GmbH* v. *Dana Gas Egypt Ltd* [2009] EWHC 2097 (Comm), [2010] Bus LR D53.

47 Case C-126/97 *Eco Swiss China Time Ltd* v. *Benetton International NV* [1999] ECR I-3055.

# 5

# Substantive law

## 1. Introduction

The purposes of this Chapter are to identify the substantive obligations undertaken by parties to the Energy Charter Treaty concerning investments and to offer some suggested answers to particular questions of construction thrown up by their drafting. This Chapter does not, however, purport to offer an analysis of all aspects of the content of the obligations which it identifies. For the ECT, as with successive investment-protection treaties, incorporates standards of treatment whose general import, though not always whose precise meaning, is well understood from earlier treaties and from the practice of states and arbitral tribunals concerning them. The body of both arbitral case law and academic writing concerning these standards is vast and it is no part of this work's ambition to attempt either a comprehensive summary or a synthesis.[1]

## 2. The scope of Part III of the ECT: investment promotion versus investment protection

The ECT's substantive provisions concerning investment are contained in Part III, entitled 'Investment Promotion and Protection'. Investment promotion and investment protection are, of course, different things: the

1 For discussions of the commonly found standards see in particular: R. Dolzer and C. Schreuer, *Principles of International Investment Law* (Oxford University Press, 2008), pp. 119–94; C. McLachlan, L. Shore and M. Weiniger, *International Investment Arbitration: Substantive Principles* (Oxford University Press, 2007), pp. 197–349; T. Grierson-Weiler and I. Laird, 'Standards of Treatment' in P. Muchlinski, F. Ortino and C. Schreuer (eds.), *The Oxford Handbook of International Investment Law* (Oxford University Press, 2008), pp. 259–303 (and see the helpful select bibliography at pp. 303–4); A. Newcombe and L. Paradell, *Law and Practice of Investment Treaties: Standards of Treatment* (Alphen aan den Rijn: Kluwer Law International, 2009); A. Reinisch (ed.), *Standards of Investment Protection* (Oxford University Press, 2008).

former is concerned with permitting, attracting and facilitating foreign investment; the latter, with the way in which an investment, once made, must be treated. As a matter of policy, the two are closely linked: the very purpose of undertaking, by treaty, to afford certain standards of treatment to foreign investments is to encourage the making of more such investments. As a matter of law, however, the ECT makes quite different provision as between promotion and protection. The provisions concerning promotion of investments are, as it is sometimes put, 'soft law', while those concerning the protection of investments are 'hard law'.[2] Focused as it is on the settlement of investment disputes between investors and states, this work concentrates on the 'hard' law concerning protection of investments, though the 'soft' law of investment promotion is briefly outlined. And, as will be seen, the policy of investment promotion – 'soft law' though it may be – cannot be ignored when construing the 'hard law' obligations concerning investment protection.

### *(a) Promotion of investment*

So far as the *promotion* of investment is concerned, Article 1(8) defines '"Make Investments" or "Making of Investments"' as 'establishing new Investments, acquiring all or part of existing Investments or moving into different fields of Investment activity'.[3] This defined expression is then deployed in paragraphs (2) and (3) of Article 10:

> (2) Each Contracting Party shall endeavour to accord to Investors of other Contracting Parties, as regards the Making of Investments in its Area, the Treatment described in paragraph (3).
> (3) For the purposes of this Article, 'Treatment' means treatment accorded by a Contracting Party which is no less favourable than that which it accords to its own Investors or to Investors of any other Contracting Party or any third state, whichever is the most favourable.

2 See K. Abbott, R. Keohane, A. Moravcsik and D. Snidal, 'The Concept of Legalization', (2000) 54 *International Organization* 401 where the authors argue that 'hard law' is characterised by legal obligation, precision and enforcement powers in the hands of some other body (e.g., an arbitral tribunal) and 'soft law' by the absence of some or all of these features.

3 In Australia (which has not ratified the Treaty and does not apply it provisionally, so the point is academic at the moment) 'the establishment of a new mining or raw materials processing project in Australia with total investment of $A10 million or more by a foreign interest, even where that foreign interest is already operating a similar business in Australia, is considered as the making of a new investment': see the fourth of the Understandings.

The 'Treatment', as defined here, is, of course, the treatment generally described as national and 'most-favoured nation' (MFN) treatment.[4] As regards the Making of Investments the obligation is to 'endeavour' to afford such Treatment to Investors (or, one might more accurately say, would-be Investors). That these paragraphs are not intended to create a 'hard' obligation actually to afford such treatment is confirmed by paragraph (4) of Article 10, which envisages a supplementary treaty which 'shall, subject to conditions to be laid down therein, oblige each party thereto to afford to Investors of other parties, as regards the Making of Investments in its Area, the Treatment described in paragraph (3) . . . .'[5] No such supplementary treaty has been concluded.[6]

Further provision concerning the Making of Investments appears in paragraphs (5), (6) and (9)(a) of Article 10. Paragraph (5) obliges Contracting Parties to endeavour to limit the number of exceptions to MFN treatment as regards the making of Investments and to endeavour to remove progressively existing restrictions to the making of Investments affecting Investors of other Contracting Parties. Paragraph (6) allows for a declaration of intention not to introduce any new exceptions to MFN treatment as regards the making of Investments and for a voluntary commitment, notifiable to the Secretariat, to refrain from introducing any more such restrictions.[7] Paragraph (9)(a) requires Contracting Parties to report to the Secretariat on signature of or accession to the Treaty concerning their laws, regulations or other measures relevant to exceptions to MFN treatment as regards the making of Investments.

Apart from the drafting in Article 10, there is a second reason why none of the obligations (in so far as they can properly be so called) imposed by Part III concerning the promotion of investment is enforceable by an aggrieved would-be investor, at least in some cases which might arise in practice. As has already been noted,[8] one of the conditions which must exist in order for a claimant to bring a claim against a Contracting Party under Article 26 is that the complaint be a complaint by an

4 As to which see Dolzer and Schreuer, *Principles of International Investment Law*, pp. 178–91; McLachlan *et al.*, *International Investment Arbitration: Substantive Principles*, pp. 251–7; P Acconci, 'Most-Favoured-Nation Treatment' in P. Muchlinski, F. Ortino and C. Schreuer (eds.), *The Oxford Handbook of International Investment Law* (Oxford University Press, 2008), pp. 363–404.

5 This ambition is also stated in the Treaty's Preamble.

6 See Chapter 1.

7 No such notifications have been made: see Annex VC.

8 See pp. 45ff.

Investor relating to an Investment. By definition, a person whose complaint is of an inability to make an investment at all cannot fulfil such a condition.

### *(b) Protection of investments*

So far as the *protection* of investments is concerned, Article 10(1) imposes five distinct obligations upon Contracting Parties as regards Investments. These may be illustrated by annotations to the text of Article 10(1), as follows:

> PROMOTION, PROTECTION AND TREATMENT OF INVESTMENTS
>
> (1) Each Contracting Party shall, in accordance with the provisions of this Treaty, encourage and create stable, equitable, favourable and transparent conditions for Investors of other Contracting Parties to make Investments in its Area. Such conditions shall include a commitment *[i] to accord at all times to Investments of Investors of other Contracting Parties fair and equitable treatment.* Such Investments shall also *[ii] enjoy the most constant protection and security* and *[iii] no Contracting Party shall in any way impair by unreasonable or discriminatory measures their management, maintenance, use, enjoyment or disposal. [iv] In no case shall such Investments be accorded treatment less favourable than that required by international law, including treaty obligations. [v] Each Contracting Party shall observe any obligations it has entered into with an Investor or an Investment of an Investor of any other Contracting Party.*
>
> ... [emphasis added].

The opening words of Article 10(1) have not here been identified as creating a distinct obligation for two reasons: first, they are simply too vague; and second, they are concerned with the promotion of investments, something which, as discussed above, is in the scheme of Part III a matter of 'soft law'. As will be seen, however, these opening words do play an important role in helping to elucidate the meaning of the five 'hard law' obligations, breach of any of which gives rise (subject to the various necessary jurisdictional conditions) to liability under Article 26.

Each of these five obligations will now be briefly considered in turn, together with the national treatment and MFN treatment obligation, which, as will be seen, is contained in Article 10(7), the obligation in Article 10(12) to provide effective means for the assertion of claims and the enforcement of rights, and certain other obligations also laid down in Part III.

### (i) Fair and equitable treatment[9]

The requirement that foreign investors be guaranteed 'fair and equitable treatment' or some variant thereof has a pedigree going back at least as far as the 1948 Havana Charter for an International Trade Organization.[10] It appears in numerous investment-protection treaties[11] and is the most frequently invoked, and most frequently *successfully* invoked, standard in international investment disputes.[12]

In contrast to other standards to be considered later in this Chapter, the standard of fair and equitable treatment is objective: the claimant succeeds by proving treatment which in its own right is to be regarded as unfair and inequitable, not by showing that some other person receives, or would receive, better treatment.

This much is clear. However, the content of the standard has been the subject of some debate. In particular, it is controversial whether a treaty obligation to accord fair and equitable treatment is really anything more than a codification of, or a codification of an aspect of, the obligation (or supposed obligation) under customary international law to uphold the 'international minimum standard' for the treatment of aliens.[13]

The classic formulation of the international minimum standard was given in 1926 by the US–Mexico Claims Commission. It is notably undemanding of host states:

9 See, as to this standard generally: Dolzer and Schreuer, *Principles of International Investment Law*, pp. 119–49; R. Dolzer, 'Fair and Equitable Treatment: A Key Standard in Investment Treaties', (2005) 39 *International Law* 87; McLachlan *et al.*, *International Investment Arbitration: Substantive Principles*, pp. 226–47; Newcombe and Paradell, *Law and Practice of Investment Treaties: Standards of Treatment*, pp. 255–97; K. Yannaca-Small, 'Fair and Equitable Treatment Standard: Recent Developments' in A. Reinisch (ed.), *Standards of Investment Protection* (Oxford University Press, 2008), pp. 111–30.

10 Article 11(2)(a), ('. . . just and equitable treatment for . . . enterprise, skills, capital, arts and technology . . . ').

11 See OECD, *International Investment Law: A Changing Landscape* (Paris: OECD, 2008), pp. 75–80.

12 Dolzer and Schreuer, *Principles of International Investment Law*, p. 119.

13 See UNCTAD, *Fair and Equitable Treatment* (UNCTAD Series on issues in international investments) (New York: United Nations, 1999), pp. 10–15.

> [T]he propriety of governmental acts should be put to the test of international standards, and . . . the treatment of an alien, in order to amount to an international delinquency, should amount to an outrage, to bad faith, to wilful neglect of duty, or to an insufficiency of governmental action so far short of international standards that every reasonable and impartial man would readily recognize its insufficiency.[14]

The argument that fair and equitable treatment merely equates to, or is an element of, this standard finds support in various sources.[15] Explaining the fair and equitable treatment obligation in the OECD Draft Convention on the Protection of Foreign Property (1967), the OECD Committee wrote that: 'The standard required conforms in effect to the "minimum standard" which forms part of customary international law.'[16] Article 1105(1) of the NAFTA, headed 'Minimum Standard of Treatment', provides that: 'Each Party shall accord to investments of investors of another Party treatment in accordance with international law, including fair and equitable treatment and full protection and security', which strongly suggests that fair and equitable treatment (along with full protection and security) is to be regarded merely an aspect of the customary international minimum standard. After the decisions of NAFTA arbitral tribunals in *S. D. Myers*[17] and *Pope & Talbot*,[18] which gave different interpretations of Article 1105(1), the states parties to the treaty (Canada, Mexico and the US), acting together as the NAFTA Free Trade Commission, issued a binding interpretative note[19] stating that: 'Article 1105(1) prescribes the customary international law minimum standard of treatment of aliens as the minimum standard of treatment to be afforded to investments of investors of another Party' and that '[t]he concepts of "fair and equitable treatment" and "full protection and security"[20] do not require treatment

14 *Neer* (*United States of America* v. *Mexico*) (1926) 4 RIAA 60, 61–2. For descriptions of what the international minimum standard entails in the context of NAFTA Article 1105, see *Waste Management Inc* v. *Mexico*, Final Award, 30 April 2004, paragraph 98.

15 For more extensive discussion see J. Thomas, 'Reflections on Article 1105 of NAFTA: History, State Practice and the Influence of Commentators' (2002) 17 *ICSID Review–Foreign Investment Law Journal* 21.

16 OECD, Draft Convention on the Protection of Foreign Property and Resolution of the Council of the OECD on the Draft Convention (1968) 7 ILM 118, 120. See also the statement of the Swiss Ministry of Foreign Affairs, (1980) 36 *Annuaire suisse de droit international* 178.

17 *S. D. Myers Inc* v. *Canada*, First Partial Award, 13 November 2000.

18 *Pope & Talbot Inc* v. *Canada*, Award on the Merits, 10 April 2001.

19 Under Article 1131(2) of the NAFTA (1993) 32 ILM 289. There is no equivalent provision for binding interpretative notes under the ECT.

20 Full protection and security is discussed below at p. 115.

in addition to or beyond that which is required by the customary international law minimum standard of treatment of aliens'.[21] NAFTA arbitral tribunals have adhered to this interpretation since[22] and the US and Canada 2004 Model BITs are both to this effect.[23]

However, this interpretation of the fair and equitable treatment standard is not without its problems. First, it seems odd to interpret a treaty provision by reference to a customary law standard first elucidated over eighty years ago (in the *Neer* award). This was the criticism made by the arbitral tribunal in *Pope & Talbot*.[24] This is not an insurmountable problem for (as conceded by all three NAFTA states parties and pointed out by the tribunal in *ADF Group*[25]) the international minimum standard may evolve: what might not have been seen as outrageous in 1927 might be viewed as such today.[26] But, second and more fundamentally, it is by no means clear that there *is* in fact a generally agreed international minimum standard of treatment of aliens of which fair and equitable treatment is an element. The existence, let alone the content, of such a standard (undemanding though it is) has long been contested between capital-exporting and capital-importing states.[27] Indeed, part of the impetus for the development of treaty standards for the treatment of foreign investment came from the lack of agreement between states as to the content of the relevant customary rules. From this perspective, the NAFTA jurisprudence serves, at best, as evidence of an agreement between the three states parties to the NAFTA that such a standard exists and that its content includes fair and equitable treatment. But it is far from constituting the extensive and virtually uniform practice, accompanied by a belief that such practice is

21 FTC Note of Interpretation, 31 July 2001.

22 See *ADF Group* v. *United States of America*, Award, 9 January 2003, paragraph 178; *Mondev International Ltd* v. *United States of America*, Award, 11 October 2002, paragraph 121. M. Sornarajah, *The International Law on Foreign Investment* (Cambridge University Press, 2004) declares at p. 236 that 'the resulting practice makes the phrase "fair and equitable treatment" otiose'.

23 See Article 5 of the US Model BIT (2004) and Article 5 of the Canada Model Foreign Investment Promotion and Protection Agreement (2004).

24 *Pope & Talbot Inc* v. *Canada*, Award on Damages, 31 May 2002, paragraphs 57–65.

25 *ADF Group* v. *United States of America*, Award, 9 January 2003, paragraphs 179–80. See also *Mondev International Ltd* v. *United States of America*, Award, 11 October 2002, paragraphs 114–16.

26 See *Glamis Gold Ltd* v. *United States of America*, Award, 8 June 2008, paragraphs 613–14.

27 See Sornarajah, *The International Law on Foreign Investment*, pp. 136–54 and 328–32; and see Chapter 1, above.

obligatory, necessary to show the existence of a rule of general custom binding on all states.[28]

Whatever the better view as regards 'fair and equitable treatment' as that expression is used in the instruments and draft instruments discussed above, it is submitted that the correct approach to 'fair and equitable treatment' in Article 10(1) of the Energy Charter Treaty is to start with the ordinary meaning of the text.[29] For Article 10(1) contains no suggestion that the obligation to accord relevant investments 'fair and equitable treatment' is to be regarded as anything other than a free-standing obligation. In contrast to Article 1105(1) of the NAFTA ('... international law, including fair and equitable treatment... ') there is no suggestion here that fair and equitable treatment is akin to, or an aspect of, anything else. There is thus no warrant for reading the obligation to accord such treatment other than at face value. A court or tribunal is, rather, driven to consider simply whether such conduct as the claimant proves to have occurred constituted a failure to treat the claimant's investment fairly and equitably.

A contrary reading is not impossible and may derive some support from the penultimate sentence of Article 10(1). There, it will be recalled, having mentioned fair and equitable treatment, constant protection and security and the duty to avoid unreasonable and discriminatory measures, the draftsman provides that: 'In no case shall such Investments be accorded treatment less favourable than that required by international law, including treaty obligations.'[30] The reference here to 'international law' is plainly to customary international law and this sentence may therefore perhaps be regarded as a sweeping-up clause intended to catch any breaches of the international minimum standard not already caught by the earlier specific proscriptions; proscriptions which, on this reading, merely cover some aspects of such standard. However, this is to beg the question. And the more natural reading is surely that the penultimate sentence of

28 *North Sea Continental Shelf* cases (*FRG* v. *Netherlands/FRG* v. *Denmark*), ICJ Rep 1969, p. 3, paragraph 74. For a contrary conclusion on the customary status of the fair and equitable treatment standard, see *Mondev International Ltd* v. *United States of America*, Award, 11 October 2002, paragraph 116.

29 See Article 31(1) of the Vienna Convention on the Law of Treaties (1969). See A. Wythes, 'Investor–State Arbitrations: Can the "Fair and Equitable Treatment" Clause Consider International Human Rights Obligations?' (2010) 23 *Leiden Journal of International Law* 241 at 248.

30 This standard is mentioned separately at p. 118 below.

Article 10(1) lays down a distinct standard which is not intended to inform the content of the other standards referred to earlier.[31]

This still leaves, of course, the question of what does and does not constitute 'fair and equitable' treatment. It has rightly been said that a tribunal may not apply its own idiosyncratic notion of fairness and equity but 'must be disciplined by being based upon state practice and judicial or arbitral case law or other sources of customary or general international law'.[32] This is especially important in an international context where the scope for disagreement as to what fairness and equity entail is inevitably greater. Dolzer and Schreuer, discussing fair and equitable treatment in international investment law generally,[33] identify from the arbitral case law five areas in which the standard may operate: (i) transparency, stability and the protection of legitimate expectations;[34] (ii) compliance with contractual obligations;[35] (iii) procedural propriety and due process; (iv) good faith; and (v) freedom from coercion and harassment. McLachlan, Shore and Weiniger emphasise that the fair and equitable treatment standard is concerned with the *process* of decision-making as it affects the investor rather than with the protection of substantive rights; and note that the protection of legitimate expectations and procedural fairness have

31 See *Pope & Talbot Inc* v. *Canada*, Award on the Merits, 10 April 2001, paragraph 111 where the tribunal, before turning to Article 1105(1) of the NAFTA, adopted this analysis of the provisions of various model BITs whose drafting ('Investment shall at all times be accorded fair and equitable treatment, shall enjoy full protection and security and shall in no case be accorded treatment less than that required by international law') was essentially the same as Article 10(1) of the ECT. The analysis appears to have been accepted as correct by Tysoe J in *Mexico* v. *Metalclad Corporation*, 2001 BCSC 664, (2001) 89 BCLR (3d) 359, paragraphs 64–5, though the court went on to criticise the *Pope & Talbot* tribunal for not giving effect to the differently-worded NAFTA Article 1105(1).

32 *ADF Group* v. *United States of America*, Award, 9 January 2003, paragraph 184. The same point was well put by Lord Hoffmann about 'unfair' shareholders' conduct in English corporate law: 'Parliament has chosen fairness as the criterion . . . But this does not mean that the court can do whatever the individual judge happens to think fair. The concept of fairness must be applied judicially and the content which it is given by the courts must be based upon rational principles. As Warner J. said [citation omitted]: "The court . . . has a very wide discretion, but it does not sit under a palm tree"': *O'Neill* v. *Phillips* [1999] 1 WLR 1092.

33 Dolzer and Schreuer, *Principles of International Investment Law*, pp. 133–47.

34 As to legitimate expectation, see *Suez, Sociedad General de Aguas de Barcelona* v. *Argentina*, Decision on Liability, 30 July 2010, paragraphs 211–31 and the Separate Opinion of Arbitrator Nikken ('more attention has been paid to what the claimants have considered the scope of their rights than what the Parties defined as the extent of their obligations' (paragraph 27)).

35 This is perhaps more controversial. Article 10(1) of the ECT expressly deals with compliance with obligations, as discussed below, p. 120 (the 'umbrella' clause).

been the main concerns of arbitral tribunals concerned with complaints about administrative action.[36] These observations are no less applicable to the fair and equitable treatment standard as it appears in the Energy Charter Treaty.

Any attempt to shed further light on the meaning of 'fair and equitable treatment' as the expression is used in Article 10(1) of the ECT must necessarily go beyond the ordinary meaning of the words and consider the relevant background, namely the words' context and the object and purpose of the ECT.[37]

Certain aspects of this background ought, it is submitted, to be dismissed as of little or no assistance. It does not, for example, assist to recall the Contracting Parties' desire, expressed in the ECT's Preamble, 'to catalyse economic growth by means of measures to liberalize investment . . . in energy'; or to recall that the purpose of the Treaty, as expressed in Article 2, is to '. . . promote long-term co-operation in the energy field . . .'. These might at first seem to commend an insistence on very *high* standards of fairness and equity towards investors, so as to encourage such investment and long-term co-operation. But when one recalls the Treaty's lack of binding obligations concerning the *making* of investments,[38] it may equally be thought that to impose very high standards of conduct towards investors is just as likely to deter some states from the desired liberalisation and long-term co-operation. As van Harten has written concerning BITs in general:

> These treaties do not affirm the rights and interests of international businessmen as an inherent good; they utilize investor protection as a means to an end. Read with care, . . . the preambular language of investment treaties does not provide a basis for adopting a presumption in favour of safeguarding the claimant against the state.[39]

No bias in favour of or against investors in the interpretation of what is 'fair and equitable' should thus be spelled out of the object and purpose of the Energy Charter Treaty in this regard.[40]

36 McLachlan *et al.*, *International Investment Arbitration: Substantive Principles*, pp. 260–2. Note, however, that McLachlan *et al.* regard fair and equitable treatment as 'the functional equivalent of the minimum standard of treatment at international law' (p. 260).

37 Article 31(1) of the VCLT.

38 See above, p. 105.

39 G. van Harten, *Investment Treaty Arbitration and Public Law* (Oxford University Press, 2007), p. 140.

40 See *El Paso International Energy Co* v. *Argentina*, Decision on Jurisdiction, 27 April 2006, paragraphs 68–70.

Much more relevant context is, however, to be found rather closer to home in the first sentence of Article 10(1) itself: 'Each Contracting Party shall, in accordance with the provisions of this Treaty, encourage and create stable, equitable, favourable and transparent conditions for Investors of other Contracting Parties to make Investments in its Area.' Although this refers on its face to the making of investments, a matter which is not the subject of direct binding obligation,[41] it is plain that the draftsman intends the binding obligations which follow – including the commitment to accord investors fair and equitable treatment – to constitute the steps taken 'in accordance with the provisions of this Treaty', to encourage and create the conditions mentioned.

Two matters are notable. First, that this is a positive commitment: Contracting Parties do not merely agree to refrain from undesirable conduct but positively 'to encourage and create' the desired conditions. They have decided to encourage investment in the energy sector and Article 10(1) seeks to reflect that decision by legislating for an investor-friendly environment. Article 10(1) thus differs from the international minimum standard (to the extent that it exists) which, as a customary rule, binds *all* states to provide a minimal level of protection regardless of their preferences for or against foreign investment. As the arbitral tribunal in *Saluka Investments BV* v. *Czech Republic* stated with regard to a similar provision in the Netherlands–Czechoslovakia BIT:

> [T]he customary minimum standard is in any case binding upon a State and provides a minimum guarantee to foreign investors, even where the State follows a policy that is in principle opposed to foreign investment; in that context, the minimum standard of 'fair and equitable treatment' may in fact provide no more than 'minimal' protection. Consequently, in order to violate that standard, States' conduct may have to display a relatively higher degree of inappropriateness. Bilateral investment treaties, however, are designed to promote foreign direct investment as between the Contracting Parties; in this context, investors' protection by the 'fair and equitable treatment' standard is meant to be a guarantee providing a positive incentive for foreign investors. Consequently, in order to violate the standard, it may be sufficient that States' conduct displays a relatively lower degree of inappropriateness.[42]

41 See above, p. 105.

42 Partial Award, 17 March 2006, paragraphs 292–3. For a similar view on the minimum standard, see *Glamis Gold Ltd* v. *United States of America*, Award, 8 June 2009, paragraph 615, which describes it as serving 'as a floor, an absolute bottom, below which conduct is not accepted by the international community'.

The second notable matter is that the opening sentence spells out the sort of conditions which fair and equitable treatment (along with the other standards mentioned in Article 10(1)) is intended to encourage and create: stable, favourable (to investors) and transparent conditions. Of course, these adjectives are no less abstract than 'fair' or 'equitable'. But, crucially, they are not their synonyms. They have distinct meanings. Thus, it is submitted, what is fair and equitable in any given case ought not to be ascertained in the abstract but, rather, in the light of the Contracting Parties' commitment to 'encourage and create stable, equitable, favourable and transparent conditions'.

### (ii) Most constant protection and security[43]

Article 10(1)'s requirement that the investments to which it applies 'shall also enjoy the most constant protection and security' likewise incorporates a standard long found in many other investment protection treaties (often expressed as 'full' protection and security) and, before them, in treaties of friendship, commerce and navigation.[44] Like the obligation to afford fair and equitable treatment, proof of its breach does not depend on the claimant's showing how some other investor has been or would have been treated. McLachlan, Shore and Weiniger point out that, unlike fair and equitable treatment, this standard is concerned not with the host state's decision-making processes but with a matter of substance: the state's failure to protect the investment from damage either by the state or – at least where due diligence might have afforded such protection – by others.[45]

As with fair and equitable treatment, it has been extensively debated whether the obligation to provide full protection and security is merely a facet of the obligation not to transgress the international minimum standard.[46] For essentially the reasons given above in the context of fair and equitable treatment, it is submitted that, as it appears in Article 10(1)

43 See, as to this standard generally: Dolzer and Schreuer, *Principles of International Investment Law*, pp. 149–53; McLachlan *et al.*, *International Investment Arbitration: Substantive Principles*, pp. 247–50; Newcombe and Paradell, *Law and Practice of Investment Treaties: Standards of Treatment*, pp. 307–14; G. Cordero Moss, 'Full Protection and Security' in A. Reinisch (ed.), *Standards of Investment Protection* (Oxford University Press, 2008), pp. 131–50.

44 For discussion of the history of the concept, see *Asian Agricultural Products Ltd* v. *Sri Lanka*, Final Award, 27 June 1990, 30 ILM 577, 599–601.

45 McLachlan *et al.*, *International Investment Arbitration: Substantive Principles*, p. 247.

46 Dolzer and Schreuer, *Principles of International Investment Law*, pp. 152–3.

of the ECT, the obligation to provide 'the most constant protection and security' is not so limited.

A related issue in investment protection law generally is whether an obligation to provide full (or constant) protection and security is limited to the physical security of an investor's assets or extends to legal protection for the investor. In *Azurix Corporation* v. *Argentina*, the tribunal reasoned that 'when the terms "protection and security" are qualified by "full" and no other adjective or explanation, they extend, in their ordinary meaning, the content of this standard beyond physical security'.[47] And as the tribunal in *Siemens AG* v. *Argentina* perceptively noted '. . . based on the definition of investment, which includes tangible and intangible assets, the Tribunal considers that the obligation to provide full protection and security is wider than "physical" protection and security. It is difficult to understand how the physical security of an intangible asset would be achieved.'[48] Both of these lines of reasoning apply with equal force to Article 10(1)'s stipulation that relevant investments 'shall enjoy the most constant protection and security'. At the same time, however, it is no less true under Article 10(1) than it is in international investment law generally that the question of whether there has been a failure to provide *legal* protection to an investment must take into account the extent to which the investor had access to a functioning legal system through which to seek such protection.[49]

### (iii) No unreasonable or discriminatory measures[50]

Article 10(1)'s stipulation that 'no Contracting Party shall in any way impair by unreasonable or discriminatory measures [the] management, maintenance, use, enjoyment or disposal [of Investments]' is, too, a familiar one in the law and practice of investment protection. The formula (sometimes rendered in other treaties as 'arbitrary or discriminatory' action or measures) in truth contains two distinct obligations: to avoid

47 Award, 14 July 2006, paragraph 408.

48 Award, 6 February 2007, paragraph 303. Intangibles are, of course, capable of amounting to Investments under the ECT too: see Article 1(6)(a).

49 See *Saluka Investments BV* v. *Czech Republic*, Partial Award, 17 March 2006, paragraphs 492–3.

50 See, as to this standard generally: Dolzer and Schreuer, *Principles of International Investment Law*, pp. 173–8; Newcombe and Paradell, *Law and Practice of Investment Treaties: Standards of Treatment*, pp. 298–306; V. Heiskanen, 'Arbitrary and Unreasonable Measures' in A. Reinisch (ed.), *Standards of Investment Protection* (Oxford University Press, 2008), pp. 87–110.

unreasonable measures and to avoid discriminatory measures.[51] The two are, however, closely related.

The former has been described by the International Court of Justice as

> not so much something opposed to a rule of law, as something opposed to the rule of law . . . a wilful disregard of due process of law, an act which shocks, or at least surprises, a sense of judicial propriety.[52]

More recently, it has been said by an arbitral tribunal – in a formulation which perhaps sets the bar for the claimant rather lower – that the obligation to avoid arbitrary measures is an obligation to avoid

> measures that affect the investments of nationals of the other Party without engaging in a rational decision-making process. Such process would include a consideration of the effect of a measure on foreign investments and a balance of the interests of the State with any burden imposed upon such investment.[53]

These formulations are applicable to the notion of unreasonable measures in Article 10(1) of the ECT.

As regards discriminatory measures, the ECT, in common with other investment protection treaties, cannot sensibly be thought to prohibit every act by which the state discriminates, i.e. prefers one Investor over another. But, again in common with other investment treaties, the ECT neglects to enumerate what constitutes a valid, and what an invalid, ground of discrimination. Nationality is presumably not a valid ground, but in this respect this part of Article 10(1) adds nothing to the national treatment standard spelled out expressly in Article 10(7). The absence of any further enumeration strongly suggests that the question of the validity, or otherwise, of other grounds on which a state elects to treat one Investor less favourably than another is itself a question of reasonableness in the sense described above. As the tribunal put it in *Enron Corporation and Ponderosa Assets LP* v. *Argentina*,[54] the question is whether there has been 'capricious, irrational or absurd differentiation'.

51 Dolzer and Schreuer, *Principles of International Investment Law*, p. 173.

52 *Case concerning Elettronica Sicula*, 20 July 1989, (1989) 15 ICJ Rep 76. This case concerned provisions of the US–Italy treaty of friendship, commerce and navigation.

53 *LG&E* v. *Argentina*, Decision on Liability, 3 October 2006. Such formulations in particular have rightly led to the observation that the modern system of investment protection treaties is 'a uniquely internationalized form of public law adjudication': van Harten, *Investment Treaty Arbitration and Public Law*, p. 83.

54 Award, 22 May 2007, paragraph 282.

### (iv) Treatment less favourable than that required by international law, including treaty obligations

As discussed briefly above,[55] the penultimate sentence of Article 10(1) stipulates that: 'In no case shall such Investments be accorded treatment less favourable than that required by international law, including treaty obligations.' The reference to the treatment 'required by international law' lays down no new standard of treatment but ensures, first, that (in what must surely be a rather unlikely case) a state which mistreats the claimant's investment in some manner constituting a breach of customary international law but not constituting a breach of any specific obligation in Part III of the Treaty is nonetheless vulnerable to a claim under Article 26 of the Treaty and not merely to the remedies of diplomatic protection available in customary international law in respect of such a breach.

Second, however, the additional words 'including treaty obligations' make clear that it is not merely breaches of *customary* international law which fall so to be treated.[56] Thus it would appear that the effect of this sentence in Article 10(1) is to elevate to the level of a breach of the ECT, and thus make amenable to a claim by the investor under Article 26, a breach by a Contracting Party of an obligation contained in some other treaty. The provision is an unusual one in this respect.[57] The ECT itself contains no guidance as to which particular treaty obligations might fall within its scope. However, the Understanding with respect to Articles 26 and 27 to the ECT adopted by the signatories to the Final Act provides that:

> The reference to treaty obligations in the penultimate sentence of Article 10(1) does not include decisions taken by international organizations, even if they are legally binding, or treaties which entered into force before 1 January 1970.

As an agreement 'relating to the treaty . . . made between all the parties in connection with the conclusion of the treaty',[58] the Understanding would seem to have considerable weight and is likely to be followed by arbitral

55 See p. 111.

56 It has been argued that a reference to 'international law' by itself brings in treaty obligations (see the submission summarised in *Pope & Talbot Inc* v. *Canada*, Award on the Merits of Phase 2, 10 April 2001, paragraph 107), but this is unconvincing.

57 Newcombe and Paradell, *Law and Practice of Investment Treaties: Standards of Treatment*, p. 254.

58 Article 31(2)(b) of the VCLT. For discussion of the relevance of Understandings to the interpretation of the ECT, see pp. 19ff. above.

tribunals. It makes clear that, for example, EU regulations or directives are not encompassed by the provision, and neither are any treaties which entered into force before the beginning of 1970, which rather restricts the provision's scope.

In addition it is uncertain whether the provision catches treaty obligations which themselves would not otherwise give rise to an individual cause of action on the part of an investor. It has been argued elsewhere that, under certain other investment treaties containing similar provisions, breaches of the WTO Agreement might give rise to claims by adversely affected investors, in spite of the fact that under the WTO Dispute Settlement Understanding it is generally for the affected person's state to take action and that compensation is not generally available for affected private persons.[59] Whether or not this argument is right as regards other investment treaties, it is debatable whether it holds for the ECT. For the application of GATT-inconsistent trade-related measures to existing Investments is, for the purposes of Article 26 of the ECT, expressly stipulated to constitute a breach of Part III of the Treaty: that is, it may found an individual cause of action.[60] It might be thought that this specific inclusion should lead, by application of the maxim *inclusio unius est exclusio alterius*, to the conclusion that other provisions of GATT 1994 cannot be so relied on. And, if this is the case, why should the provisions of other treaties which do not, of themselves, give rise to a right of private action be any more capable of being relied on by an Investor? The best answer may be that the words 'including treaty obligations' would be largely otiose if they referred only to obligations whose breach was already actionable by the Investor. But the point is not at all clear.

Even if an expansive view of the provision is taken, however, in principle it would seem sensible to limit its effect to treaty obligations owed by the host state to the *investor's* state: an investor should not be able to benefit under this provision from obligations undertaken by the host state to

59 G. Verhoosel, 'The Use of Investor–State Arbitration under Bilateral Investment Treaties to Seek Relief for Breaches of WTO Law' (2003) 6 *Journal of International Economic Law* 493. The ECJ has consistently refused to hold that WTO law has any direct effect in the EU legal order: see P. Hilpold, *Die EU im GATT/WTO-System* (Innsbruck: Innsbruck University Press, 3rd edn, 2009).

60 See Article 10(11) of the ECT, which provides that 'For the purposes of Article 26 [i.e. enforceability by an aggrieved Investor], the application by a Contracting Party of a trade-related investment measure as described in Article 5(1) and (2) to an Investment of an Investor of another Contracting Party existing at the time of such application shall, subject to Article 5(3) and (4), be considered a breach of an obligation of the former Contracting Party under this Part.'

some third state (though, of course, if investors of a third state are treated more favourably than the claimant investor this constitutes a distinct breach of the MFN clause under Article 10(7)[61]).

In any case, the scope of the provision would appear to be limited by Article 26, which requires that any complaint be related to an Investment.[62] This would seem to exclude, for example, most complaints under human rights treaties.[63] In consequence, it may be that, in practical terms, the penultimate sentence of Article 10(1) adds little to the MFN clause in Article 10(7).[64]

### (v) Observance of obligations – the 'umbrella' clause

Claims brought in respect of violations of provisions of Part III of the ECT are claims made to vindicate rights granted by treaty. Such rights are distinct from any other rights an Investor might enjoy by virtue of its being a party to a contract, even if there is an identity between the parties to the contract and those to the treaty claim. Facts amounting to a breach of the treaty do not necessarily amount to a breach of contract, and vice versa. This was made clear by the ICSID annulment committee in *Compañiá de Aguas del Aconquija SA and Vivendi* v. *Argentina*.[65] The applicants had entered into a concession agreement with the Province of Tucumán, a constituent sub-division of Argentina, which provided that disputes concerning the interpretation and application of the contract were subject to the exclusive jurisdiction of the Tucumán administrative courts. However, they subsequently brought a claim against Argentina claiming that the contract had been terminated as a result of actions of the Tucumán authorities in breach of substantive provisions of the France–Argentina BIT. The ICSID tribunal established to determine the

61 Discussed below at pp. 127–30.

62 It will be recalled that Article 26(1) provides that only '[d]isputes between a Contracting Party and an Investor of another Contracting Party relating to an Investment of the latter in the Area of the former' are amenable to its provisions.

63 For example, in *Blioune* v. *Ghana* the claimant alleged that he had been arbitrarily detained by the Ghanaian authorities and unlawfully expelled from the country. However, the tribunal held that it lacked 'jurisdiction to address, as an independent cause of action, a claim of violation of human rights', a conclusion that seems to have been based on the claimant's failure to establish a link between his alleged ill-treatment and his investment: *Biloune and Marine Drive Complex Ltd* v. *Ghana Investments Centre and the Government of Ghana*, Award on Jurisdiction and Liability, 27 October 1989, 95 ILR 184 at 203.

64 See pp. 127–30 below.

65 Decision on Annulment, 3 July 2003.

claim held that it had jurisdiction under the BIT.[66] However, the tribunal dismissed the claim on the ground that, on the facts of the case, it was impossible to separate breach of contract claims from BIT violations without interpreting and applying the concession agreement, which was a task that the parties had assigned to the local courts.

The claimants sought successfully to have the tribunal's award annulled. The committee agreed with the tribunal that the fact that the investment concerned a concession agreement made with a sub-division of Argentina did not mean that the dispute fell outside the scope of the BIT, and that the exclusive jurisdiction clause in the contract did not affect the jurisdiction of the tribunal. On the merits, however, it disagreed with the tribunal. The provisions of the BIT set an independent standard and, in consequence:

> whether there has been a breach of the BIT and whether there has been a breach of contract are different questions. Each of these claims will be determined by reference to its own proper or applicable law – in the case of the BIT, by international law; in the case of the Concession Contract, by the proper law of the contract, in other words, the law of Tucumán . . . In a case where the essential basis of a claim brought before an international tribunal is a breach of contract, the tribunal will give effect to any valid choice of forum clause in the contract. . . . On the other hand, where the 'fundamental basis of the claim' is a treaty laying down an independent standard by which the conduct of the parties is to be judged, the existence of an exclusive jurisdiction clause in a contract between the claimant and the respondent state or one of its subdivisions cannot operate as a bar to the application of the treaty standard. . . . In such a case, the inquiry which the ICSID tribunal is required to undertake is one governed by the ICSID Convention, by the BIT and by applicable international law. Such an inquiry is neither in principle determined, nor precluded, by any issue of municipal law, including any municipal law agreement of the parties.[67]

The existence of the exclusive jurisdiction clause in the concession agreement was irrelevant to the issue of whether there had been a breach of the BIT and, consequently, should not have prevented the tribunal from determining whether the impugned conduct amounted to a breach of treaty or not. Accordingly, the tribunal had manifestly exceeded its powers by not examining the merits of the applicants' claims for acts of the Tucumán authorities.

In most cases, however, a breach of contract by a state will not amount to a breach of treaty. As the tribunal in *Impregilo* v. *Pakistan* stated:

66 *Compañiá de Aguas del Aconquija SA and Vivendi Universal* v. *Argentina*, Award, 21 November 2000.

67 Paragraphs 96–102.

> The State, or its emanation, may have behaved as an ordinary contracting party having a difference of approach, in fact or law, with the investor. In order that the alleged breach of contract may constitute a violation of the BIT, it must be the result of behaviour going beyond that which an ordinary contracting party could adopt. Only the State in the exercise of its sovereign authority ('puissance publique'), and not as a contracting party, may breach the obligations assumed under the BIT.[68]

Thus, ordinarily, a breach of an agreement between a foreign investor and a host state does not amount to a breach of the investor's rights under any relevant investment protection treaty, at least if the state has simply acted as any private party might and has not utilised its public powers to avoid its contractual commitments (for example, by expropriating the investor's contractual rights).[69]

It follows that, generally, an investor who alleges a breach of contract not involving any exercise of sovereign authority must bring its claim before the forum provided for in the contract. (Of course, if the respondent state frustrates the proceedings (e.g., through manipulating the local courts), or prevents the investor from enjoying the fruits of its efforts (e.g., by having an award declared invalid), then a treaty claim might lie, but the claim would be not be based upon the state's initial failure to honour its contractual commitments.)

However, the last sentence of Article 10(1) consists of what is known as an 'umbrella clause': so-called because it brings claims under contracts concluded between Investors and Contracting Parties under the umbrella of the treaty:[70]

> Each Contracting Party shall observe any obligations it has entered into with an Investor or an Investment of an Investor of any other Contracting Party.

Contracting Parties may enter reservations to avoid the effects of the provision. Article 26(3)(c) provides that:

68 *Impregilo SpA* v. *Pakistan*, Decision on Jurisdiction, 22 April 2005, paragraph 260. See also *Waste Management* v. *Mexico*, Award, 30 April 2004, paragraph 174.

69 See, e.g., the allegations in *Compañiá de Aguas del Aconquija SA and Vivendi Universal* v. *Argentina*, Decision on Annulment, 3 July 2003, paragraph 106: 'incitement of consumers, by legislators and others, not to pay their water bills; unauthorized tariff changes; the incorrect imposition of fines (never in fact collected) for allegedly deficient water quality; incorrect invoicing for municipal and provincial water taxes . . . unilateral changes by the provincial Governor to the . . . agreement'.

70 For the history of umbrella clauses, see A. Sinclair, 'The Origins of the Umbrella Clause in the International Law of Investment Protection', (2004) 20 *Arbitration International* 411.

> A Contracting Party listed in Annex IA does not give such unconditional consent with respect to a dispute arising under the last sentence of Article 10(1).[71]

At present, only four states are listed in Annex IA: Australia (a signatory but not yet a Contracting Party to the ECT), Canada (neither a signatory nor a Contracting Party), Hungary (a Contracting Party) and Norway (which has also signed but not yet ratified).

The legal effect of umbrella clauses is somewhat controversial. In *Société de Surveillance SA* v. *Pakistan*[72] it was said that the rather differently worded umbrella clause there[73] did not transform contract claims into treaty claims but merely obliged the host state to enact rules and regulations to implement any statutory or contractual undertakings it has entered into vis-à-vis foreign investors.[74] However, the wording of the umbrella clause in the ECT is not capable of bearing such a limited meaning. Rather, the view taken by the arbitral tribunal in *Société de Surveillance SA* v. *Philippines*[75] seems preferable as far as the ECT is concerned. There, the tribunal held that an umbrella clause, worded similarly to that in the ECT,[76] could transform a contract claim into a treaty claim or, to be more precise, give jurisdiction to an arbitral tribunal established under the BIT to determine claims under investment contracts brought by investors of one party to the treaty against the other party.

This is not to say, however, that such contracts are governed by international law. An umbrella clause is, in its effect, simply a jurisdiction-conferring provision. The contract remains governed by its applicable law, which has to be determined by applying the relevant choice-of-law rules.

Moreover, the parties remain free to choose the forum for the determination of their contractual disputes, so that if the contract includes an exclusive forum selection clause, that clause continues to apply.[77] Thus in *Société de Surveillance SA* v. *Philippines*, the contract included a clause

71 Article 27(2) similarly excepts from inter-state arbitration provided for in Article 27 disputes arising out of the provision.

72 Decision on Jurisdiction, 6 August 2003.

73 'Either Contracting Party shall constantly guarantee the observance of the commitments it has entered into with respect to the investments of the investors of the other Contracting Party.'

74 Paragraph 172.

75 Decision of the Tribunal on Objections to Jurisdiction, 29 January 2004.

76 'Each Contracting Party shall observe any obligation it has assumed with regard to specific investments in its territory by investors of the other Contracting Party.'

77 See also the discussion in Chapter 6.

submitting disputes to the Philippine courts. The tribunal held that the general provisions of the BIT did not override this specific provision. Accordingly, even though, as a result of the effect of the umbrella clause in the Switzerland–Philippines BIT, the tribunal had jurisdiction over the claimant's contract claim, the existence of the exclusive jurisdiction clause in the contract rendered the claim inadmissible:

> SGS should not be entitled to approbate and reprobate in respect of the same contract: if it claims under the contract, it should comply with the contract in respect of the very matter which is the foundation of the claim.[78]

Accordingly, proceedings were stayed pending the outcome of proceedings in the Philippine courts.[79]

In *Société de Surveillance SA* v. *Philippines* the contract claims were for payment for customs pre-inspection services. In several other cases, however, arbitral tribunals have distinguished between commercial claims and claims arising as a result of action by the state party in its sovereign capacity, with only the latter within the scope of an umbrella clause. As the tribunal in *El Paso* v. *Argentina* reasoned:

> In view of the necessity to distinguish the State as a merchant, especially when it acts through instrumentalities, from the State as a sovereign, the Tribunal considers that the 'umbrella clause' in the Argentine–US BIT, which prescribes that '[e]ach Party shall observe any obligation it may have entered into with regard to investments', can be interpreted in the light of Article VII(1), which clearly includes among the investment disputes under the Treaty all disputes resulting from a violation of a commitment given by the State as a sovereign State, either through an agreement, an authorization, or the BIT . . . Interpreted this way, the umbrella clause, read in conjunction with Article VII, will not extend the Treaty protection to breaches of an ordinary commercial contract entered into by the State or a State-owned entity, but will cover additional investment protections contractually agreed by the State as a sovereign – such as a stabilization clause – inserted in an investment agreement.[80]

78 *Société de Surveillance SA* v. *Philippines*, Decision of the Tribunal on Objections to Jurisdiction, paragraph 155.

79 See *Société de Surveillance SA* v. *Philippines*, Order of the Tribunal on Further Proceedings, 17 December 2007.

80 *El Paso Energy International Company* v. *Argentina*, Decision on Jurisdiction, 27 April 2006, paragraph 81. Article VII(1) read as follows: 'For purposes of this Article, an investment dispute is a dispute between a Party and a national or company of the other Party arising out of or relating to (a) an investment agreement between that Party and such national or company; (b) an investment authorization granted by that Party's foreign investment authority (if any such authorization exists) to such national or company; or

Under the ECT, the inclusion within the definition of an Investment in Article 1(6) of 'any right conferred by law or contract or by virtue of any licences and permits granted pursuant to law to undertake any Economic Activity in the Energy Sector'[81] could perhaps be assimilated to the relevant provisions of Article VII of the Argentina–US BIT so as, by the same reasoning, to restrict the ECT's umbrella clause to obligations entered into by the host state *qua* sovereign. It is submitted, however, that such a conclusion would be mistaken. The plain meaning of Article 10(1) does not admit such a restriction. The better view is that expressed by the tribunal in *Eureko* v. *Poland* with regard to a similarly-worded provision:[82]

> The plain meaning – the 'ordinary meaning' – of a provision prescribing that a State 'shall observe any obligations it may have entered into' with regard to certain foreign investments is not obscure. The phrase 'shall observe' is imperative and categorical. 'Any' obligations is capacious; it means not only obligations of a certain type, but 'any' – that is to say, all obligations entered into with regards to investments of investors of the other Contracting Party.[83]

However, although an 'umbrella clause' is capable of converting a breach of a contractual obligation into a breach of the treaty, it does not change the criteria by which the question whether there has been a breach of this contractual obligation is assessed. In other words, the 'obligations', which, in the last sentence of Article 10(1), the state undertakes to observe, are obligations arising under the applicable law of the agreement under which those obligations have been entered into and, just as the content of the obligation falls to be determined under the applicable law, so does the question whether or not it has or has not been observed. Failure to observe a relevant obligation gives rise to a breach of the umbrella clause and it is only that latter breach which is a breach of international law.[84]

(c) an alleged breach of any right conferred or created by this Treaty with respect to an investment.' See also *Pan American Energy LLC and BP Argentina Exploration Company* v. *Argentina*, Decision on Preliminary Objections, 27 July 2006, paragraph 110.

81 Article 1(6)(f).

82 Article 3.5 of the Netherlands–Poland BIT provided that each Contracting Party 'shall observe any obligations it may have entered into with regard to investments or investors of the other Contracting Party'.

83 *Eureko BV* v. *Poland*, Partial Award, 19 August 2005, paragraph 246. See also *Noble Ventures Inc* v. *Romania*, Award, 12 October 2005, paragraphs 50–61; and *Siemens* v. *Argentina*, Award, 6 February 2007, paragraph 206.

84 See *Noble Ventures, Inc* v. *Romania*, Award, 12 October 2005, paragraph 85.

The umbrella clause in Article 10(1) (as with its counterparts in many BITs) only refers to obligations entered into by the Contracting Party. What counts as an obligation entered into by the Contracting Party is, however, not clear. In *Impregilo* v. *Pakistan* the claimant attempted to rely on an umbrella clause (which, it argued, had been imported into the Italy–Pakistan BIT by virtue of the treaty's MFN provision). However, the relevant contracts were not with Pakistan but with the Pakistan Water and Power Development Authority ('WAPDA'), which possessed separate legal personality under Pakistani law. The claimant argued that WAPDA was an instrumentality of Pakistan whose actions and omissions were attributable to Pakistan under international law. This was rejected:

> In the Tribunal's view, given that the Contracts were concluded by Impregilo with WAPDA, and not with Pakistan, Impregilo's reliance upon Article 3 of the BIT [the MFN provision] takes the matter no further. Even assuming *arguendo* that Pakistan, through the MFN clause and the Swiss–Pakistan BIT [which included an umbrella clause], has guaranteed the observance of the contractual commitments into which it has entered together with Italian investors, such a guarantee would not cover the present Contracts – since these are agreements into which it has not entered. On the contrary, the Contracts were concluded by a separate and distinct entity.[85]

Similarly, in *Azurix* v. *Argentina* the tribunal held that contracts with the Province of Buenos Aires were not covered by an umbrella clause. This seems to have been based on a decision not to apply the customary international law rules on attribution.[86] In neither case, however, was it made clear what law the tribunal did apply to determine the issue (although the implication seems to be that it was left to municipal law).

However, in *Noble Ventures* v. *Romania* the tribunal did apply international law to find that the acts of the Romanian State Ownership Fund (SOF) were attributable to Romania. Contracts between the claimant and SOF were covered by the umbrella clause in the Romania–US BIT because, although possessing separate legal personality under Romanian law, SOF had acted as a governmental agency.[87] The decision was based on the tribunal's application of the ILC Articles on State Responsibility, which

85 *Impregilo SpA* v. *Pakistan*, Decision on Jurisdiction, 22 April 2005, paragraph 223 (footnote omitted).

86 *Azurix* v. *Argentina*, Award, 14 July 2006, paragraphs 50–2. Under Article 4(1) of the ILC Articles on State Responsibility (International Law Commission, Responsibility of States for Internationally Wrongful Acts (2001) (GA res. 56/83 (2002), Annex)), conduct of a territorial unit of the state is considered an act of the state.

87 *Noble Ventures Inc* v. *Romania*, Award, 12 October 2005, paragraphs 69–86.

it considered reflected customary international law.[88] Although SOF was not an organ of the Romanian state, it was empowered by that state's law to exercise elements of governmental authority and on all relevant occasions, including when entering into contracts with the claimant, it had been acting in that capacity.[89]

It is submitted that the approach taken by the tribunal in *Noble Ventures* is the correct one. Given that the ECT is a treaty, the reference to '[e]ach Contracting Party' in Article 10(1) should be taken to mean that the conduct covered by the provision is conduct attributable to the relevant Contracting Party as a matter of international law. However, *Impregilio* and *Azurix* both illustrate a reluctance to hold governments (which, of course, represent the state in foreign affairs) liable for the actions of entities (whether constituent sub-divisions or state enterprises) whose day-to-day activities they cannot control.

### (vi) National and most-favoured nation treatment[90]

Article 10(7) of the ECT provides that:

> (7) Each Contracting Party shall accord to Investments in its Area of Investors of other Contracting Parties, and their related activities including management, maintenance, use, enjoyment or disposal, treatment no less favourable than that which it accords to Investments of its own Investors or of the Investors of any other Contracting Party or any third state and their related activities including management, maintenance, use, enjoyment or disposal, whichever is the most favourable.[91]

Article 10(7) thus adopts two further concepts from the 'standard repertoire of bilateral investment treaties':[92] national treatment – treating investors no less favourably than investors of the host state's own nationality; and most-favoured nation (MFN) treatment – treating investors no less favourably than investors of any other state are treated. There is no

88 At paragraph 70. 89 Article 5 of the ILC Articles on State Responsibility.

90 See, as to these standards generally: Dolzer and Schreuer, *Principles of International Investment Law*, pp. 178–91, 253–7; McLachlan *et al.*, *International Investment Arbitration: Substantive Principles*, pp. 254–7; Newcombe and Paradell, *Law and Practice of Investment Treaties: Standards of Treatment*, pp. 147–232; A. Bjorklund, 'National Treatment' in A. Reinisch (ed.), *Standards of Investment Protection* (Oxford University Press), pp. 29–58, and A. Ziegler, 'Most-Favoured-Nation (MFN) Treatment' in A. Reinisch (ed.), *Standards of Investment Protection* (Oxford University Press, 2008), pp. 59–86.

91 It is characteristic of the rather haphazard drafting of the ECT that the draftsman here repeats at length ('treatment no less favourable than that which [etc] . . . ') a description of a concept already established, four paragraphs earlier in Article 10(3), as the defined term 'the Treatment'.

92 Dolzer and Schreuer, *Principles of International Investment Law*, p. 178.

reason to believe that the concepts as they appear in the ECT ought to receive any different treatment from when they appear in other bilateral and multilateral investment treaties.[93]

A controversial issue in international investment law generally is whether and, if so, to what extent a claimant may take advantage of an MFN clause in an investment protection treaty so as to circumvent restrictions on the bringing of a claim under that same treaty.[94] Thus the claimant in *Maffezini* v. *Spain* persuaded the tribunal that his failure to comply with the conditions of the dispute resolution clause in the Argentina–Spain BIT under which he purportedly brought his claim was of no consequence: Spain was precluded by the MFN clause in the BIT from relying on the conditions since no such conditions appeared in Spain's BIT with Chile.[95]

One may imagine a hypothetical example under the Energy Charter Treaty. An investor of the Republic of Ireland invests in the energy industry in Mongolia; suffers allegedly unfair and inequitable treatment at the hands of the Mongolian authorities; initially submits the dispute under Article 26(2)(a) of the ECT to the Mongolian courts alleging a breach of Part III of the ECT (Mongolian law adopts the 'monist' approach to treaties,[96] so the ECT has direct effect in the domestic law of Mongolia); then discontinues this claim and instead seeks international arbitration under Article 26(3) of the ECT. Mongolia is one of the states listed in Annex ID which, under Article 26(3)(b)(i), does not give its unconditional consent to such international arbitration where the investor has previously submitted the dispute under Article 26(2)(a). It therefore denies that the ECT tribunal has jurisdiction. As it happens, Mongolia has no bilateral investment treaty with the Republic of Ireland. But it does have a treaty with Japan,[97] which provides for similar substantive protections for investments as those in the ECT, provides for international arbitration, but has no equivalent of ECT Article 26(3)(b)(i). May the investor in these circumstances point, in support of his alleged entitlement to arbitration under Article 26, to Mongolia's obligation under Article 10(7) to afford him MFN treatment, arguing that Mongolia's reliance on ECT

93 See, however, the discussion of the effect of Article 25 in Chapter 4.

94 See Dolzer and Schreuer, *Principles of International Investment Law*, pp. 253–7; McLachlan *et al.*, *International Investment Arbitration: Substantive Principles*, pp. 254–7.

95 Award on Jurisdiction, 25 January 2000. See also *Tecnicas Medioambientales Tecmed SA* v. *Mexico*, Award, 29 May 2003, *Siemens AG* v. *Argentina*, Award on Jurisdiction, 3 August 2004.

96 Constitution of Mongolia (1992), Article 10(3).

97 Japan–Mongolia BIT (2001).

Article 26(3)(b)(i) is a breach of this obligation since a Japanese investor, bringing a claim under the Japan–Mongolia BIT, would face no such obstacle?

Plainly not, it is submitted. Such an argument only succeeds if one regards the right granted by Article 10(7) of the ECT as having a life of its own and as prevailing over any inconvenient features (from the investor's point of view) in Article 26 of the ECT's express provisions as to how that same right (with others) is to be vindicated. However, this is a fundamental error, for the duty of any tribunal construing a treaty is to construe the treaty *as a whole.* As it has been well put, '[o]ne of the corollaries of the "general rule of interpretation" in the Vienna Convention is that interpretation must give meaning and effect to all the terms of a treaty. An interpreter is not free to adopt a reading that would result in reducing whole clauses or paragraphs of a treaty to redundancy or inutility.'[98] In Part III of the ECT, the Contracting Parties have undertaken to afford certain protections to investors. In Article 26(3) they have offered, subject to certain conditions, to submit to international arbitration disputes about whether their undertakings have been complied with. To accept that the undertaking to afford MFN treatment can require a Contracting Party to consent to arbitration under the ECT even where the conditions of its offer to do so are not met can only be done by giving no effect to the plain words of Article 26(3)(b)(i) (or whichever other part of Article 26 appears in the particular case to present an impediment to jurisdiction). But there is nothing in the ECT to suggest or compel such a construction.

The decision in *Maffezini* has been described as 'heretical'[99] and it was not followed in *Plama Consortium* v. *Bulgaria.*[100] It is not inconceivable that there are nevertheless treaties on whose proper construction the MFN clause – read in the light of some more investor-friendly dispute resolution arrangements in a treaty with a different state – does indeed override wording in the dispute resolution provisions, though the MFN

98 WTO Appellate Body Report, United States – Standards for Reformulated and Conventional Gasoline, WT/DS2/AB/R (Apr. 29, 1996), quoted in W. Burke-White and A. von Staden, 'Investment Protection in Extraordinary Times: The Interpretation and Application of Non-Precluded Measures Provisions in Bilateral Investment Treaties' (2008) 48 *Virginia Journal of International Law* 307 at 323.

99 C. McLachlan *et al.*, *International Investment Arbitration: Substantive Principles*, p. 254. See also Douglas's convincing demolition of the heresy: *The International Law of Investment Claims* (Cambridge University Press, 2009), pp. 344–62.

100 Decision on Jurisdiction, 8 February 2005; see also *Salini Costruttori* v. *Jordan*, Decision on Jurisdiction, 15 November 2004.

clause would need to be very clearly worded to have such an effect.[101] But the ECT is not one of them.

Finally, Article 10(10) qualifies the effects of Article 10(7) (and Article 10(3)) as regards intellectual property rights, providing that:

> Notwithstanding any other provision of this Article, the treatment described in paragraphs (3) and (7) shall not apply to the protection of Intellectual Property; instead, the treatment shall be as specified in the corresponding provisions of the applicable international agreements for the protection of Intellectual Property rights to which the respective Contracting Parties are parties.

'Intellectual Property' is elsewhere defined as including 'copyrights and related rights, trademarks, geographical indications, industrial designs, patents, layout designs of integrated circuits and the protection of undisclosed information'.[102] The provision seems to remove the level of protection granted to intellectual property rights from the ambit of Article 10(7). However, it does not seem to preclude the use of Article 26 to determine complaints that the respondent state has failed to accord to the claimant the treatment specified in the 'corresponding provisions of the applicable international agreements'.[103]

### (vii) Effective means for the assertion of claims and the enforcement of rights

Article 10(12) provides that:

> Each Contracting Party shall ensure that its domestic law provides effective means for the assertion of claims and the enforcement of rights with respect to Investments, investment agreements, and investment authorizations.

This provision plainly overlaps to a significant extent with Article 10(1)'s obligation to accord fair and equitable treatment, one of whose elements is an obligation to avoid denying justice to the claimant or, as it has

101 It has been suggested that the United Kingdom Model BIT is such a treaty because its MFN clause expressly provides that 'the treatment provided for in [this clause] shall apply to the provisions of Articles 1 to 11 of this Agreement [which include the dispute settlement provisions]'. See also S. Fietta, 'Most Favoured Nation Treatment and Dispute Resolution under Bilateral Investment Treaties: A Turning Point?' (2005) 8 *International Arbitration Law Review* 131.

102 Article 1(12) of the ECT.

103 A failure to accord the treatment required by the applicable international agreement concerning intellectual property would on the face of it also seem actionable under the penultimate sentence of Article 10(1) ('In no case shall such Investments be accorded treatment less favourable than that required by international law, including treaty obligations'), discussed above.

been put, such behaviour in the state's judicial process as may give rise, 'on reflection, to justified concerns as to the judicial propriety of the outcome, bearing in mind on one hand that international tribunals are not courts of appeal, and on the other hand [that investment treaties are] intended to provide a real measure of protection'.[104] However, it is rather more specific in its terms. Article 10(12) was directly considered by the tribunal in *AMTO* v. *Ukraine*.[105] In a passage which bears quotation at length, the tribunal stated that:

> The fundamental criteria of an 'effective means' for the assertion of claims and the enforcement of rights within the meaning of Article 10(12) is [sic] law and the rule of law. There must be legislation for the recognition and enforcement of property and contractual rights. This legislation must be made in accordance with the constitution, and be publicly available. An effective means of the assertion of claims and the enforcement of rights also requires secondary rules of procedure so that the principles and objectives of the legislation can be translated by the investor into effective action in the domestic tribunals. . . . Article 10(12) requires a State not only to ensure legislation and rules are promulgated to recognise and enforce property and contractual rights, but also that the quality of the legislation meets minimum international standards. . . . Accordingly, Article 10(12) is not only a rule of law standard, but also a qualitative standard.
>
> The difficulty is to identify the criteria by which to assess the effectiveness of the legislation and rules called into question under Article 10(12) ECT. Bearing in mind the context and the object and purpose of the ECT, the Tribunal considers that 'effective' is a systematic, comparative, progressive and practical standard. It is systematic in that the State must provide an effective framework or system for the enforcement of rights, but does not offer guarantees in individual cases. Individual failures might be evidence of systematic inadequacies, but are not themselves a breach of Article 10(12). It is comparative in that compliance with international standards indicates that imperfections in the law might result from the complexities of the subject matter rather than the inadequacies of the legislation. It is progressive in the sense that legislation ages and needs to be modernized and adapted from time to time, and results might not be immediate. Where a State is taking the appropriate steps to identify and address deficiencies in its legislation – in other words improvement is in progress – then the progress should be recognized in assessing effectiveness. Finally, it is a practical standard in that some areas of law, or the application of legislation in certain circumstances, raise particular difficulties which should not be ignored in assessing effectiveness.

104 *Mondev International Ltd* v. *United States of America*, Award, 11 October 2002, paragraph 127.

105 Award, 26 March 2008, paragraphs 87–8.

It is not altogether clear why a state should escape liability to an Investor whose interests have been damaged by the lack of any effective means for the assertion of claims on the ground that it is working on the problem. But otherwise it is submitted that this is as good a description as any of what is required by Article 10(12).

### (viii) Other obligations

Finally, a further five other obligations contained in Part III of the Treaty must briefly be mentioned.

**Article 10(11): trade-related investment measures** Article 10(11) provides that

> For the purposes of Article 26, the application by a Contracting Party of a trade-related investment measure as described in Article 5(1) and (2) to an Investment of an Investor of another Contracting Party existing at the time of such application shall, subject to Article 5(3) and (4), be considered a breach of an obligation of the former Contracting Party under this Part.

Article 5(1) and (2) describe trade-related measures which are inconsistent with relevant provisions of the GATT (or, by virtue of the Amendment to the Trade-Related Provisions of the Energy Charter Treaty,[106] the WTO). Thus the effect of Article 10(11) is, in practice, to translate the obligations created by these provisions into obligations owed to, and enforceable by, Investors under the ECT. This is important insofar as the obligations which Article 10(11) imports into Part III are not enforceable by private persons before the WTO's dispute settlement procedures,[107] which can only be accessed by members, or considered to have direct effect in national legal orders.[108] As a result, Article 10(11) permits vindication of these provisions by the mechanisms provided to Investors under Article 26.

As most ECT Contracting Parties are now also WTO Members,[109] in most cases it means that Investors can rely on the WTO Agreement

106 See Chapter 1 at p. 11.

107 See Articles XXII and XXIII, General Agreement on Tariffs and Trade, and the WTO Understanding on Rules and Procedures Governing the Settlement of Disputes, reproduced in World Trade Organization, *The Legal Texts: The Results of the Uruguay Round of Multilateral Trade Negotiations* (Cambridge University Press, 1999).

108 Including in EU law, for which see Hilpold. *Die EU im GATT/WTO-System.*

109 Only Azerbaijan, Bosnia-Herzegovina, Kazakhstan, Kyrgyzstan, Turkmenistan and Uzbekistan are not also WTO Members.

on Trade-Related Investment Measures ('TRIMs'), which considerably develops Articles III (National Treatment) and XI (General Elimination of Qualitative Restrictions) of the GATT, in particular by providing an illustrative list of trade-related investment measures which are inconsistent with those two provisions. Indeed, the list in the Annex to the TRIMS Agreement is reproduced in Article 5(2) of the ECT, which defines as incompatible with Articles III and XI GATT:

> . . . any investment measure which is mandatory or enforceable under domestic law or under any administrative ruling, or compliance with which is necessary to obtain an advantage, and which requires:
>
> (a) the purchase or use by an enterprise of products of domestic origin or from any domestic source, whether specified in terms of particular products, in terms of volume or value of products, or in terms of a proportion of volume or value of its local production; or
> (b) that an enterprise's purchase or use of imported products be limited to an amount related to the volume or value of local products that it exports;
>
> or which restricts:
>
> (c) the importation by an enterprise of products used in or related to its local production, generally or to an amount related to the volume or value of local production that it exports;
> (d) the importation by an enterprise of products used in or related to its local production by restricting its access to foreign exchange to an amount related to the foreign exchange inflows attributable to the enterprise; or
> (e) the exportation or sale for export by an enterprise of products, whether specified in terms of particular products, in terms of volume or value of products, or in terms of a proportion of volume or value of its local production.

It can be seen that such measures can, and frequently are, conditions imposed on persons wishing to make an investment, as well as for obtaining advantages (for example subsidies) once an investment has been made.[110] However, Article 10(1) specifically restricts the scope of Article 5 to 'the application by a Contracting Party of a trade-related investment measure . . . to an Investment of an Investor of another Contracting Party

110 Although Article 5(3) permits the use of such measures as conditions of eligibility for export promotion, foreign aid, government procurement or preferential tariffs or quota programmes.

existing at the time of such application'.[111] Article 10(11) is thus consistent with the general approach in Chapter III, which does not impose enforceable obligations with regard to the Making of Investments.[112] In addition, for a trade-related investment measure to be inconsistent with the provisions of Articles III or XI GATT it must be related to trade in goods.[113]

**Article 11: key personnel** Article 11 requires each Contracting Party, subject to its laws, to

> examine in good faith requests by Investors of another Contracting Party, and key personnel who are employed by such Investors or by Investments of such Investors, to enter and remain temporarily in its Area to engage in activities connected with the making or the development, management, maintenance, use, enjoyment or disposal of relevant Investments, including the provision of advice or key technical services;

and to

> permit Investors of another Contracting Party which have Investments in its Area, and Investments of such Investors, to employ any key person of the Investor's or the Investment's choice regardless of nationality and citizenship provided that such key person has been permitted to enter, stay and work in the Area of the former Contracting Party and that the employment concerned conforms to the terms, conditions and time limits of the permission granted to such key person.

**Article 12: non-discrimination in payments for losses caused by war etc.** Article 12 requires the non-discriminatory payment of compensation for losses caused by war or other armed conflict, state of national emergency, civil disturbance or other similar event.

**Article 13: expropriation** Article 13, mirroring widespread and long-established provisions in many other treaties, prohibits nationalisation, expropriation or measures having similar effect except where such nationalisation etc. is for a purpose which is in the public interest, not discriminatory, carried out under due process of law and accompanied by the

111 Although this restriction, only being for the purposes of Article 26, would not prevent the bringing of such a claim by the Investor's state of nationality in some other forum.

112 See pp. 105–7 above.

113 See Article 1 (Coverage), WTO Agreement on Trade-Related Investment Measures, reproduced in World Trade Organization, *The Legal Texts*.

payment of prompt, adequate and effective compensation.[114] In practice, this is an important and frequently-pleaded type of provision. Article 13, however, displays no unusual features requiring specific elucidation.[115]

**Article 14: transfer of funds** Finally, Article 14, likewise mirroring many other treaties, makes detailed provision requiring the free transfer of funds in and out of the host state.[116]

114 See, as to expropriation: Dolzer and Schreuer, *Principles of International Investment Law*, pp. 89–118; McLachlan *et al.*, *International Investment Arbitration: Substantive Principles*, pp. 265–313; Newcombe and Paradell, *Law and Practice of Investment Treaties: Standards of Treatment*, pp. 321–98; A. Reinisch, 'Legality of Expropriations' in A. Reinisch (ed.), *Standards of Investment Protection* (Oxford University Press, 2008), pp. 171–204.

115 Article 18 reaffirms Contracting Parties' sovereignty over their energy resources. However, this does not conflict with the protections granted Investors in Article 13, as it is generally agreed that states' permanent sovereignty over natural resources is preserved by permitting expropriation provided that the interests of investors are respected. For discussion of the topic, see N. Schrijver, *Sovereignty over Natural Resources: Balancing Rights and Duties* (Cambridge University Press, 1997). Similarly, Article 19 (environmental aspects) cannot serve to avoid the application of Article 13. If measures taken to protect the environment constitute, or are tantamount to, an expropriation, full compensation must be paid; see *Compañiá del Desarrollo de Santa Elena SA* v. *Costa Rica*, Award (Final), 17 February 2000, paragraph 71.

116 See, as to transfer of funds: Dolzer and Schreuer, *Principles of International Investment Law*, pp. 191–4; McLachlan *et al.*, *International Investment Arbitration: Substantive Principles*, pp. 265–313; Newcombe and Paradell, *Law and Practice of Investment Treaties: Standards of Treatment*, pp. 399–436; A. Kolo and T. Wälde, 'Capital Transfer Restrictions under Modern Investment Treaties' in A. Reinisch (ed.), *Standards of Investment Protection* (Oxford University Press, 2008), pp. 205–44.

# 6

# Procedure

## 1. Introduction

Article 26(1) provides that the disputes to which it applies[1] 'shall, if possible, be settled amicably'. By Article 26(2):

> If such disputes can not be settled according to the provisions of paragraph (1) within a period of three months from the date on which either party to the dispute requested amicable settlement, the Investor party to the dispute may choose to submit it for resolution:
>
> (a) to the courts or administrative tribunals of the Contracting Party party to the dispute;
> (b) in accordance with any applicable, previously agreed dispute settlement procedure; or
> (c) in accordance with the following paragraphs of this Article [i.e. paragraphs (3) to (8), which contain the provisions for investor–state arbitration considered in more detail below].

## 2. Amicable settlement

The restriction of the right to choose one of these options for formal dispute settlement to those cases which 'can not be settled according to the provisions of paragraph (1) within a period of three months from the date on which either party to the dispute requested amicable settlement' is similar to the provisions of many investment treaties.[2] On one reading it imposes a jurisdictional hurdle: since it is only if the dispute is one which cannot be settled amicably within three months of a request for amicable settlement that an investor may proceed to formal dispute settlement, the investor must first make such a request and then allow three

1 See Chapter 3 as to the disputes covered by Article 26.

2 See generally C. Schreuer, 'Travelling the BIT Route – Of Waiting Periods, Umbrella Clauses and Forks in the Road' (2004) 5 *Journal of World Investment & Trade* 231; R. Dolzer and C. Schreuer, *Principles of International Investment Law* (Oxford University Press, 2008), pp. 247–9.

months to elapse; an investor who purports to move to formal dispute settlement sooner has no entitlement to use any of the dispute resolution mechanisms.

Arbitral tribunals have given conflicting indications as to the meaning of similar provisions in other instruments. Some have treated such provisions as merely directory and thus as not precluding the bringing of a claim in breach of them.[3] Others point the other way, treating such provisions as going to the jurisdiction of the tribunal to entertain the claim at all.[4] It is submitted that the better view, at least so far as Article 26 of the ECT is concerned, is that it does indeed present a jurisdictional hurdle. This follows from its plain wording, which unambiguously makes the right to elect for formal dispute settlement conditional on the dispute being one which cannot be settled within three months.[5] This wording cannot simply be brushed aside. This is clearest in the context of the third option, arbitration '(c) in accordance with the following paragraphs of this Article'. Article 26(3)(a) expressly provides that the state's unconditional consent is given to such arbitration 'in accordance with the provisions of this Article'. As has rightly been said: 'Consent of the respondent host state to investor/state arbitration in the investment treaty is the most important condition for the vesting of adjudicative power in

3 *Ethyl Corporation* v. *Canada*, Decision on Jurisdiction, 24 June 1998, paragraphs 76–88: the most relevant provision was Article 1120 of the NAFTA, '. . . provided that six months have elapsed since the events giving rise to a claim . . . '; *Ronald S Lauder* v. *Czech Republic*, Award (Final), 3 September 2001, paragraph 187: the relevant provision was Article VI(3)(a) of the United States–Czech Republic BIT, 'At any time after six months from the date on which the dispute arose, the [claimant] may choose to consent in writing to the submission of the dispute for settlement . . . '; *SGS Société Générale de Surveillance SA* v. *Pakistan*, Decision on Jurisdiction, 6 August 2003, paragraph 184: the relevant provision was Article 9 of the Switzerland–Pakistan BIT, ' . . . consultations shall take place between the parties concerned . . . If these consultations do not result in a solution within twelve months . . . '.

4 *Goetz* v. *Burundi*, Award, 10 February 1999, paragraph 93: the relevant provision was Article 8, paragraph 3 of the Belgium–Burundi BIT, '*Si le différend ne peut être réglé dans les trois mois à compter de la notification écrite . . .* '; *Enron Corporation and Ponderosa Assets LP* v. *Argentina*, Decision on Jurisdiction, 14 January 2004, paragraph 88: the relevant provision was Article VII, paragraph 3(a) of the US–Argentina BIT, 'Provided that . . . six months have elapsed from the date on which the dispute arose . . . '.

5 Of the decisions mentioned above, only in *Ethyl Corporation* v. *Canada* did the tribunal really engage with *why* the amicable settlement provision did not mean what it appeared to mean. The tribunal suggested that a literal reading would lead to a manifestly absurd result (see Article 32(b)) of the Vienna Convention on the Law of Treaties (1969)('VCLT'). Holding the claimant in that case to the terms of the NAFTA would undoubtedly have been inconvenient, but it is submitted that this was not necessarily a reason to override the plain meaning of the words.

the tribunal.'[6] That consent is simply not given unless the dispute is one which 'can not be settled according to the provisions of paragraph (1) [i.e. amicably] within a period of three months from the date on which either party to the dispute requested amicable settlement'.

Some degree of flexibility perhaps derives from the fact that Article 26(2), in contrast with the instruments considered in many of the other cases, does not purport to impose an absolute time-bar. The pre-condition for submission of the dispute to formal dispute settlement is not that the specified period has elapsed but, rather, that the dispute 'can not be settled' within it. There may be cases where it is quite plain, well within the period of three months, that the dispute is one which 'can not be settled . . . within a period of three months'. Arguably, in such circumstances there is no need for the claimant to wait the full three months before initiating formal dispute settlement; though a sensible claimant is likely wherever possible to wait three months all the same so as to spare the necessity of having the argument.

It is submitted that this reading of Article 26(2) better gives effect[7] to the ordinary meaning of its terms in their context and in the light of the object and purpose of the ECT than a reading which denies any real force to the requirement to wait three months. Of course there may be cases where a jurisdictional reading gives rise to inconvenience. But this does not make the reading itself absurd or unreasonable. On the contrary, a strong and enforceable requirement that the parties attempt amicable settlement before moving to formal dispute resolution is a salutary one for host states and investors alike.[8]

## 3. No requirement of exhaustion of remedies

As is the position under most BITs, there is no rule in the ECT that an aggrieved investor must exhaust all remedies in the host state's courts under the host state's domestic law[9] before making a complaint under the

6 Z. Douglas, *The International Law of Investment Claims* (Cambridge University Press, 2009), p. 151.

7 In accordance with Article 31 of the VCLT.

8 It is, of course, consistent with the trend in the common law world towards much greater emphasis on resolution of disputes, where possible, without formal dispute resolution.

9 In this context 'domestic law' means domestic law not including the ECT. As discussed below, the ECT may take effect in, or have been expressly incorporated into, the domestic laws of some Contracting Parties.

Treaty.[10] In general,[11] therefore, the investor may (subject to the amicable settlement requirement) move directly to court or arbitral proceedings under one of the options provided for in Article 26(2), paragraphs (a), (b) and (c).

### *(a) Exceptions to the right to move directly to proceedings under Article 26(2)*

Equally, however, as under most BITs, the investor may not disregard the local courts in all circumstances.

#### (i) Exclusive jurisdiction clauses

First, where there is a dispute in good faith as to the content of the rights constituting the Investment in respect of which the host state is alleged to have breached its obligations under Part III, and those rights derive from a contract which gives exclusive jurisdiction to determine such disputes to some court or arbitral tribunal, the body chosen by the claimant under Article 26(2) ought to stay its jurisdiction in favour of such court or arbitral tribunal.[12] This follows from the principle that a body charged with determining the international lawfulness, under a treaty, of a host state's behaviour towards an investment should begin by analysing what rights the investment consists of in the law of the host state.[13] If those rights stem from an agreement which also confers exclusive jurisdiction on some other body to resolve disputes about them, it is wrong to allow the claimant to take advantage of the rights without being bound by

10 See C. McLachlan, L. Shore and M. Weiniger, *International Investment Arbitration: Substantive Principles* (Oxford University Press, 2007), p. 88. For criticism of this feature of international investment law, see G. van Harten, *Investment Treaty Arbitration and Public Law* (Oxford University Press, 2007), pp. 110–13.

11 An exception is when a complaint alleges a denial of justice, in which case failure of domestic remedies is a substantive component of the cause of action, not a procedural requirement for bringing the claim: see p. 141 below.

12 This formulation draws in particular on *Compañia de Aguas del Aconquija SA and Vivendi Universal* v. *Argentina*, Decision on Annulment, 3 July 2002 paragraph 98; and on Rule 44 in Douglas, *The International Law of Investment Claims*, p. 370. As discussed below, the body chosen under Article 26(2) may in fact be a court in the host state. If so, it is not unlikely that the court so seised will also be the court stipulated in the exclusive jurisdiction clause. In such circumstances there will be no question of the court staying its jurisdiction, but it ought to resolve the bona fide dispute about the contractual rights before it considers any allegation of Treaty infringement in relation to the Investment constituted by those rights.

13 See Chapter 3, above, at p. 49.

his agreement as to who should determine disputes about them (at least where the dispute is raised in good faith).[14]

This important principle appears to have been overlooked, in the context of an ECT claim, by the tribunal in *Nykomb Synergetics Technology Holding AB* v. *Latvia*.[15] Somewhat simplified, the facts were that the claimant's Investment was its ownership of a Latvian company, Windau. Windau contracted with Latvenergo, a Latvian state energy company, to build a power plant. The contract gave the Latvian courts exclusive jurisdiction to determine disputes arising under it. A dispute arose between Windau and Latvenergo over the price to be paid to Windau, in particular as to whether a higher or lower multiplier should be applied to certain quantities. Rather than cause Windau to do as it had contracted to do – to submit this dispute to the Latvian courts – the claimant brought a claim by arbitration under the ECT against Latvia. The claimant alleged that it, as an investor in Latvia, had suffered loss by virtue of Latvenergo's failure to pay Windau the higher price to which Windau was entitled; this failure (for which Latvia was internationally responsible) was said to have been discriminatory, contrary to Article 10(1) of the Treaty, because comparable companies *had* received the higher price. Latvia responded that the alleged contractual entitlement to the higher price (the *sine qua non* of the claim) was disputed; and that this dispute was a matter for the Latvian courts in accordance with exclusive jurisdiction clause.[16] This objection was dismissed by the tribunal with the short observation that the claimant was not a party to the contract and therefore not bound by the jurisdiction clause.[17] The tribunal proceeded to decide the contractual dispute itself and, having decided that the claimant's entitlement was indeed to the higher price, it awarded compensation for Latvia's discriminatory failure to cause Latvenergo to pay it to the claimant.[18] Thus the claimant was permitted to rely on the part of Windau's contract with Latvenergo which helped it – the part contended to give rise to the higher price – while being

14 Of course, there may be cases in which this rule is inapplicable on the facts. For example, if the court or tribunal designated in the exclusive jurisdiction clause would be *bound* to determine the nature or content of the rights constituting the investment in a certain way by virtue of some new legislative provision whose enactment is itself the basis of the alleged treaty violation, there is no point in making the claimant wait while the court or tribunal goes through the motions. Douglas, *The International Law of Investment Claims*, p. 394, gives another example: there should be no stay if the claimant adduces compelling evidence that he can expect a denial of justice in the court or tribunal designated in the exclusive jurisdiction clause.

15 Award, 16 December 2003.

16 Award, section 2.4(a).

17 Award, section 2.4(a).

18 Award, sections 3.8 and 4.3.2(a).

free to ignore the part which did not – Windau's agreement to submit disputes about such contentions to the Latvian courts. The tribunal ought instead to have stayed its proceedings until and unless the claimant had caused Windau to honour its agreement to have the contractual dispute resolved in court; only then, if the dispute had been resolved in favour of Windau,[19] would it have been appropriate to return to argue about Latvia's alleged breach of Part III of the Treaty.

### (ii) Acts of the local courts as violations of Part III of the Treaty

It is well established that the acts of a host state's courts may themselves, if so objectionable as to amount to a denial of justice, constitute a breach of an investment-protection treaty.[20] However, denial of justice 'arises where a national legal *system* fails to provide justice – not where there is a single procedural irregularity or misapplication of the law at some level of the judicial system'.[21] It follows that a claimant will be unable to claim that there has been a denial of justice until he has exhausted all reasonably available routes of appeal.[22] This requirement is not a procedural bar to the bringing of a claim. Rather, it is an ingredient of the substantive cause of action: 'Since a denial of justice occurs only where "there is no reasonably available national mechanism to correct the challenged action," the exhaustion of local remedies becomes an inherent and material element of every denial of justice claim.'[23] There is no reason to think that this reasoning does not apply equally to claims under the ECT.[24]

19 Or had been resolved against Windau in a way itself alleged to constitute a violation by Latvia of Part III of the Treaty.

20 See Article 4(1) of the International Law Commission Articles on Responsibility of States for Internationally Wrongful Acts (2001); *Mondev International Ltd* v. *United States of America*, Award, 11 October 2002, *Loewen* v. *United States of America*, Decision on Jurisdiction, 9 January 2001.

21 A. Newcombe and L. Paradell, *Law and Practice of Investment Treaties: Standards of Treatment* (Alphen aan den Rijn: Kluwer Law International, 2009), pp. 241–2.

22 *Loewen* v. *United States of America*, Decision on Jurisdiction, 9 January 2001.

23 Newcombe and Paradell, *Law and Practice of Investment Treaties: Standards of Treatment*, p. 241. The internal quotation is from J. Paulsson, *Denial of Justice in International Law* (Cambridge University Press, 2005), p. 100.

24 It has been suggested that an unsuccessful attempt to obtain redress in the local courts may constitute an ingredient of other substantive claims under investment-protection treaties, e.g., expropriation: see Dolzer and Schreuer, *Principles of International Investment Law*, pp. 215–16 and the cases there cited.

## 4. The claimant's choice between options under Article 26(2)

The choice between the options is solely for the claimant to make. Moreover, subject only to an express exception for claims against certain Contracting Parties,[25] the commencement of proceedings under one option does not of itself preclude their commencement under another.

However, this general statement must be qualified in two ways. First, if, having opted to take one of the available options, the claimant pursues his claim all the way to a final hearing but is unsuccessful, he is likely to be precluded from trying again for a better result by running the same claim via another of the options. This follows not from anything in the Treaty but from the principle of *res judicata*.[26] Second, a claimant is likely to be precluded from seeking simultaneously to run the same claim along more than one of the routes provided for in Article 26(2) by the principle of *lis alibi pendens*, under which a respondent is likely to obtain a stay of all but one of the sets of proceedings.[27]

Against this background it is now proposed to discuss the various methods by which Article 26(2) allows for the disputes to which it applies to be resolved (if amicable settlement has not proved possible).

### *(a) Article 26(2)(a): 'to the courts or administrative tribunals of the Contracting Party party to the dispute'*

Most discussions of investor–state disputes, the current work included, focus principally on their resolution by international arbitration.[28] However, the option for resolution in the host state's courts ought not to be overlooked by a claimant. Two principal factors, one legal and one practical, are likely to determine whether the option is a realistic one in a given case.

The legal factor is whether or not alleged breaches of the host state's obligations under Part III of the Treaty are in fact justiciable in the host state's courts. This cannot be assumed, for the ECT is, of course, a treaty between states (plus the EU) and has no necessary place in the domestic

25 Article 26(3)(b), discussed below, pp. 146–9.

26 See McLachlan *et al.*, *International Investment Arbitration: Substantive Principles*, pp. 121–5; *Waste Management Inc* v. *Mexico (No. 2)*, Decision on Preliminary Objections, 26 June 2002, paragraph 39.

27 McLachlan, *et al.*, *International Investment Arbitration: Substantive Principles*, pp. 121–5.

28 This is where all the reported investment claims have been advanced: Douglas, *The International Law of Investment Claims*, p. 157.

law of any state. This is made explicit by the sixteenth of the Understandings adopted by the signatories to the ECT: 'Article 26(2)(a) should not be interpreted to require a Contracting Party to enact Part III of the Treaty into its domestic law.' In the domestic law of some jurisdictions the conclusion of a treaty (if done in accordance with the constitution) binds the courts automatically without the need for any specific act of incorporation.[29] But in others a treaty is only part of domestic law if the legislature so provides.[30] So the question whether Part III of the ECT is justiciable in the domestic courts of the host state depends first upon whether or not the state in question is one under whose constitutional law the ECT, as an international treaty, takes effect automatically; and second, if not, on whether the ECT has nevertheless been expressly incorporated into domestic law.[31]

The first factor likely to determine whether a claimant opts for litigation in the courts of the host state, where this is a legal option, is the claimant's perception of the independence, calibre and administrative efficiency of such courts. Given that the claimant's allegation of breach of Part III of the ECT is likely to have flowed from a perception of unlawful conduct by the host state's governmental authority, the claimant is unlikely to entrust the same state's courts with the task of providing redress unless strongly convinced about all three qualities.[32] Other factors likely to be taken into account include the publicity attendant on court proceedings,[33] the greater likelihood of any decision being potentially amenable to one

29 See I. Brownlie, *Principles of Public International Law* (Oxford University Press, 7th edn, 2008), p. 48.

30 England and Wales is one such jurisdiction: *J. H. Rayner (Mincing Lane) Ltd* v. *Department of Trade and Industry* [1990] 2 AC 418, HL.

31 In the UK the ECT has been expressly incorporated into domestic law by the European Communities (Definition of Treaties) (The Energy Charter Treaty) Order 1996 under which the ECT is defined as a 'Community Treaty' with the consequence that (by section 2(1) of the European Communities Act 1972), 'All such rights, powers, liabilities, obligations and restrictions... arising by or under the [ECT], and all such remedies and procedures... provided for by or under the [ECT], as in accordance with the [ECT] are without further enactment to be given legal effect or used in the United Kingdom shall be recognised and available in law, and be enforced, allowed and followed accordingly...'.

32 In some cases, of course, it is the host state's courts themselves whose conduct is impugned by the claimant as a breach of Part III of the ECT: see, e.g., *Petrobart* v. *Kyrgyz Republic* Award, 29 March 2005.

33 Of the fifty-one state signatories to the ECT which apply it, all but eight (Belarus, Japan, Kazakhstan, Kyrgyzstan, Mongolia, Tajikistan, Turkmenistan and Uzbekistan) are also parties to the European Convention on Human Rights and consequently bound to provide for judgment to be pronounced publicly except in very limited circumstances (Article 6).

or more layers of appeal[34] and, importantly, the fact that a court judgment is unlikely to share with an arbitral award the advantage of widespread enforceability throughout the world.[35]

### (b) *Article 26(2)(b): 'in accordance with any applicable, previously agreed dispute resolution procedure'*

This option allows for the fact that many pairs of Contracting Parties to the ECT already have in force between them bilateral investment treaties with their own dispute settlement provisions. In most cases these provisions are likely to add nothing to the other options provided by Article 26. However, there may be circumstances in which a claimant prefers to enforce rights under Part III of the ECT by means of a claim brought under the dispute settlement provisions of a BIT. For example, a British company with a claim against Azerbaijan, if it had already brought but abandoned proceedings in the Azerbaijani courts for substantially the same relief, might face difficulty in bringing a claim by arbitration under Article 26(2)(c) because Azerbaijan does not give its unconditional consent to ECT arbitration in such circumstances.[36] However, Azerbaijan's consent, in Article 8(1) of the UK–Azerbaijan BIT, to ICSID arbitration of 'any legal dispute . . . concerning an investment' (including therefore a claim concerning alleged breach of Part III of the ECT) is subject to no such qualification.

### (c) *Article 26(2)(c): 'in accordance with the following paragraphs of this Article': international arbitration under the ECT itself*

The remainder of Article 26 is concerned with the institution and conduct of arbitral proceedings under the ECT itself.

Article 26(3)(a) provides that:

> Subject only to subparagraphs (b) and (c), each Contracting Party hereby gives its unconditional consent to the submission of a dispute to international arbitration or conciliation in accordance with the provisions of this Article.

34 A further factor may be the availability and effectiveness of interim measures within the jurisdiction of the host state's courts as compared to interim measures directed by an arbitral tribunal.

35 Enforceability of awards under the ECT is discussed below, p. 153.

36 See Article 26(3)(b)(i) and Annex ID, discussed below, pp. 146–9.

This paragraph provides one half of the 'indispensable requirement',[37] namely the host state's consent, for an arbitral tribunal's jurisdiction. The other half is provided by Article 26(4):

> In the event that an Investor chooses to submit the dispute for resolution under subparagraph (2)(c), the Investor shall further provide its consent in writing for the dispute to be submitted to:
>
> (a) (i) The International Centre for Settlement of Investment Disputes, established pursuant to the Convention on the Settlement of Investment Disputes between States and Nationals of other States opened for signature at Washington, 18 March 1965 (hereinafter referred to as the 'ICSID Convention'), if the Contracting Party of the Investor and the Contracting Party party to the dispute are both parties to the ICSID Convention; or
> (ii) The International Centre for Settlement of Investment Disputes, established pursuant to the Convention referred to in subparagraph (a)(i), under the rules governing the Additional Facility for the Administration of Proceedings by the Secretariat of the Centre (hereinafter referred to as the 'Additional Facility Rules'), if the Contracting Party of the Investor or the Contracting Party party to the dispute, but not both, is a party to the ICSID Convention;[38]
> (b) a sole arbitrator or *ad hoc* arbitration tribunal established under the Arbitration Rules of the United Nations Commission on International Trade Law (hereinafter referred to as 'UNCITRAL'); or
> (c) an arbitral proceeding under the Arbitration Institute of the Stockholm Chamber of Commerce.

Article 26(5)(a)(i) expressly provides (lest there be any doubt on the point) that the consent given by the host state in Article 26(3) and by the Investor when, pursuant to Article 26(4), it submits the dispute to arbitration under Article 26(2)(c) 'shall be considered to satisfy the requirement for . . . written consent of the parties to a dispute for the purposes of Chapter III of the ICSID Convention[39] and for purposes of the Additional Facility Rules.[40] Article 26(5)(a)(iii) expressly provides that these consents 'shall be considered to satisfy the requirement for . . . "the parties to a

37 C. Schreuer, 'Consent to Arbitration' in P. Muchlinski, F. Ortino and C. Schreuer (eds.), *Oxford Handbook of International Investment Law* (Oxford University Press, 2008), p. 831.

38 Only four signatories to the ECT are not also parties to the ICSID Convention: Liechtenstein, Poland, Tajikistan and the European Union (source: http://icsid.worldbank.org, accessed March 2010).

39 See Article 25(1) of the ICSID Convention: ' . . . which the parties to the dispute consent in writing to submit to the Centre'.

40 See Article 2 of the Additional Facility Rules.

contract [to] have agreed in writing"' for the purposes of Article 1 of the UNCITRAL Arbitration Rules.[41]

## 5. Exceptions to host states' consent

The Contracting Parties' unconditional consent to arbitration is qualified, it will be noted, in two respects ('Subject only to subparagraphs (b) and (c) . . .').

### *(a) Article 26(3)(b): the fork-in-the-road clause*

Article 26(3)(b) provides that:

> (b) (i) The Contracting Parties listed in Annex ID[42] do not give such unconditional consent where the Investor has previously submitted the dispute under subparagraph (2)(a) or (b).

This 'fork-in-the-road' provision, like others in bilateral investment treaties, is of somewhat uncertain effect.[43] Plainly it ought only to have effect where the person who submitted the previous dispute was the Investor who now seeks arbitration under Article 26(2)(c). The difficulty, however, lies in defining 'the dispute', prior submission of which to another forum under subparagraphs 2(a) and 2(b) removes the state's unconditional consent to its being arbitrated under subparagraph 2(c).[44] At one end of the spectrum, a claimant who has instituted arbitral proceedings against an Annex ID state under a bilateral investment treaty (as permitted by Article 26(2)(b) of the ECT), complaining expressly of

41 'Where the parties to a contract have agreed in writing that disputes in relation to that contract shall be referred to arbitration under the UNCITRAL Arbitration Rules, then such disputes shall be settled in accordance with these Rules subject to such modification as the parties may agree in writing.'

42 Namely Australia (which had not ratified the Treaty when this work went to press), Azerbaijan, Bulgaria, Croatia, Cyprus, the Czech Republic, the European Union, Finland, Greece, Hungary, Republic of Ireland, Italy, Japan, Kazakhstan, Mongolia, Norway (which had not ratified the Treaty when this work went to press), Poland, Portugal, Romania, Russia (which applied the Treaty provisionally until 18 October 2009 inclusive and for which the Treaty will remain in effect with respect to Investments in existence at that date until 18 October 2029 (see Article 45(3)(b))), Slovenia, Spain, Sweden, Turkey.

43 On 'fork-in-the-road' provisions, see: Douglas, *The International Law of Investment Claims*, pp. 152–7; McLachlan *et al.*, *International Investment Arbitration: Substantive Principles*, pp. 103–7; Dolzer and Schreuer, *Principles of International Investment Law*, pp. 216–17; Schreuer, 'Consent to Arbitration', pp. 848–9.

44 As discussed below (p. 148), Article 26(3)(b)(i), where it applies, does not remove the state's 'consent' to arbitration but its 'unconditional consent'.

breaches of Part III of the ECT, may not subsequently bring arbitral proceedings as of right against the same state under the ECT itself (Article 26(2)(c)) in respect of the same complaint. At the other, a claimant should not be potentially precluded from bringing such proceedings merely by the fact that some matter distantly related to the alleged breach of Part III has previously been submitted to another forum under subparagraphs (a) or (b). The question is where to draw the line in cases nearer the middle of this spectrum.

Schreuer argues, in relation to 'fork-in-the-road' provisions generally, that the parties and causes of action in the two sets of proceedings must be identical in order for the second to be precluded by the first.[45] However, this absolute statement of the position is not without its difficulties. For example, if the step said to preclude arbitration against the Annex ID state under the ECT were a court action to enforce the Treaty in a state into whose domestic law it had been incorporated (being a state under whose constitution the ECT would otherwise have no effect in domestic law),[46] the cause of action could rightly be regarded as not identical: not breach of the Treaty per se but breach of the domestic law which provided for the substance of the Treaty to have effect.[47] It surely cannot have been intended that such a distinction should thus deprive Article 26(3)(b) of much of its effect. Yet if one accepts that the causes of action in the two sets of proceedings do not have to be completely identical, it is not easy to see why certain other proceedings in a forum specified in subparagraph 2(a) or 2(b) ought not also to qualify as 'previously submit[ing] the dispute'. For example, most ECT Contracting Parties have probably complied, to at least some extent, with Article 10(12)'s requirement to 'ensure that its domestic law provides effective means for the assertion of claims and the enforcement of rights with respect to Investments, investment agreements, and investment authorizations'. Such means may include remedies in public law for unreasonable or

45 Schreuer, 'Travelling the BIT Route – Of Waiting Periods, Umbrella Clauses and Forks in the Road', 248; Schreuer, 'Consent to Arbitration', p. 849. See also the discussion of the ECT's fork-in-the-road in the *Yukos* cases (*Yukos Universal Ltd* v. *Russia*, *Hulley Enterprises Ltd* v. *Russia* and *Veteran Petroleum Ltd* v. *Russia*, Interim Awards on Jurisdiction and Admissibility, 30 November 2009, paragraphs 587–600. On the facts it was clear that the claimants had not previously submitted the same dispute.

46 See the discussion above, p. 143.

47 See (in the analogous case of EU law in its effect in England and Wales), *Thoburn* v. *Sunderland City Council* [2002] EWHC 195 (Admin), [2003] QB 151: 'what is the legal foundation within which those substantive provisions [of EU law] enjoy their primacy . . . ? The foundation is English law' (*per* Laws LJ at [69]). See also McLachlan *et al.*, *International Investment Arbitration: Substantive Principles*, p. 107.

discriminatory behaviour. Many Contracting Parties are parties to the European Convention on Human Rights,[48] with its provisions in Article 1 of the First Protocol for the protection of property, and have provided means to enforce Convention rights in the domestic courts. If a claimant uses one of these means, in a forum specified in subparagraph 2(a) or 2(b), to complain of an act by the host state which coincidentally also amounts to a contravention of Part III of the Treaty, the better view is probably that a subsequently-commenced arbitration claim about the same act under subparagraph 2(c) does indeed constitute a second submission of 'the dispute' so as to engage the fork-in-the-road in favour of an Annex ID state. What matters is whether the substance of the factual complaint is the same; and whether the substance (but not necessarily the juridical source) of the right relied on is the same. This reading, it is submitted, better gives effect to the ordinary meaning, in context, of the words 'has previously submitted the dispute' than one which, in addition, demands formal identity.

It should be noted that Article 26(3)(b)(i) refers to the Annex ID states withholding not their 'consent' but their 'unconditional consent'. Thus an Annex ID state may yet consent to the submission to ECT arbitration of a dispute previously submitted elsewhere, provided that its conditions for so doing are met. Article 26(3)(b)(ii) provides that:

> (ii) For the sake of transparency, each Contracting Party that is listed in Annex ID shall provide a written statement of its policies, practices and conditions in this regard to the Secretariat . . .

Thus there is no constraint on whether the Annex ID state does or does not offer to give consent to arbitrate a previously-submitted dispute subject to conditions, or on what any such conditions may be. But the position must be made clear to the Secretariat and thus accessible to an Investor who is contemplating first commencing proceedings other than by arbitration under the ECT.[49] So, for example, Spain's statement under Article 26(3)(b)(ii) indicates that it *will* consent to arbitration under the ECT of a previously-submitted dispute provided that the Investor 'withdraws from any other previous procedure before the responsible authority issues a decision' and 'renounces [any right] to submit the same dispute to any other procedure of dispute settlement'. Italy's statement likewise provides

48 See the list at n. 33.

49 The statements of policies, practices and conditions submitted to the Secretariat are available at www.encharter.org/fileadmin/user_upload/document/Annex_ID.pdf (accessed June 2010).

that: 'if a resolution of the dispute has not yet been made by internal judicial or conciliation bodies, the Investor may revoke his judicial action or arbitral procedure by procedural or lateral renouncement and apply to other forms of dispute settlement'. By contrast, the statement of (for example) the European Communities indicates an absolute refusal of consent to arbitration of any dispute previously submitted to the European Court of Justice.[50]

Although this is not expressly spelled out in the Treaty, it is submitted that a Contracting Party must be held to its statement under Article 26(3)(b)(ii). Such a statement, if it contains an offer to consent to the arbitration of previously-submitted disputes provided certain conditions are met, is as much a standing offer of arbitration, if those conditions are met, as if it were contained in the Treaty itself.

Unfortunately not all of the statements which have been submitted under Article 26(3)(b)(ii) enable the investor to tell whether and in what circumstances consent might be given to international arbitration of a dispute previously submitted to the domestic courts. The following rather disarming statement from Slovenia is perhaps the most egregiously unhelpful:

> ... Slovenia is of the view that disputes should not be transferred to international institutions once they have been submitted to the courts or tribunals of a Contracting Party. Such a transfer should only be possible on the basis of an agreement between both parties to the dispute. However, Slovenia does not have sufficient relevant experience to be able to define the conditions enabling a subsequent transfer of dispute settlement to international arbitration.

### *(b) Article 26(3)(c)*

Article 26(3)(c) contains a substantive, rather than procedural, limitation on the consent to arbitration under subparagraph 2(c). It provides that the Contracting Parties listed in Annex IA[51] do not give their consent to such arbitration 'with respect to a dispute arising under the last sentence of Article 10(1)'. The last sentence of Article 10(1) is the 'umbrella' clause: 'Each Contracting Party shall observe any obligations it has entered into

50 'Statement submitted by the European Communities to the Secretariat of the Energy Charter pursuant to Article 26(3)(b)(ii) of the Energy Charter Treaty', OJ (L69) 115, 9.3.1998.

51 Australia and Norway (neither of which had ratified the Treaty when this work went to press) and Hungary.

with an Investor or an Investment of an Investor of any other Contracting Party.'[52]

### *(c) Contracting out of the right to proceed to international arbitration under Article 26(3)?*

An issue in international investment protection law generally, which has yet to receive a complete answer, is whether an investor can waive his rights under an investment protection treaty.[53] In the nineteenth and twentieth centuries, Latin American governments, in particular, sought to include clauses (known as 'Calvo clauses') in their contracts with foreign parties, binding them to litigate their disputes in the local courts and not to seek the diplomatic protection of their states of nationality. Such clauses were held to be effective in requiring contractual disputes to be litigated in the state party's courts but not to prevent the exercise of diplomatic protection and the bringing of international claims by the foreign party's home state for breach of the international minimum standard.[54] This was because in such cases the claim was seen as belonging to the investor's home state, whose rights had been infringed by the host state. The investor could only bind himself, not his state of nationality.

In *Compañiá de Aguas del Aconquija SA and Vivendi Universal* v. *Argentina*[55] and the earlier case of *Lanco International Inc* v. *Argentina*,[56] exclusive jurisdiction clauses in contracts between the foreign investor and the host state (in *Lanco*) or a constituent sub-division of the host state (in *Compañiá de Aguas*) were held ineffective to prevent a treaty arbitration tribunal from determining treaty (as opposed to contract) claims. The annulment committee in *Compañiá de Aguas* noted that the exclusive jurisdiction clause in the concession agreement:

> did not in terms purport to exclude the jurisdiction of an international tribunal arising under Article 8(2) of the [France–Argentina] BIT: at the very least, a clear indication of an intention to exclude that jurisdiction would be required.[57]

52 See Chapter 4, p. 120.

53 See O. Spiermann, 'Individual Rights, State Interests and the Power to Waive ICSID Jurisdiction under Bilateral Investment Treaties' (2004) 20 *Arbitration International* 179.

54 See *Woodruff* case (1903–5) IX RIAA 213; and *North American Dredging Co* v. *Mexico* (1926–7) IV RIAA 26.

55 Decision on Annulment, 3 July 2003.

56 Decision on Jurisdiction, 8 December 1998.

57 *Compañiá de Aguas del Aconquija SA and Vivendi Universal* v. *Argentina*, Decision on Annulment, 3 July 2003, paragraph 76.

It is not clear whether, provided that such a 'clear indication' is given,[58] an investor may contract out of its right to bring a claim to arbitration under Article 26(3) of the ECT. The justification given in *Woodruff* and *North American Dredging* for declining to give effect to such an indication – that the claim in question is the state's and incapable of being waived by the investor – loses its force if, as has been forcefully argued, the claim is the investor's rather than the state's.[59] A more fundamental objection might be that the ECT contains no express provision permitting its terms to be subjected to contrary agreement. And it may be thought undesirable in policy terms to permit a state to contract out of its treaty obligations.

However, as has been seen, the ECT itself sets out not one but three options for the vindication of the rights in Part III: (i) a claim in the host state's courts or administrative tribunals; (ii) arbitration under some other, previously agreed procedure; or (iii) arbitration under Article 26 itself (Article 26(2)). Plainly an alleged waiver of all three would be unlikely to be upheld. But it is much less obvious why a clear and freely made choice to limit potential claims to one of these forums should not be upheld.[60] If the position were that the investor had not sought to advance the claim (for example, a complaint of unfair and inequitable treatment contrary to Article 10(1)) by the agreed method – say, litigation in the host state's courts – but instead sought to commence immediate arbitration under Article 26(3), there would seem no objection in principle to holding the investor to its agreement. The position would be different if the investor had brought proceedings in the host state but the treatment of these proceedings by the host state (e.g., by its courts) had been such as to amount to a distinct breach of Part III of the Treaty. In those circumstances it would seem unlikely that an agreement, however clearly drawn, to allege breaches of Part III only in the host state's courts would be upheld.

58 Suppose, for example, an agreement which read: 'All disputes between [the host state and the investor], whether arising out of or in relation to this contract or not and including any claims made under Part III of the Energy Charter Treaty, shall be referred to the exclusive jurisdiction of the courts of [the host state] and, in particular, [the investor] waives all its rights under Article 26(3) of the Energy Charter Treaty.'

59 See Douglas, *The International Law of Investment Claims*, pp. 1–38.

60 Under the European Convention on Human Rights, persons, by agreeing to arbitrate their disputes, can validly waive their Article 6 rights provided that the waiver is made without undue compulsion, in an unequivocal manner and does not run contrary to any important public interest: see *Stretford* v. *Football Association* [2007] EWCA Civ 238, [2007] 2 Lloyd's Rep 31, paragraphs 43–67.

## 6. Factors determining the claimant's choice of international arbitration forum[61]

The factors likely to determine the claimant's choice of forum for international arbitration of his claims may conveniently be divided into: first, factors which determine which forums are available in the particular case; and, second, factors which may influence the choice from among the available options. The former derive solely from the identity of the parties. The latter range more widely.

### *(a) Available forums*

Ad hoc arbitration under the UNCITRAL Arbitration Rules and arbitration under the Arbitral Institute of the Stockholm Chamber of Commerce (SCC) are available in respect of any claim. By contrast, ICSID arbitration requires various hurdles to be overcome.

First, for arbitration under the ICSID Convention to be an available option, both the Contracting Party of the investor and the Contracting Party respondent to the dispute must be parties to the ICSID Convention. This requirement arises both under the ECT[62] and under the ICSID Convention itself.[63] Moreover, it should be noted that the claimant must be an investor 'of' the relevant Contracting Party as that term is understood both under the ECT and under the ICSID Convention. Notably, whereas mere lawful permanent residency in a Contracting Party will suffice to make a natural person an investor of that Contracting Party under the ECT,[64] the only connection between putative claimant and Contracting State which qualifies under the ICSID Convention is nationality.[65]

Second, the ICSID Convention is limited in its application to a 'legal dispute arising directly out of an investment'.[66] The term 'investment' as used (though not expressly defined) in the ICSID Convention has often been understood to have an autonomous meaning which is not necessarily coincident with the meaning of 'investment' as it appears in the relevant

61 This section draws on J. Blanch, A. Moody and N. Lawn, 'Investment Dispute Resolution and the Energy Charter Treaty' in G. Coop and C. Ribeiro (eds.), *Investment Protection and the Energy Charter Treaty* (New York: JurisNet, 2008), pp. 8–15.

62 Article 26(4)(a)(i) of the ECT.

63 Article 25(1) of the ICSID Convention. This requirement rules out arbitration under the ICSID Convention against the EU, which is not a party to it. The Additional Facility Rules are available where only one party is a party to the ICSID Convention: see Article 26(4)(a)(ii) of the ECT.

64 Article 1(7)(a)(i) of the ECT.

65 Article 25(2)(a) of the ICSID Convention.

66 Article 25(1) of the ICSID Convention.

investment-protection treaty.[67] Thus it is theoretically possible that a putative investment may count as such for the purposes of the ECT but not for the purposes of the ICSID Convention, thereby precluding arbitration under the ICSID Convention.[68] However, in practice this is most unlikely to occur, particularly if one regards the definition of 'investment' in the relevant treaty as tending to inform the meaning of that term in the ICSID Convention.[69]

Arbitration under the ICSID Additional Facility Rules is available, whether or not the dispute arises out of an 'investment' within the meaning of the ICSID Convention,[70] as long as either the claimant is a national (not just a permanent resident) of, or the host state is, a party to the ICSID Convention.[71] Since the ICSID Convention does not apply to arbitration under the Additional Facility Rules,[72] such arbitration may be assimilated to SCC and ad hoc UNCITRAL arbitration for the purposes of considering questions concerning challenge and enforcement.

### *(b) Choice among available arbitral forums*

It has been said that '[t]he end should actually be the beginning for any Investor considering which arbitral route to take...'[73] In other words, the first consideration should always be the practical enforceability of any award which the Investor may obtain.

If the chosen forum for the Investor's claim is an ICSID arbitration, any resulting award is enforceable (at least as to the pecuniary obligations which it contains) under Article 54 of the ICSID Convention in any

67 See Dolzer and Schreuer, *Principles of International Investment Law*, pp. 60–2 and the cases there cited.

68 It might be thought that *Petrobart Ltd* v. *Kyrgyz Republic*, Award, 29 March 2005 (discussed in Chapter 3 at p. 60), where the claim was in fact brought under the SCC rules rather than the ICSID Convention, was such a case, though the better view is that it was simply wrongly decided: there was no investment either under the ICSID Convention or under the ECT.

69 For an emphatic endorsement of this approach, see the majority opinion in *Malaysian Historical Salvors Sdn Bhd* v. *Malaysia*, Decision on Application for Annulment, 16 April 2009.

70 Although if there is no investment within Article 25 of the ICSID Convention the Secretary-General must be 'satisfied... that the underlying transaction has features which distinguish it from an ordinary commercial transaction' (Additional Facility Rules, Article 4(3)); and of course there must be an Investment within the meaning of the ECT.

71 Article 26(4)(a)(ii) of the ECT; Article 2 of the Additional Facility Rules.

72 Article 3 of the Additional Facility Rules.

73 Blanch *et al.*, 'Investment Dispute Resolution and the Energy Charter Treaty', p. 10.

state which is a party to that Convention.[74] If the chosen forum is an ad hoc UNCITRAL arbitration, an SCC arbitration or arbitration under the ICSID Additional Facility Rules, the principal enforcement mechanism is likely to be the New York Convention,[75] Article III of which compels contracting states to recognise and enforce awards arising out of 'an agreement in writing under which the parties undertake to submit to arbitration all or any differences which have arisen or which may arise between them in respect of a defined legal relationship, whether contractual or not, concerning a subject matter capable of settlement by arbitration'.[76] Article 26(5)(a)(ii) of the ECT expressly confirms that the consent given by host state and Investor to arbitration under Article 26 of the ECT constitutes an 'agreement in writing' for the purposes of the New York Convention.

Article 26(5)(b) of the ECT caters for two respects in which contracting parties to the New York Convention may seek, under Article I(3) of the Convention, to limit their obligations under it. First, by the so-called 'reciprocity reservation', Article 1(3) permits states to declare that they will recognise and enforce only arbitral awards obtained in another contracting state to the Convention. Several states have made such declarations.[77] Article 26(5)(b) of the ECT deals with this by permitting either party to insist that the arbitration be held in a state which is party to the New York Convention. Second, Article I(3) of the New York Convention permits states to declare that they will apply the Convention 'only to differences arising out of legal relationships, whether contractual or not, which are considered as commercial under the national law of the State'. Some states have so declared.[78] Article 26(5)(b) of the ECT deals with this by providing that claims submitted under Article 26 of the ECT 'shall be considered to arise out of a commercial relationship for the purposes of article I . . . '.

Since there are currently over 150 parties to the ICSID Convention[79] and over 140 Contracting Parties to the New York Convention[80] there

74 Article 54(1) requires a Contracting State to recognise any award rendered pursuant to the Convention as binding and to enforce any pecuniary obligations imposed by an award within its territories as if it were a final judgment of a court of that state.

75 Convention on Recognition and Enforcement of Foreign Arbitral Awards (1958).

76 New York Convention, Article II(1).

77 See www.uncitral.org/uncitral/en/uncitral_texts/arbitration/NYConvention_implementation.html (accessed March 2010) for a partial list.

78 See www.uncitral.org/uncitral/en/uncitral_texts/arbitration/NYConvention_implementation.html (accessed March 2010).

79 See http://icsid.worldbank.org for a list.

80 See www.uncitral.org for a list.

is unlikely to be a great deal to choose between the various forms of arbitration permitted by Article 26 of the ECT in terms of finding a state in which the respondent has assets and in which enforcement is possible in practice. The choice between ICSID, ICSID Additional Facility, SCC and ad hoc UNCITRAL arbitration does, however, have some further important consequences.

### (i) Challenges to awards

First, there are consequences as regards the amenability of awards to challenge. With any form of arbitration other than arbitration under the ICSID Convention, the award will be amenable to challenge in the courts at the seat of the arbitration under whatever is the relevant law applicable in that jurisdiction.

If the claimant chooses SCC arbitral proceedings, the seat of the arbitration is likely to be Stockholm.[81] An SCC award is thus likely to be amenable to challenge under the Arbitration Act 1999 (Sweden)[82] which provides in material part that:

> An award . . . shall . . . be wholly or partially set aside upon motion of a party:
>
> 1. if it is not covered by a valid arbitration agreement between the parties;
> 2. if the arbitrators have made the award after the expiration of the period decided on by the parties, or where the arbitrators have otherwise exceeded their mandate; . . .
> 4. if an arbitrator has been appointed contrary to the agreement between the parties or this Act;
> 5. if an arbitrator was unauthorized due to any circumstance set forth in sections 7 or 8 [incapacity, lack of impartiality etc]; or
> 6. if, without fault of the party, there otherwise occurred an irregularity in the course of the proceedings which probably influenced the outcome of the case. . . .[83]

81 Though not inevitably so: see Articles 9 and 20 of the Arbitration Rules of the Arbitration Institute of the Stockholm Chamber of Commerce adopted by the Stockholm Chamber of Commerce and in force as of 1 January 2010, which give the Board of the Chamber of Commerce power to determine the seat unless the parties expressly agree where it is to be.

82 Available at www.sccinstitute.com (accessed March 2010). See generally F. Madsen (translated R. Ben-Dor), *Commercial Arbitration in Sweden: A Commentary on the Arbitration Act (1999:116) and the Rules of the Arbitration Institute of the Stockholm Chamber of Commerce* (New York: Oxford University Press, 2007).

83 Section 34.

Although this is, consistently with the modern approach, a limited power of review, it does, importantly, permit review on the ground of jurisdiction ('not covered by a valid arbitration agreement'). Since, as has been seen,[84] the conditions for the availability of arbitration under Article 26 of the ECT are numerous and have the potential to be both factually and legally complex, the prospect of a challenge on jurisdiction is unlikely to be attractive to a claimant.[85]

If the arbitral law at the seat of the arbitration is based on the UNCITRAL Model Law,[86] as it is in twenty-six jurisdictions which are signatories to the ECT,[87] the grounds will likewise be limited, but again not so as to exclude or restrict a challenge to the tribunal's jurisdiction. Article 34 of the Model Law[88] provides:

> Application for setting aside as exclusive recourse against arbitral award
>
> (1) Recourse to a court against an arbitral award may be made only by an application for setting aside in accordance with paragraphs (2) and (3) of this article.
>
> (2) An arbitral award may be set aside by the court . . . only if:
>
> (a) the party making the application furnishes proof that:
>
> (i) a party to the arbitration agreement . . . was under some incapacity; or the said agreement is not valid under the law to which the parties have subjected it or, failing any indication thereon, under the law of this State; or
>
> (ii) the party making the application was not given proper notice of the appointment of an arbitrator or of the arbitral proceedings or was otherwise unable to present his case; or
>
> (iii) the award deals with a dispute not contemplated by or not falling within the terms of the submission to arbitration,

84 See Chapter 3.

85 Although, as discussed in Chapter 3 at p. 63, the Svea Court of Appeal dealt with the respondent's challenge to jurisdiction in *Petrobart* v. *Kyrgyz Republic* somewhat cursorily.

86 UNCITRAL Model Law on International Commercial Arbitration 1985, amended 2006 (United Nations documents A/40/17, annex I and A/61/17, annex I).

87 Armenia, Australia, Austria, Azerbaijan, Belarus, Bulgaria, Croatia, Cyprus, Denmark, Estonia, Germany, Greece, Hungary, Republic of Ireland, Japan, Lithuania, Malta, Norway, Poland, Russia, Scotland (as part of the United Kingdom), Slovenia, Spain, the former Yugoslav Republic of Macedonia, Turkey, Ukraine (source: www.uncitral.org (accessed March 2010)).

88 Which reflects the limited grounds for refusal of enforcement under Article V of the New York Convention.

or contains decisions on matters beyond the scope of the submission to arbitration, provided that, if the decisions on matters submitted to arbitration can be separated from those not so submitted, only that part of the award which contains decisions on matters not submitted to arbitration may be set aside; or

(iv) the composition of the arbitral tribunal or the arbitral procedure was not in accordance with the agreement of the parties, unless such agreement was in conflict with a provision of this Law from which the parties cannot derogate, or, failing such agreement, was not in accordance with this Law; or

(b) the court finds that:

(i) the subject-matter of the dispute is not capable of settlement by arbitration under the law of this State; or

(ii) the award is in conflict with the public policy of this State.

(3) An application for setting aside may not be made after three months have elapsed from the date on which the party making that application had received the award . . .

(4) The court, when asked to set aside an award, may, where appropriate and so requested by a party, suspend the setting aside proceedings for a period of time determined by it in order to give the arbitral tribunal an opportunity to resume the arbitral proceedings or to take such other action as in the arbitral tribunal's opinion will eliminate the grounds for setting aside.

The arbitral law of states which have not adopted the UNCITRAL Model Law may permit of further challenges.[89]

By contrast, an award under the ICSID Convention is not amenable to challenge in the courts at the seat of the arbitration. For by Article 53 of the Convention: 'The award shall be binding on the parties and shall not be subject to any appeal or to any other remedy except those provided

89 So, for example, R. Chapaev and V. Bradautanu, 'International and Commercial Arbitration in the CIS and Mongolia', (2006) 17(3) *American Review of International Arbitration* 411 at 442–3, suggest that the arbitral law of Moldova permits a challenge on the ground that the award is 'contrary to the principles of Moldovan law . . . '; that under Uzbek law the award may be set aside 'if the award was not made on the basis of Uzbek law'; and that Turkmenistan permits a general right of appeal to the courts. Under Section 69 of the English Arbitration Act 1996 either party may (with the leave of the court and subject to severe limitations) appeal against the arbitral tribunal's decision on a point of law, though the point must be one of English law (section 82(1) and see *Reliance Industries Ltd* v. *Enron Oil and Gas India Ltd* [2002] 1 Lloyd's Rep. 645).

for in this Convention.' The sole remedy provided for is an application[90] under Article 52 of the Convention for the Secretary-General to appoint an ad hoc Committee to consider that party's request for annulment of the award on one or more of five grounds:

(a) that the Tribunal was not properly constituted;
(b) that the Tribunal has manifestly exceeded its powers;
(c) that there was corruption on the part of a member of the Tribunal;
(d) that there has been a serious departure from a fundamental rule of procedure; or
(e) that the award has failed to state the reasons on which it is based.[91]

It is well established that this is a closed list of grounds. Nothing less will do than establishing at least one of them. Even if a ground is established, it does not follow that the matter in question is sufficiently serious to warrant annulment of the award.[92]

As to the approach to be taken by a Committee convened to consider a request for annulment, it has been rightly stated that:

> An *ad hoc* committee should not be concerned with upholding the finality of an award or [conversely, with] ensuring that the review of the award is as extensive as possible given that the annulment proceeding is the only possibility open to the parties, but should simply act within the confines of the task devolved upon it by the ICSID Convention. It may annul the award if, but only if it deems that one or more of the grounds for annulment set out in Article 52(1) of the ICSID Convention obtain.[93]

The most frequently fought-over ground in the ICSID case law is (b), 'that the Tribunal has manifestly exceeded its powers'. It is settled that an excess of powers consists both in a tribunal assuming a jurisdiction it does not have and in declining to exercise a jurisdiction which it does have.[94] But a challenge even to jurisdiction is significantly limited in the ICSID system. Where the question for the ad hoc committee turns on the correctness or otherwise of the arbitral tribunal's decision that the claimant did, or did not, comply with the five conditions identified in Chapter 3 as necessary

90 Made within 120 days except where the ground alleged is corruption: Article 52(2) of the ICSID Convention.

91 See the discussion in Dolzer and Schreuer, *Principles of International Investment Law* at pp. 279–86.

92 See *Compañiá de Aguas del Aconquija SA and Vivendi Universal* v. *Argentina*, Decision on Annulment, 3 July 2002, paragraph 66.

93 *Rumeli Telekom AS* v. *Kazakhstan*, Decision of the ad hoc Committee, 25 March 2010, paragraph 73.

94 *Ibid.* at paragraph 86.

to found jurisdiction under Article 26 of the ECT, the following statement is likely to be pertinent:

> An *ad hoc* committee is not a court of appeal and cannot therefore enter, within the bounds of its limited mission, into an analysis of the probative value of the evidence produced by the parties. An in-depth analysis of the evidence[95] . . . lies outside the scope of the Committee's powers. Indeed, this is why the Award can only be annulled for a *manifest* excess of powers. Such lack of jurisdiction should have been evident on the face of the award and should not require the Committee to reconsider the evidence put before the Tribunal. An *ad hoc* committee will not annul an award if the tribunal's approach is reasonable or tenable, even if the committee might have taken a different view on a debatable point of law. Where . . . the question of jurisdiction depends not on a question of law but rather on an appreciation of the evidence, it would not be proper for an *ad hoc* committee to overturn a tribunal's treatment of the evidence to which it was referred.[96]

The restrictive nature of Article 52 is such that it may reasonably be concluded in most cases that an ICSID arbitral tribunal's decision on jurisdiction is less likely to be subsequently reversed than that of a tribunal constituted under any of the other available regimes.

An ad hoc committee's sole power is to annul an award or any part of it and, if asked to do so by either party, to remit the dispute to a fresh arbitral tribunal.[97]

### (ii) Challenges to enforcement

There is a similarly wide divergence between ICSID Convention awards and other awards when it comes to enforcement.

Enforcement of a non-ICSID award is a matter of law of the jurisdiction in which enforcement is sought. If the jurisdiction in question is a party to the New York Convention, its law ought to provide for only the limited grounds for refusal of enforcement listed in Article V:

> 1. Recognition and enforcement of the award may be refused, at the request of the party against whom it is invoked, only if that party furnishes to the competent authority where the recognition and enforcement is sought, proof that:

95 In that case, of alleged fraud by the claimant. On claimants' misconduct under the ECT see Chapter 3 at p. 87.

96 *Rumeli Telekom AS* v. *Kazakhstan*, Decision of the ad hoc Committee, 25 March 2010, paragraph 96 (emphasis added; internal citations omitted).

97 Article 52(3), Article 52(6) of the ICSID Convention.

(a) the parties to the agreement . . . were, under the law applicable to them, under some incapacity, or the said agreement is not valid under the law to which the parties have subjected it or, failing any indication thereon, under the law of the country where the award was made; or

(b) the party against whom the award is invoked was not given proper notice of the appointment of the arbitrator or of the arbitration proceedings or was otherwise unable to present his case; or

(c) the award deals with a difference not contemplated by or not falling within the terms of the submission to arbitration, or it contains decisions on matters beyond the scope of the submission to arbitration, provided that, if the decisions on matters submitted to arbitration can be separated from those not so submitted, that part of the award which contains decisions on matters submitted to arbitration may be recognized and enforced; or

(d) the composition of the arbitral authority or the arbitral procedure was not in accordance with the agreement of the parties, or, failing such agreement, was not in accordance with the law of the country where the arbitration took place; or

(e) the award has not yet become binding on the parties, or has been set aside or suspended by a competent authority of the country in which, or under the law of which, that award was made.

2. Recognition and enforcement of an arbitral award may also be refused if the competent authority in the country where recognition and enforcement is sought finds that:

(a) the subject matter of the difference is not capable of settlement by arbitration under the law of that country; or

(b) the recognition or enforcement of the award would be contrary to the public policy of that country.

These grounds (which correspond to the grounds for challenge in the courts under the UNCITRAL Model Law[98]), though limited – in particular, of course, in that they do not permit a challenge on the merits – permit a challenge to the jurisdiction of the arbitral tribunal. It has been held in England that a respondent may challenge enforcement on one of the Article V grounds notwithstanding that he failed to challenge the award in the courts at the seat of the arbitration; and, importantly and in stark contrast to annulment under the ICSID Convention, that to decide such challenge the court may undertake a wholesale rehearing of the question raised by the ground relied on, giving the arbitral tribunal's

98 See above, p. 156.

reasons no more than 'as much persuasive weight as their cogency gives them'.[99]

By contrast, Article 54 of the ICSID Convention simply requires parties to the Convention 'to recognize an award rendered pursuant to this Convention as binding and [to] enforce the pecuniary obligations imposed by that award within its territories as if it were a final judgment of a court in that State'. Thus, subject only to the fact that enforcement is limited to pecuniary obligations, the court in the state in which enforcement is sought is bound to enforce an ICSID award regardless of any question concerning its correctness on any point, including jurisdiction.

## 7. Powers of a tribunal constituted pursuant to Article 26

The powers of a tribunal constituted pursuant to Article 26 are largely delineated by the applicable rules: the ICSID Convention, the Additional Facility Rules, the SCC arbitration rules or the UNCITRAL Arbitration Rules as the case may be. Each of these is a subject in its own right and beyond the scope of this work. However, certain points may be briefly highlighted concerning the application of these rules to an arbitration under the ECT.

First, the ECT itself places no limits on the exercise by an arbitral tribunal of such powers as it may possess to make interim orders or orders for provisional measures.[100]

Second, so far as final relief is concerned, Article 26(8) expressly confirms an arbitral tribunal's power to award interest.[101]

Third, unlike (for example) the US Model BIT (2004),[102] the ECT does not generally limit the tribunal to awards for monetary damages and restitution of property. Indeed, Article 26(8) (second sentence) provides that:

99 *Dallah Estate and Tourism Holding Company* v. *Ministry of Religious Affairs, Government of Pakistan* [2009] EWCA Civ 755, [2010] 2 WLR 805, paragraph 21 (affirmed [2010] UKSC 46, [2010] 3 WLR 1472).

100 See, e.g., Article 47 (provisional measures) of the ICSID Convention; Article 32 (interim measures) and Appendix II (emergency arbitrator) of the Arbitration Rules of the Arbitration Institute of the Stockholm Chamber of Commerce adopted by the Stockholm Chamber of Commerce and in force as of 1 January 2010; Article 26 (interim measures) of the UNCITRAL Arbitration Measures.

101 See, as to the award of interest, McLachlan *et al.*, *International Investment Arbitration: Substantive Principles*, pp. 343–6.

102 Article 34(1).

> An award of arbitration concerning a measure of a sub-national government or authority of the disputing Contracting Party shall provide that the Contracting Party may pay monetary damages in lieu of any other remedy granted.

Though this provision plainly precludes the grant of non-monetary relief as a sole remedy in the particular circumstances in which it applies, it is premised on the general availability of an order for non-monetary relief – e.g., an injunction – without the option of paying damages in lieu.[103] In practice, however, investment arbitral tribunals have proved reluctant to make such orders, even in cases where non-pecuniary remedies have been requested.

103 See, as to non-pecuniary remedies, C. Schreuer, 'Non-pecuniary Remedies in ICSID Arbitration' (2004) 20 *Arbitration International* 325; McLachlan *et al.*, *International Investment Arbitration: Substantive Principles*, pp. 341–3.

# 7

# Contracting Parties' international responsibility for breaches of Part III of the ECT

## 1. Introduction

A Contracting Party is only liable for breach of Part III of the Energy Charter Treaty if it is responsible in law for the conduct constituting such breach. The general international law rules on state responsibility are customary in nature but have been codified by the International Law Commission.[1] Articles 22 and 23 of the ECT make particular provision as to state responsibility under the Treaty. These are examined in this Chapter although it will be concluded that they do not ultimately change the applicable rules of attribution.

In addition, unlike most investment protection treaties, the ECT includes among its parties not only states, including all of the members of the European Union (EU), but also the EU itself, an international organisation. There is therefore a question as to whether conduct complained of by a claimant should be attributed to an international organisation alone, to or to one or more of that organisation's member states, or to both. Relevant to this question are the International Law Commission's draft Articles on the International Responsibility of International Organisations.[2]

## 2. State responsibility under the ECT

The respondent to an investor's claim under an international investment treaty must invariably be a party to the treaty, that is (in almost all cases) a state. Equally invariably, in practice, the conduct of the state's response to a claim is in the hands of the executive branch of the state's national government, as the body responsible for the state's international relations.

1 International Law Commission's Articles on Responsibility of States for Internationally Wrongful Acts (2001) GA res. 56/83 (2002), Annex.

2 See International Law Commission, Draft Articles on the Responsibility of International Organizations (Report of the Sixty-First Session (2009), UN Doc. A/64/10) ('draft IO Articles').

The paradigm complaint advanced by an investor is that that same body has, by its own acts or omissions, violated the treaty's guarantees of protection of the investment. However, since the real world of investment is rarely so simple, it is also necessary to consider the extent to which liability can be fixed to a host state in respect of the acts or omissions of bodies and persons other than the executive branch of the national government.

There is a temptation, when considering this question, to go straight to the International Law Commission's Articles on Responsibility of States for Internationally Wrongful Acts (2001)[3] ('ILC Articles') in which the rules of public international law on this subject are sought to be codified, and the accompanying Commentary on the draft Articles.[4] This will often be the right destination but it is not the right starting-point. The starting-point ought always to be a proper analysis of the claim advanced by the claimant. A tribunal which is asked to attribute an act or omission to the respondent state needs to identify what obligation of the state is in issue. If the obligation is one which arises under the treaty, then the applicable rules of attribution are indeed those of international law, supplemented, where specific provision is made in the relevant treaty, by the treaty's own rules of attribution. However, if on analysis it transpires that the obligation is in truth a contractual one, then international law has no part to play in attributing to the respondent the act or omission said to constitute a breach of this contractual obligation.[5] The following discussion therefore assumes that the relevant obligation is indeed one arising under the Energy Charter Treaty.

The Commentary to the draft Articles draws attention to the distinction between the rules of state responsibility, which are 'secondary rules' which explain when a state is to be considered responsible for wrongful acts or omissions, and the 'primary rules', in which the content of international obligations may be found.[6] It is helpful to keep this distinction in mind when considering the Treaty's provisions on state responsibility.

3 GA res. 56/83 (2002), Annex.

4 'Draft Articles on Responsibility of States for Internationally Wrongful Acts, with Commentaries' (2001) II *Yearbook of the International Law Commission.*

5 Z. Douglas, *The International Law of Investment Claims* (Cambridge University Press, 2009), p. 80. See *AMTO* v. *Ukraine*, Award, 26 March 2008, paragraphs 109–12, in which an attempt to attribute a state-owned energy company's contractual defaults to the state under Article 22(1) of the ECT foundered. Rightly, the claimant did not even attempt to argue that general principles of public international law could support the attribution.

6 See paragraphs (1), (2) and (4), 'Draft Articles on Responsibility of States for Internationally Wrongful Acts with Commentaries'.

### (a) *Responsibility of a Contracting Party for acts of all organs of government: Article 23*

Article 4 of the ILC Articles[7] provides that:

> 1. The conduct of any State organ shall be considered an act of that State under international law, whether the organ exercises legislative, executive, judicial or any other functions, whatever position it holds in the organization of the State, and whatever its character as an organ of the central Government or of a territorial unit of the State.
> 2. An organ includes any person or entity which has that status in accordance with the internal law of the State.

This general principle, which is well established in public international law generally,[8] applies equally in the law of international investment claims.[9]

The ECT makes specific provision in respect of regional and local governments and authorities in Article 23(1):

> OBSERVANCE BY SUB-NATIONAL AUTHORITIES
>
> (1) Each Contracting Party is fully responsible under this Treaty for the observance of all provisions of the Treaty, and shall take such reasonable measures as may be available to it to ensure such observance by regional and local governments and authorities within its Area.

7 Article 4 is in Part One of the ILC Articles, which is concerned with what amounts, in international law, to the act of a state. There is no reason to regard Part One as inapplicable to investor–state claims. However, as Douglas, *The International Law of Investment Claims* points out (at p. 96), Part Two of the ILC Articles, which is concerned with the consequences of state responsibility, is not directly applicable to claims under international investment treaties since it is expressly limited to 'obligations . . . owed to another State, to several States, or to the international community as a whole' (Article 33(1)). Part Three is also inapplicable, being about the invocation of responsibility by an injured state.

8 See, e.g., *LaGrand (Germany* v. *United States of America)*, Judgment, ICJ Rep 2001, p. 466, (noted X. Yang, 'Thou Shalt not Violate Provisional Measures' (2001) *Cambridge Law Journal* 441) in which the ICJ held that the US had committed breaches of its treaty obligations by acts done by its federal government and its Supreme Court and by the Governor of the State of Arizona.

9 See, e.g., *Nykomb Synergetics Technology Holding* v. *Latvia*, Award, 16 December 2003 (legislature and executive), *Mondev International Ltd* v. *United States of America*, Award, 11 October 2002 (City of Boston and Massachusetts Supreme Judicial Court), *Loewen* v. *United States of America*, Decision on Jurisdiction, 9 January 2001 (Mississippi State Court judge and jury); *Amco* v. *Indonesia*, Award, 20 November 1984 (armed forces and police).

This paragraph[10] contains both a secondary rule of attribution – 'Each Contracting Party is fully responsible . . . for the observance of all provisions of the Treaty' – and a primary rule of obligation – 'shall take such reasonable measures as may be available to it to ensure such observance by regional and local governments and authorities within its Area'. The two rules are plainly independent of each other. By the secondary rule, the acts of a state's regional or local authorities (of whatever character) are attributable to the state, so that an act amounting to a breach of the investor-protection parts of the Treaty which is done by a regional or local authority is treated as an act of the state. A state cannot diminish its responsibility for a non-observance of the Treaty by pleading that it was not the fault of its national authorities, even if it occurred in spite of those national authorities' reasonable measures to prevent it. The rule thus replicates the rule of customary international law codified as Article 4 of the ILC Articles. And, lest there be any doubt that the effect of the secondary rule in Article 23(1) is to make a Contracting Party whose local or regional authorities have done acts amounting to breaches of Part III of the Treaty amenable to arbitration under Article 26, Article 23(2) adds that:

> (1) The dispute settlement provisions in Parts II, IV and V of this Treaty [Article 26 is in Part V] may be invoked in respect of measures affecting the observance of the Treaty by a Contracting Party which have been taken by regional or local governments or authorities within the Area of the Contracting Party.

The second sentence of Article 26(8), however, places a limit on what an arbitral tribunal may order as regards the acts of regional and local governments or authorities. It provides that: 'An award of arbitration concerning a measure of a sub-national government or authority of the disputing Contracting Party shall provide that the Contracting Party may pay monetary damages in lieu of any other remedy granted.'

The premise is that an arbitral tribunal has the power not only to award monetary compensation but also to grant injunctive relief. Assuming this to be right, there would, but for this provision, be nothing to preclude a tribunal from making an order against a federated state simply requiring

10 Which mirrors that of the Understanding on the Interpretation of Article XXIV of the General Agreement on Tariffs and Trade 1994, paragraph 13: 'Each Member is fully responsible under GATT 1994 for the observance of all provisions of GATT 1994, and shall take such reasonable measures as may be available to it to ensure such observance by regional and local governments and authorities within its territory.'

(say) that some continuing, treaty-infringing, practice on the part of one of its state governments cease. Such an order could be made regardless of whether or not the federal government was in any position to compel compliance with it by the state government.[11] This course is precluded by the obligation to offer the respondent state the alternative of paying monetary damages in lieu.

By the primary rule in Article 23(1), if the national authorities do fail to take reasonable measures to prevent the non-observance of the treaty by a local or regional authority, the state commits a distinct breach of Article 23(1). It is not obvious, however, that this rule is of much utility in the context of investor–state disputes. First, it is hard to envisage a case in which a claimant investor which can prove itself to be the victim of a breach of an obligation in Part III of the Treaty at the hands of local or regional authorities, and which therefore has a claim against the state under the secondary rule in Article 23(1) regardless of the culpability or otherwise of the state's national authorities, would wish to take on the burden of proving such culpability (i.e., their failure to take reasonable measures to prevent the non-observance of the Treaty by the local or regional authorities). Second, since Article 23(1) is in Part IV of the Treaty, the rule is not enforceable by arbitration under Article 26, which applies only to disputes which 'concern an alleged breach of an obligation . . . under Part III'.[12] The rule is more likely to be relevant at the stage when a local or regional authority is threatening, or is in the process of committing, some infringement of an investor's rights under Part III: the investor can legitimately remind the host state's national authorities – albeit without the threat of direct means of enforcement under Article 26 – of the rule's existence and their obligation under it to take reasonable measures to stop the infringement.

The ECT contains no express provision about the effect of an excess of jurisdiction on the part of an organ of government. However,

11 See, by analogy (but only by analogy for the reasons discussed above, n. 4) ILC Articles 30–2, summarised in paragraph (2) of the Commentary to Article 32 as follows: 'international law does not . . . allow internal law to count as an excuse for non-performance of the obligations of cessation and reparation [in respect of internationally wrongful acts]'. I. Brownlie, *Principles of Public International Law*, (Oxford University Press, 7th edn., 2008), p. 463, suggests, however, that a remedy 'which accommodates the internal competence of governments . . . is to be preferred'.

12 T. Wälde and P. Wouters, 'State Responsibility in a Liberalised World Economy: "State, Privileged and Sub-National Authorities" under the 1994 Energy Charter Treaty: An analysis of Articles 22 and 23', (1996) 26 *Netherlands Yearbook of International Law* 143 suggest the contrary on the basis of 'context and history' but for reasons discussed below in the context of Article 22 it is submitted that this is wrong.

international law is clear on this subject and there is no reason to think that the principle embodied in Article 7 of the ILC Articles does not apply:

> The conduct of an organ of a State or of a person or entity empowered to exercise elements of the governmental authority shall be considered an act of the State under international law if the organ, person or entity acts in that capacity, even if it exceeds its authority or contravenes instructions.

In *Kardassopoulos* v. *Georgia*, this principle precluded the respondent from avoiding the consequences of a concession granted in alleged excess of power by a state-owned enterprise.[13]

### (b) *State and privileged enterprises: Article 22*

Article 5 of the ILC Articles provides that:

> The conduct of a person or entity which is not an organ of the State under article 4 but which is empowered by the law of that State to exercise elements of the governmental authority shall be considered an act of the State under international law, provided the person or entity is acting in that capacity in the particular instance.

Article 8 of the ILC Articles provides that:

> The conduct of a person or group of persons shall be considered an act of a State under international law if the person or group of persons is in fact acting on the instructions of, or under the direction or control of, that State in carrying out the conduct.

The principles codified in these Articles are also well established, both in international law generally and under international investment treaties.[14] Under the Energy Charter Treaty the relevant provision is Article 22:

> STATE AND PRIVILEGED ENTERPRISES
> (1) Each Contracting Party shall ensure that any state enterprise which it maintains or establishes shall conduct its activities in relation to the sale or provision of goods and services in its Area in a manner

13 *Kardassopoulos* v. *Georgia*, Decision on Jurisdiction, 6 July 2007, discussed at p. 51 above).

14 For a short summary in the investment context, see R. Dolzer and C. Schreuer, *Principles of International Investment Law* (Oxford University Press, 2008), pp. 198–204.

consistent with the Contracting Party's obligations under Part III of this Treaty.

(2) No Contracting Party shall encourage or require such a state enterprise to conduct its activities in its Area in a manner inconsistent with the Contracting Party's obligations under other provisions of this Treaty.

(3) Each Contracting Party shall ensure that if it establishes or maintains an entity and entrusts the entity with regulatory, administrative or other governmental authority, such entity shall exercise that authority in a manner consistent with the Contracting Party's obligations under this Treaty.

(4) No Contracting Party shall encourage or require any entity to which it grants exclusive or special privileges to conduct its activities in its Area in a manner inconsistent with the Contracting Party's obligations under this Treaty.

(5) For the purposes of this Article, 'entity' includes any enterprise, agency or other organization or individual.

It will be noted that in form this Article consists entirely of primary rules of obligation rather than secondary rules of attribution. Moreover, like Article 23, it is not contained in Part III of the Treaty and the obligations which it contains are, therefore, not obligations of whose breach a claimant can complain by notice of arbitration under Article 26.

So far as paragraphs (2) to (4) of Article 22 are concerned, these matters of drafting are unlikely to be significant. Any state which encouraged or required a state enterprise to act inconsistently with the state's obligations under Part III of the Treaty would surely be guilty of a breach of those obligations in its own right:[15] Article 22(2) is thus arguably otiose anyway. Likewise, any state which did the same as regards 'any entity to which it grants exclusive or special privileges' would be committing a direct breach of Part III irrespective of Article 22(4). Article 22(3) (which is similar in form to the second rule in Article 23(1))[16] obliges the state to ensure that an entity entrusted with governmental authority exercises that authority consistently with the state's obligations under the Treaty (including, therefore, the obligations in Part III). Although this rule, too, is not enforceable directly by arbitration (because of Article 22's location in Part IV, not in Part III), this is of little consequence since breaches of obligations under Part III by an entity entrusted with governmental authority will be attributable to the state anyway on ordinary principles

15 See Article 8 of the ILC Articles. 16 See above, p. 166.

of attribution in customary international law (see Article 5 of the ILC Articles).[17]

More problematic is Article 23(1) ('shall ensure that any state enterprise which it maintains or establishes shall conduct its activities *in relation to the sale or provision of goods and services* in its Area in a manner consistent with the Contracting Party's obligations under Part III of this Treaty' (emphasis added)). Now the rule of attribution under Article 5 of the ILC Articles is clearly limited to the exercise of 'elements of the governmental authority'. The Commentary to the draft Articles explains that:

> The justification for attributing to the state under international law the conduct of 'parastatal' entities lies in the fact that the internal law of the state has conferred on the entity in question the exercise of certain elements of the governmental authority. If it is to be regarded as an act of the state for purposes of international responsibility, the conduct of an entity must accordingly concern governmental activity and not other private or commercial activity in which the entity may engage.[18]

In the light of this, one might read Article 22(1) of the ECT as applying only to 'activities [by state enterprises] in relation to the sale or provision of goods and services' which amount to activities of a governmental type. Yet there is no warrant for such a reading in the words of Article 22(1), and it is not obvious that it is necessary to find yet further redundant words in Article 22 (redundant because the attribution of the exercise of governmental authority is already covered, both by Article 5 of the ILC Articles and by Article 22(3) of the ECT). The better view is that Article 22(1) of the ECT means what it says: thus it requires states not merely to ensure that state enterprises exercise any governmental authority they might have consistently with Part III, but that they do so generally 'in relation to the sale or provision of goods and services in [the state's] Area'. Moreover, the obligation is not to take reasonable steps to ensure that the state enterprise 'conduct[s] its activities . . . in a manner consistent with the Contracting Party's obligations under Part III of this Treaty'; but, rather, to *ensure* that it does so. This is potentially a far-reaching and onerous obligation and it is easy to imagine the scope for allegations of breach. Suppose, for example, there was a serious breakdown in the functioning

17 Above, p. 168.

18 See paragraph (5) of the Commentary to Article 5. The tribunal in *Noble Ventures* v. *Romania*, Award, 12 October 2005 appears at paragraph 82 to reject the importance of the distinction between acts of the governmental authority and commercial acts by state entities. However, it is clear from the award as a whole that the tribunal was concerned on the facts with acts of the governmental authority.

of a state-owned postal service, or sudden and substantial changes in the goods rates charged by a state-owned railway, neither of which were the result of anything other than commercial factors, but which nevertheless had a serious adverse impact on investors. These might be said to amount to failures by the state to ensure that the relevant enterprise did not act inconsistently with the state's obligations under Article 10(1) (fair and equitable treatment, most constant protection and security, no impairing of management of Investments by unreasonable measures etc.).

However, much of the utility of Article 22(1) from an Investor's point of view is removed, it is submitted, by the fact of its location, in common with all of the primary rules of obligation contained in Articles 22 and 23, in Part IV of the Treaty, for which there is no provision for enforcement by Investors under Article 26. It is, of course, arguable that a strained construction should be given to the Treaty so as to avoid this conclusion, inconvenient as it is for an Investor. One might perhaps construe Part III as including by implication the further obligations in Articles 22 and 23. But it is submitted that such a construction is untenable. The ordinary meaning[19] to be given to the relevant terms of Article 26(1), namely 'an obligation . . . under Part III', is 'the obligations expressly contained in Part III and not elsewhere'. Neither the context nor the Treaty's object and purpose[20] compel any other reading.

## 3. International responsibility of international organisations under the ECT

The European Communities (as they then were) were able to become parties to the ECT because the ECT defines 'Contracting Party' as 'a state or Regional Economic Integration Organization which has consented to be bound by this Treaty . . . '.[21] A Regional Economic Integration Organization (REIO) is:

> An organization constituted by states to which they have transferred competence over certain matters a number of which are governed by this Treaty, including the authority to take decisions binding on them in respect of these matters.[22]

The European Communities were (and the European Union (EU) is) a REIO and, to date, the only REIO party to the ECT.

19 Article 31 of the Vienna Convention on the Law of Treaties (1969) ('VCLT').

20 As to which see the Preamble and Article 2.

21 Article 1(2).

22 Article 1(3).

The basis on which the Communities were competent, as a matter of Community law (i.e., as between themselves and the member states), to enter into the ECT may be discerned from the Communities' Decision to do so, which sets out (in accordance with the usual practice in such instruments) the various legal bases for the Decision.[23] However, this is of little assistance in discerning, in respect of any matter about which an Investor might complain, who is to be held responsible to the Investor under the ECT. Unlike certain other instruments, the ECT contains no obligation for a REIO to make a declaration specifying the matters governed by the treaty in respect of which competence has been transferred to the REIO by its member states.[24] This is unsurprising given the numerous ways in which an act of the Communities might adversely affect Investors and their Investments.

Eilmansberger has suggested a typology of such acts.[25] They include (i) acts under Articles 64, 66 and 75 TFEU[26] restricting free movement of capital with respect to non-EU member states,[27] and (ii) EU rules permitting – or requiring – preferential treatment for EU companies, both of which apply only in relation to Investors of non-EU member state parties to the ECT; as well as (iii) a much broader category, which would seem to apply with regard to all Investors, including nationals of member states: provisions of EU law which compromise the value of an Investor's Investment. Within this category, Eilmansberger argues,

23 98/181/EC, ECSC, Euratom: Council and Commission Decision of 23 September 1997 on the conclusion, by the European Communities, of the Energy Charter Treaty and the Energy Charter Treaty Protocol on energy efficiency and related environmental aspects, OJ L 069, 9.3.1998, p. 1. Foreign direct investment was formerly a matter within the competence of the member states. However, the Lisbon Treaty has brought direct foreign investment within the Common Commercial Policy: see Article 207 of the Treaty on the Functioning of the European Union (Consolidated Version), OJ C 115/47, 9.5.2008 (TFEU).

24 Compare, for example, United Nations Convention on the Law of the Sea, 1833 UNTS 396 (1982), Annex IX, Article 2; Constitution of the Food and Agriculture Organization of the United Nations, Article II(5); (Cape Town) Convention on International Interests in Mobile Equipment (2001), Article 48(2).

25 See T. Eilmansberger, 'Bilateral Investment Treaties and EU Law' (2009) 48 *Common Market Law Review* 383, 407.

26 Formerly Articles 57(2), 59 and 60(1) of the TEC.

27 The incompatibility of these provisions and the capital transfer clauses in certain BITs has led to the Commission bringing infringement proceedings against several member states: see Case C-205/06 *Commission of the European Communities* v. *Austria* [2009] 2 CMLR 50; Case C-249/06 *Commission of the European Communities* v. *Sweden* [2009] 2 CMLR 49; Case C-118/07 *Commission of the European Communities* v. *Finland* [2010] All ER (EC) 558.

> two different subcategories can be distinguished. The first subcategory would comprise EC norms which prevent a member state from honouring specific guarantees given to the investor or made specifically in connection with a particular investment; the second category would capture Community law provisions which generally alter, possibly in a negative and unexpected way, the legal environment in which the investor operates.[28]

As Eilmansberger points out, in this third category 'a myriad of examples are conceivable'.[29] The measures in dispute in *AES*[30] and *Electrabel*,[31] for example, fall within its first subcategory; the claimants' complaints being that power supply agreements they had entered into were rewritten, allegedly to ensure their compatibility with EU law on state aid.

However, the EU frequently acts through the governments of its member states, which apply EU law through the acts of their own authorities. The issue thus arises as to whether, in such a situation, the EU or the member state, or both, are internationally responsible for the particular act. Here, Eilmansberger argues that:

> Responsibility for a breach ... by the European side could ... internally be organized according to the principle of attribution of breaching acts, possibly with the nuance that liability falls upon the EU if the member state's organs were implementing EU/EC law. Externally, i.e. with regard to potential claimants under a dispute resolution [mechanism] provided for in the agreement, the agreement would have to provide for the possibility that the European side first determines the respondent party before such proceedings are initiated.[32]

As an approach to the problem, this might perhaps be workable. But it is not the approach taken in the ECT, which contains no provision for any such determination as to the proper respondent.[33] In this context, however, the statement of the European Communities pursuant to Article 26(3)(b)(ii) of the ECT is notable. As discussed elsewhere,[34] Article 26(3)(b)(i) provides that the Contracting Parties listed in Annex ID do not consent unconditionally to arbitration where the Investor has previously submitted the dispute to the Contracting Party's own courts

28 Eilmansberger, 'Bilateral Investment Treaties and EU Law', 413.

29 *Ibid.* Eilmansberger goes on to provide a very full list of potential scenarios, most of which concern the application of EC competition law: *ibid.*, 414–15.

30 *AES Summit Generation Ltd and AES-Tisza Erőmű Kft.* v. *Hungary*, Award, 23 September 2010.

31 *Electrabel SA* v. *Hungary*, ICSID Case No. ARB/07/19.

32 *Ibid.*, 396.

33 Eilmansberger's suggestion to the contrary ('Bilateral Investment Treaties and EU Law') is mistaken.

34 See Chapter 5, p. 146.

or administrative tribunals, or in accordance with any applicable previously agreed dispute settlement procedure. The European Communities are listed in Annex ID and therefore had to provide a written statement, pursuant to Article 26(3)(b)(ii), of their relevant 'policies, practices and conditions in this regard'. The European Communities' statement also addresses, however, the issue of international responsibility, providing in relevant part:

> The European Communities are a regional economic integration organisation within the meaning of the Energy Charter Treaty. The Communities exercise the competences conferred on them by their member states through autonomous decision-making and judicial institutions.
>
> The European Communities and their member states have both concluded the Energy Charter Treaty and are thus internationally responsible for the fulfilment of the obligations contained therein, in accordance with their respective competences.
>
> The Communities and the member states will, if necessary, determine among them who is the respondent party to arbitration proceedings initiated by an Investor of another Contracting Party. In such case, upon the request of the Investor, the Communities and the member states concerned will make such determination within a period of 30 days.[35]

It is submitted that, having made and communicated any such determination, the EU or the relevant member state would be estopped from resiling from it and claiming in any consequent proceedings that it was the incorrect respondent. Indeed, in such cases, international responsibility would appear to follow from the fact that either the EU or the member state had acknowledged and adopted the conduct as its own.[36] However, there is no requirement in the ECT that a claimant seek such a declaration. Nor, even if a claimant were to seek and receive one, would it appear to be bound by the EU and the member states' identification of the proper respondent to the claim. Indeed, a footnote to the statement acknowledges that any determination by the Communities and the member states is not binding on the Investor, who may initiate proceedings against both[37] or (it is suggested) either.

35 Statement submitted by the European Communities to the Secretariat of the Energy Charter Treaty pursuant to Article 26(3)(b)(ii) of the Energy Charter Treaty, OJ L 336, 23.12.1994, p. 115 (footnotes omitted).

36 See Article 11 of the ILC Articles, and article 8 of the draft IO Articles.

37 The footnote provides that a determination made by the EC (now EU) and the member states concerned as to which of them should be the respondent is 'without prejudice to the right of the investor to initiate proceedings against both the Communities and their member states'.

Nor is it correct to say, as the statement does, that the EU and its member states are only internationally responsible for the fulfilment of the obligations contained in the ECT 'in accordance with their respective competences'. Insofar as this suggests that international responsibility derives from their competences under EU law, it is plainly wrong. Parties to a treaty generally undertake to observe all the obligations contained therein, unless the treaty itself provides otherwise or the party has made a valid reservation. This is usually seen as based upon the duty of good faith which parties to treaties undertake.[38]

A number of commentators,[39] as well as Advocate General Jacobs in his Opinion in *European Parliament* v. *Council of the European Union*,[40] have argued that (in the latter's words): 'Under a mixed agreement [i.e. an agreement 'concluded by the Community and its member states jointly'] the Community and member states are jointly liable unless the provisions of the agreement point to the opposite.' There being no provision *of the ECT* which expressly purports to allocate responsibility as between a state Contracting Party and a REIO of which that state is a member, it may be concluded that joint liability is indeed the norm.

This general statement is admirable as a starting-point but may be a poor substitute for what is really required in any given case involving potential liability of either or both of a state and a REIO, namely a close focus on the act alleged by the claimant to constitute a breach of an obligation in Part III of the Treaty. For the question which falls to be answered is not an abstract but a concrete one. It is whether, on the particular facts of the case and under this particular Treaty, the act complained of is attributable to the state, or to the REIO, or to both.

38 'Every treaty is binding on the parties to it and must be performed by them in good faith.' The same provision appears in Article 27 of the VCLT and in Article 46 of the 1986 Vienna Convention on the Law of Treaties between States and International Organizations or between International Organizations, 25 ILM 543 (1986). However, the obligation of good faith can be seen as cutting both ways: see M. Björklund, 'Responsibility in the EC for Mixed Agreements – Should Non-Member Parties Care?' (2001) 70 *Nordic Journal of International Law* 373, 389–400.

39 See G. Gaja, 'The European Community's Rights and Obligations under Mixed Agreements' in D. O'Keefe and H. Schermers (eds.), *Mixed Agreements* (Deventer: Kluwer Law & Taxation Publishers and Leiden: the Europa Instituut, 1983); E. Stein, 'External Relations of the European Community: Structure and Process', (1991) 1 *Collected Courses of the Academy of European Law* 115 and I. MacLeod, I. Hendry and S. Hyett, *The External Relations of the European Communities* (Oxford University Press, 1996). See also C. Hillion and P. Koutrakos (eds.), *Mixed Agreements Revisited* (Oxford: Hart Publishing, 2010).

40 Case C-316/91, *European Parliament* v. *Council of the European Union* [1994] ECR I-625, 646, paragraph 69.

It is easy to envisage a case in which the REIO bears no liability: the obvious example is a complaint about the enactment by a member state of a law when that enactment had nothing to do with the REIO. An obvious case in which a REIO does bear liability is equally easy to envisage: the enactment of a law by a member state which was obliged to do so under the rules of the REIO (e.g., the passing of primary legislation in order to comply with an EU Directive).[41]

More problematic, it is submitted, is finding a case in which a REIO is liable but the member state (or states) in which the relevant Investment was located is (or are) not. For a complaint under Article 26 of a breach of Part III must almost invariably be about some aspect of the exercise of governmental authority, be it executive, legislative or judicial,[42] and a REIO, by definition, has none of its own, but only the authority conferred on it by member states: accordingly, any executive, legislative or judicial act in a member state, whether or not instigated by (or compelled by the rules of) the REIO, is arguably always to be regarded as an act of the member state, even if also an act of the REIO. The argument follows not from any rule about how acts of international organisations are to be attributed to states but from the fact that an act by a REIO is, by its nature, ultimately an act in the exercise of states' governmental authority.

One can best test the argument by an example. Suppose that the European Parliament and Council, acting under Article 64(2) of the TFEU, adopt, by simple majority, over the opposition of the UK, a Regulation precluding the investment in the EU of any capital from persons in a particular ECT Contracting Party outside the EU. An Investor of that Contracting Party with an Investment in the UK complains that its rights under Article 10 of the ECT have thereby been infringed. Against whom should it bring its complaint? The EU is presumably liable as the instigator of the measure in question. But can the government of the UK escape responsibility on the ground that the infringing measure was not its measure but that of the EU? Arguably, it can. Since under EU law a regulation has direct effect without more in the law of the member states,[43] the infringing measure ought to be regarded as solely that of the EU. Moreover, the UK can point to the fact that it positively opposed the passing of the infringing measure. There is perhaps some support for this

41 In circumstances where the Directive could only be complied with in ways which deprived the claimant's investment of the treatment to which it was entitled under Part III. Plainly the EU might have a defence if the member state could have found a non-infringing way of enacting the Directive.

42 See above, p. 163.

43 Article 288 of the TFEU (formerly Article 249 TEC).

view in the wording of Article 1(3) of the ECT, where a REIO is defined as 'an organization . . . to which [states] have transferred competence over certain matters . . . including the authority to take decisions binding on them in respect of those matters'. Thus the ECT expressly contemplates circumstances in which a decision which binds member states is taken by a REIO, and (it might be argued) caters for this by expressly having the REIO as a Contracting Party and thus responsible to the Investor. If this is right, there is no reason for the member state in addition to be held responsible.

However, from the perspective of the Investor, the matter looks quite different. The obligations under Article 10 are owed by 'each Contracting Party'. There is no proviso to the effect that a Contracting Party is not liable to the extent that it has transferred control over the relevant matter to a REIO. Moreover, the infringing measure – here, the Regulation – only has any effect at all on the Investor's Investment in the UK because it is given force by the law of the UK, which provides that EU laws (such as the Regulation in this example) which, under EU law, are to have effect without further enactment shall have the immediate force of law in the UK.[44] The Investor may with some force argue that its Investment has been damaged by a law of the UK and that it should not be concerned with the provenance of that law. Any argument by the UK that it was not responsible for the Regulation involves the impermissible step of relying on internal law (here, the UK law that regulations have the immediate force of law in the United Kingdom) as justification for breach of an international obligation.[45]

Of some relevance to this question, arguably, is the fact that the Lisbon Treaty specifically provides that the EU has legal personality, replacing and succeeding the EC.[46] When an international organisation has international legal personality it has an identity distinct from that of its member states. It has been argued, largely on the strength of two cases – *Arab Organization for Industrialization* v. *Westland Helicopters*

44 Section 2(1) of the European Communities Act 1972; see *Thoburn* v. *Sunderland City Council* [2002] EWHC 195 (Admin), [2003] QB 151; and see the German Federal Constitutional Court's re-assertion of the principle that the EU has only the powers conferred on it by its members: Judgment of the second senate of 30 June 2009, 2 BvE 2/08, 2 BvE 5/08, 2 BvR 1022/08, 2 BvR 1259/08 and 2 BvR 182/09.

45 Contrary to Article 32 of the ILC Articles.

46 Articles 1 and 47 of the Treaty on European Union (Consolidated Version), OJ C 115/13, 9.5.2008. Thus the EU clearly falls within the definition of an 'international organization' in the International Law Commission's draft Articles on responsibility of International Organizations: see Article 2(a) of the draft IO Articles.

*Ltd*[47] and *J. H. Rayner (Mincing Lane) Ltd* v. *Department of Trade and Industry*[48] – that member states of an international organisation with legal personality are not, or not generally, liable for that organisation's wrongful acts.[49] However, these cases are of limited assistance in determining the extent to which a member state of the EU may be liable under the ECT for acts of the EU. They concern the quite different question whether a contract entered into by an international organisation with legal personality may be enforced against member states not expressly made parties to the contract. In any event, the rule that member states are not generally liable for the acts of international organisations with separate legal personality is (if it exists) a rule about secondary liability. The rule cannot strip a member state of liability if, following the reasoning outlined above, the state is itself directly liable to an Investor for what are on analysis its own acts.

The ILC Articles are of no help here. Article 57 provides that they 'are without prejudice to any question of the responsibility under international law of an international organization, or of any State for the conduct of an international organization'. However, in August 2009 the International Law Commission provisionally adopted on first reading draft Articles on the Responsibility of International Organizations ('draft IO Articles'). The draft IO Articles represent a work in progress,[50] the utility of which has been criticised,[51] but can be seen as a snap-shot of the current stage in the continuing debate on the accountability of international organisations. They do not give a full picture, particularly with regard to questions of the responsibility of member states for conduct required, authorised or recommended by an international organisation. Nevertheless it may be helpful to consider the question of the liability of REIOs and their member states under the ECT in their light. At the same time it is helpful

47 80 ILR 652 (1988) (Swiss Federal Supreme Court).

48 [1990] 2 AC 418 (House of Lords).

49 G. Gaja, Fourth Report on Responsibility of International Organizations, Addendum, UN Doc A/CN.4/564/Add.2. The principle is now reflected in Article 61 of the draft IO Articles '1. . . . a State member of an international organization is responsible for an internationally wrongful act of that organization if: (a) it has accepted responsibility for that act; or (b) it has led the injured party to rely on its responsibility'.

50 They are currently being submitted to governments and international organisations for their comments and observations.

51 See, e.g., J. Alvarez, 'International Organizations: Accountability or Responsibility?', Luncheon Address, Canadian Council of International Law, 35th Annual Conference on Responsibility of Individuals, States and Organizations, 26 October 2006 (text available at www.asil.org/aboutasil/documents/CCILspeech061102.pdf): Alvarez calls them 'a slow motion train wreck', and worse.

to consider briefly some of the European case law which bears, however indirectly, on the problem.

The draft IO Articles provide that: 'Every internationally wrongful act of an international organization entails the international responsibility of the international organization.'[52] For an internationally wrongful act to exist, conduct constituting a breach of an international obligation of the organisation must be attributable to it under international law.[53] The general rule on the attribution of conduct to international organisations is set out in Article 5 of the draft IO Articles:

> 1. The conduct of an organ or agent of an international organization in the performance of functions of that organ or agent shall be considered as an act of that organization under international law whatever position the organ or agent holds in respect of the organization.
> 2. Rules of the organization shall apply to the determination of the functions of its organs and agents.

Article 5(2) of the draft IO Articles would seem to give a role to the internal law of the organisation. However, Article 7 of the draft IO Articles provides that:

> The conduct or an organ or agent of an international organisation shall be considered an act of that organization if the organ or agent acts in that capacity, even though the conduct exceeds the authority of that organ or agent or contravenes instructions.[54]

Examples of conduct attributable to the EU under these rules would seem to include actions of the European Commission (e.g., in the context of competition law or state aid investigations), judgments of the European Court of Justice and the General Court and legislation enacted by the European Parliament:[55] these bodies are all 'organs' of the EU.

However, the point made above in the course of the discussion concerning the hypothetical Regulation prohibiting direct investment from a

52 Article 3, Draft IO Articles.

53 Article 4, Draft IO Articles.

54 See also Case C-327/91, *France* v. *Commission of the European Communities* [1994] ECR I-3641, where the ECJ held that an *ultra vires* act of the Commission nevertheless bound the EC.

55 However, difficult issues arise with regard to EU legislation. First, it is generally the application of legislation rather than its promulgation that engages international responsibility (although this would not be an issue if the national authorities implementing the measures were seen as agents of the EU, as discussed below). Second, Directives require implementation via national legislation, giving rise to questions whether any discrepancies with other international obligations arise as a result of action at the EU or at the national level.

particular ECT Contracting Party[56] would appear to hold good in respect of each of these examples: each of the acts mentioned only has any legal force in the member state where the Investment is located by virtue of the principle of that member state's law giving effect to EU law. Sometimes effect is given without more, as in the case of a Regulation. Sometimes, there is a further step which must be taken by the member state: the legislature passing legislation to give effect to a Directive, for example; or the court deciding a case in the light of the European Court's ruling. In either case (though more obviously in the case where some further step is to be taken by an organ of the member state's government) the act complained of by the Investor may therefore arguably be regarded as that of the member state as well as of the EU.

An answer to this perhaps lies in Article 2(c) of the draft IO Articles where the term 'agent' is defined as including 'officials and other persons or entities through whom the organization acts'. It might consequently be argued that, as regards the matter complained of by an Investor, particularly when it consists of the implementation of some measure within the EU's exclusive competence under EU law (or within an area of shared competence where the EU has exercised its competence), the member state Contracting Party is simply acting as an agent of the EU, which is consequently internationally responsible (and internationally responsible alone) for its actions. Moreover, it might be argued, by virtue of Article 7 of the draft IO Articles this is so even if the member state Contracting Party acts *ultra vires* the relevant EU law.[57]

A member state Contracting Party might also pray in aid Article 6 of the draft IO Articles:

> The conduct of an organ of a State ... that is placed at the disposal of another international organization shall be considered under international law an act of the latter organization if the organization exercises effective control over that conduct.

Thus, it might be argued, the organ of the member state Contracting Party which gave effect to the EU matter complained of – the legislature, in giving effect to the Directive; the national court, deciding a case in compliance with the European Court's ruling on the law; or even simply the legal system as a whole recognising as immediately effective the

56 See above, p. 176.

57 Although this is especially dubious: to put it in English law terms, a principal may sometimes be liable for the acts of his agent outside the scope of his authority but it does not follow that the agent is not personally liable too.

Regulation – had previously been placed under the 'effective control' of the EU so that its acts were attributable only to that organisation.[58]

The notion of 'effective control' was decisive for the Grand Chamber of the European Court of Human Rights in *Behrami* v. *France*.[59] The applicants sought to sue, for breaches of their rights under the European Convention on Human Rights, a number of the states which had contributed forces to KFOR in Kosovo. The Court attributed the acts complained of to KFOR (in one instance) and UNMIK (in the other) and ultimately (in both cases) to the United Nations.[60] As the UN is not a party to the European Convention on Human Rights, the Court declared the claims inadmissible for lack of jurisdiction.

In reaching this conclusion, the Court made specific reference to the International Law Commission's 2003 draft Articles on the Responsibility of International Organizations, in particular draft Article 5 (now Article 6 of the draft IO Articles).[61] The Court went on:

> The key question is whether the UNSC [United Nations Security Council] retained ultimate authority and control so that operational command only was delegated...
>
> ... UNSC Resolution 1244 gave rise to the following chain of command. The UNSC was to retain ultimate authority and control over the security mission and it delegated to NATO ... the power to establish, as well as the operational command of, the international presence, KFOR...
>
> [T]he necessary ... donation of troops by willing TCNs [Troop Contributing Nations] means that, in practice, those TCNs retain some authority over those troops (for reasons, *inter alia*, of safety, discipline and accountability) and certain obligations in their regard (material provision including uniforms and equipment)
>
> ...
>
> The Court is not persuaded that TCN involvement, either actual or structural, was incompatible with the effectiveness (including the unity) of NATO's operational command.
>
> ...

58 See also Article 14 of the draft IO Articles (direction and control exercised over the commission of an internationally wrongful act).

59 *Behrami* v. *France; Saramati* v. *France, Germany and Norway*, Application No. 71412/01 2 May 2007, (2007) 45 EHRR SE10.

60 KFOR (Kosovo Force) was the NATO force deployed in Kosovo. UNMIK (United Nations Mission in Kosovo) was the UN mission responsible for the civil administration of the province.

61 *Behrami* v. *France*; *Saramati* v. *France, Germany and Norway*, Application No. 71412/01 2 May 2007, (2007) 45 EHRR SE10, paragraphs 30–3.

> In such circumstances, the Court observes that KFOR was exercising lawfully delegated Chapter VII [of the Charter of the United Nations] powers of the UNSC so that the impugned action was, in principle, 'attributable' to the UN...

However, in the context of the ECT it is submitted that neither the argument based on agency (Articles 2(c) and 5 of the draft IO Articles), nor that based on 'effective control' (Article 6 of the draft IO Articles) is altogether convincing. For it is surely somewhat unreal to regard an EU member state Contracting Party to the ECT as nothing more than an 'agent' of the EU or as a body under its 'effective control'. Moreover, the premise of both arguments is that: 'When an organ of a State is placed at the disposal of an international organization, the organ may be fully seconded to that organization. In this case the organ's conduct would clearly be attributable only to the receiving organization.'[62] This premise is not necessarily sound, at least not for all purposes. As Brownlie put it, 'it would be contrary to good sense if a State could avoid responsibility by creating an international organization'.[63] (And it is questionable in any event whether 'effective control' in the chain-of-command sense, as described by the Court in *Behrami*, exists over member states' implementation of their obligations under EU law.[64]) Moreover, the internal rules of an international organisation and the international law of attribution are in principle quite distinct. As Milanoviç and Papiç forcefully (and, it is suggested, convincingly) put it concerning *Behrami*:

> Why is the Court's reliance on the notion of delegation so inappropriate in the context of attribution? The answer to this question is quite simple. The rules of attribution, and the rules of international responsibility in general, are secondary rules, which continue to apply in an identical fashion across multiple fields of primary rules unless a *lex specialis* is shown to exist. The delegation model, on the other hand, is a part of the institutional law of international organizations and has nothing to do with the law of responsibility. Its purpose is to determine whether an organ of an international organization can lawfully empower some other entity, according

62 International Law Commission, Report of the Sixty-first session (2009), UN Doc. A/64/10 at p. 62.

63 Brownlie, *Principles of Public International Law*, p. 684.

64 In any case, the Court's reasoning seems to apply only to the delegation of powers by the UN, specifically by the Security Council acting under Chapter VII of the Charter: see *Behrami* v. *France*, paragraphs 146–51. See also J. Klabbers, *An Introduction to International Institutional Law* (Cambridge University Press, 2009), pp. 280–1.

> to the rules of its own internal law. It does not, and conceptually cannot, establish whether a state, or an international organization, or both, are responsible for a given act or not.[65]

Other aspects of the draft IO Articles tend in any event to contradict the proposition that a member state may avoid liability for the acts of an international organisation. The draft IO Articles provide that an international organisation incurs international responsibility when it circumvents one of its international obligations by adopting a decision binding on a member state to commit an act that would be internationally wrongful if committed by the former.[66] Indeed, circumvention through authorisations and recommendations given to member states also engages international responsibility, providing that the member state acts on the authorisation or recommendation.[67] It appears implicit in such situations that the member state cannot itself avoid international responsibility by arguing that it acted pursuant to the decision, authorisation or recommendation.[68] In addition, a member state of an international organisation incurs international responsibility when it seeks to circumvent one of its international obligations by availing itself of the separate legal personality of the international organisation of which it is a member.[69] In consequence, although the point is not made in terms, the draft IO Articles in fact appear to support the idea that states cannot avoid their international obligations by transferring competences to an international organisation.

In this respect, the draft IO Articles follow the jurisprudence of the European Court of Human Rights when, on a number of occasions, it has grappled with issues arising out of the membership of the EC of states parties to the European Convention on Human Rights. In *Matthews* v. *United Kingdom*,[70] which concerned the applicant's inability, as an inhabitant of Gibraltar, to participate in elections to the European Parliament, the UK argued that:

65 M. Milanoviç and T. Papiç, 'As Bad as It Gets: The European Court of Human Rights' *Behrami and Saramati* Decisions and General International Law' (2009) 58 *International and Comparative Law Quarterly* 267, 281.

66 Article 16(1) of the draft IO Articles.

67 Article 16(2) of the draft IO Articles.

68 Although the provisions are subject to a 'without prejudice' clause: Article 18 of the draft IO Articles provides that: 'This chapter [Articles 9–18 of the draft IO Articles] is without prejudice to the international responsibility of the State or international organization which commits the act in question'.

69 See Articles 57–61 of the draft IO Articles.

70 Application No. 24833/94, 18 February 1999, (1999) 28 EHRR 361.

> acts adopted by the Community or consequent to its requirements could not be imputed to the member States, together or individually... [T]o engage the responsibility of any State under the Convention, that State must have a power of effective control over the act complained of.[71]

The Grand Chamber of the European Court of Human Rights rejected this argument:

> The [European] Convention [on Human Rights] does not exclude the transfer of competences to international organisations *provided that Convention rights continue to be 'secured'*. Member states' responsibility therefore continues even after such a transfer.[72]

The Court took the same approach in *Bosphorus* v. *Republic of Ireland*.[73] The complaint was of the government's seizure of an aircraft, in compliance with an EC regulation but arguably in breach of the applicant's rights under the European Convention on Human Rights. As the Court explained:[74]

> The [European] Convention [on Human Rights] does not, on the one hand, prohibit Contracting Parties from transferring sovereign power to an international organisation in order to pursue co-operation in certain fields of activity.... On the other hand, it has also been accepted that a Contracting Party is responsible under Article 1 of the Convention for all acts and omissions of its organs regardless of whether the act or omission in question was a consequence of domestic law or of the necessity to comply with international legal obligations. Article 1 makes no distinction as to the type of rule or measure concerned and does not exclude any part of a Contracting Party's 'jurisdiction' from scrutiny under the Convention.

The analogy with the position of a EU member state Contracting Party to the ECT is obvious. The converse, which the draft IO Articles seem to argue, is that international organisations cannot avoid their international responsibility by acting through their member states.

In conclusion, whether particular conduct falls within the competence of the EU (or any other REIO which might become a Contracting Party) is probably not decisive. On the one hand, it can be argued that, if it does, the member state's national authorities act as agents of the EU (Article 5 of the draft IO Articles) or that the EU has effective control over the conduct in question (Article 6 of the draft IO Article). On the other hand (and it is submitted that this is the better view), both the EU and the member state implementing the particular measure can be seen as concurrently

71 *Ibid.*, paragraph 26. 72 *Ibid.*, paragraph 32 (emphasis added).
73 Application No. 45036/98, 30 June 2005, (2006) 42 EHRR 1 74 *Ibid.*, paragraph 152.

liable for any breach (Articles 57 and 60 of the draft IO Articles). Every case must, of course, be closely considered on its own facts.

One way round the question would be for a claimant to take up the Communities' offer in the statement under Article 26(3)(b)(ii) of the ECT to 'determine among them who is the respondent party to arbitration proceedings initiated by an Investor of another Contracting Party'. Tactically, however, this may not be ideal, not least because it is not clear what should happen if the tribunal subsequently takes a different view as to who is responsible. Another way might be to bring a claim against both. Since the EU is neither a party to the ICSID Convention nor a state, this would rule out resort to the ICSID or to the ICSID Additional Facility, leaving only the options of SCC arbitration or ad hoc arbitration under the UNCITRAL Rules. It would also permit the European Commission to participate in proceedings as of right, rather than having to request leave from the tribunal to make third-party submissions.[75] The third option, which has so far been the one chosen by Investors and which permits resort to ICSID, is to claim against the particular member state Contracting Party only.

75 See L. Peterson, 'ICSID Tribunal will Permit European Commission to File Legal Brief in Energy Charter Treaty Arbitration', (2008) 16(1) *Investment Arbitration Reporter*, 11 December 2008.

# 8

# Taxation

## 1. Introduction

Tax regimes and levels of taxation are major concerns of investors, as they have direct and obvious effects on the profitability of their investments. The ECT, however, includes a major 'carve out' for taxation measures, taking them largely outside of the scope of the protections accorded by the Treaty. Such provisions are common in investment treaties. They are motivated, first, by a belief that taxation measures are more properly covered by bilateral tax conventions[1] and, second and more fundamentally, by states' reluctance to abandon their fiscal prerogatives. Given, however, the use of taxation measures not only to raise revenue but also to regulate corporate behaviour and to promote a variety of social and political objectives – and their potential for abuse in order to 'squeeze' foreign investors – such exclusions have potentially far-reaching effects.[2]

Part III of the ECT includes nothing specifically about taxation issues. Article 21 (Taxation), however, has rather a lot to say on the subject. Article 21 appears in Part IV of the Treaty and it will be recalled that, under Article 26, Investors can only bring claims for breach of obligations in Part III. However, despite its location, Article 21 affects Investors' rights under Article 26 because it serves to define the extent of the obligations which Contracting Parties incur in Part III. It is, however, a provision of Byzantine complexity.

Article 21(1) provides that:

1 There are believed (the number has not been verified) to be some 2,000 bilateral tax conventions in existence, making them as common as bilateral investment treaties.

2 See T. Wälde and A. Kolo, 'Coverage of Taxation in Modern Investment Treaties' in P. Muchlinski, F. Ortino and C. Schreuer (eds), *The Oxford Handbook of International Investment Law* (Oxford University Press, 2008), pp. 306–11.

> Except as otherwise provided in this Article, nothing in this Treaty shall create rights or impose obligations with respect to Taxation Measures of the Contracting Parties. In the event of any inconsistency between this Article and any other provision of the Treaty, this Article shall prevail to the extent of the inconsistency.

In consequence, Taxation Measures are governed exclusively by Article 21 and no other provisions of the ECT (including Part III) apply to them except as provided therein. It is this that renders Article 21 such a crucial provision. The provisions of Article 21 which specifically address Part III of the Treaty are contained in paragraphs (3), (5) and (6), which will be examined subsequently. Before doing so, however, it is necessary to consider to what measures Article 21 applies. 'Taxation Measures' are described in Article 21(7)(a) as including:

> (i) any provision relating to taxes of the domestic law of the Contracting Party or of a political subdivision thereof or a local authority therein; and
>
> (ii) any provision relating to taxes of any convention for the avoidance of double taxation or of any other international agreement or arrangement by which the Contracting Party is bound.

The terms 'tax provisions' and 'taxes', as utilised in Article 21, do not include customs duties,[3] so it can be deduced that Taxation Measures do not include provisions relating to customs duties in the domestic law of a Contracting Party or to any provision relating to customs duties of any international agreement or arrangement by which a Contracting Party is bound.[4] Beyond that, however, no real definition is provided. There is simply a reference back to the definitions given, respectively, in national law and in other relevant treaties. This is perhaps unfortunate, with the *renvoi* to national law, in particular, seeming open to abuse.[5] Even if it is argued that the term 'taxes' in Article 21(7)(a) has an autonomous

3 Article 21(7)(7)(d) of the ECT.

4 Although such agreements and arrangements might fall within Article 25 (Economic Integration Agreements).

5 Indeed, one might see the reference to double taxation conventions as not entirely satisfactory, as these can refer back to national law: see Articles 2(3) and 3(2) of the OECD Model Tax Convention on Income and on Capital (2010 Revision) and Articles 2(3) and 3(2) of the UN Model Double Taxation Convention between Developed and Developing Countries (1999 Revision). However, in both cases a general definition of taxes on income and on capital is given, with the existing taxes listed being only particular examples, and reference back to national tax laws is only permitted when the context of the treaty does not otherwise require.

meaning, no indication is given as to what that meaning might be. For example, no indication is given as to how to distinguish taxes from fees or charges (that is, payments for a public service, even if compulsory),[6] nor whether penalties and interest (e.g., for late payment of taxes) are included within the definition.[7] However, these issues are perhaps less problematic than they might appear. Doctrine is clear: fees are paid for a precise consideration whereas taxes are paid without concrete consideration.[8] Moreover, at least according to the Commentary to the OECD Model Tax Convention on Income and on Capital, penalties and interest for late payment of taxes are considered to be taxes in the sense of Article 2(2) of the Convention.[9] Indeed, given that the definition of Taxation Measures in Article 21(7)(a) includes 'any provision *relating* to taxes',[10] one might consider that the text of the provision itself provides warrant for the inclusion of such payments, despite this providing even further scope for abuse.[11]

## 2. Taxation and most-favoured nation and national treatment (Article 10(2) and (7))

Article 21(3) provides that:

> Article 10(2) and (7) [which, it will be recalled, concern most-favoured nation and national treatment] shall apply to Taxation Measures of the Contracting Parties other than those on income or on capital, except that such provisions shall not apply to:
>
> (a) impose most favoured nation obligations with respect to advantages accorded by a Contracting Party pursuant to the tax provisions of any convention, agreement or arrangement described in subparagraph (7)(a)(ii) or resulting from membership of any Regional Economic Integration Organization; or

6 Indeed, this is a problem not only in the investment treaty context but also elsewhere, for example under Article 34 of the Vienna Convention on Diplomatic Relations (1961) 500 UNTS 95, which exempts diplomatic agents from 'dues and taxes' but not from 'charges levied for specific services rendered': see H. Mulholland, 'Foreign Diplomats Owe £23m over London Congestion Charge', *The Guardian*, 19 November 2008.

7 See Wälde and Kolo, 'Coverage of Taxation under Modern Investment Treaties', pp. 317–19.

8 See, e.g., the discussion in *San Juan Cellular Telephone Co* v. *Public Service Commission* 967 F.2d 683 (1st Cir.1992).

9 OECD, Commentaries on the Articles of the Model Tax Convention, July 2008, p. 64, available at: www.oecd.org/dataoecd/14/32/41147804.pdf (accessed 28 November 2010)

10 Emphasis added.

11 The Yukos cases, in particular, spring to mind in this context: see *OAO Neftyanaya Kompaniya Yukos* v. *Russia*, ECHR appl no. 14902/04, Admissibility Decision, 29 January 2010.

(b) any Taxation Measure aimed at ensuring the effective collection of taxes, except where the measure arbitrarily discriminates against an Investor of another Contracting Party or arbitrarily restricts benefits accorded under the Investment provisions of this Treaty.

In consequence, Articles 10(2) and (7) do not apply to Taxation Measures on income and capital. Article 21(7)(b) defines what is meant by taxes on income and capital:

> There shall be regarded as taxes on income or on capital all taxes imposed on total income, on total capital or on elements of income or of capital, including taxes on gains from the alienation of property, taxes on estates, inheritances and gifts, or substantially similar taxes, taxes on the total amounts of wages or salaries paid by enterprises, as well as taxes on capital appreciation.

Articles 10(2) and (7) do, however, apply to other Taxation Measures: provisions relating to indirect taxes such as VAT, sales tax, excise tax, stamp duty, services tax, registration duty and transaction tax. This difference in treatment would seem to arise from the fact that double taxation agreements usually cover taxes on income and capital,[12] so the intention was to avoid conflict between the provisions of such agreements and Articles 10(2) and (7) of the ECT.[13] Indeed, the definition of taxes on income and capital in Article 21(7)(b) is identical to that in the OECD Model Tax Convention on Income and on Capital.[14]

Even in cases relating to taxes other than on income and on capital, matters within the ambit of applicable double taxation agreements are excluded. Consequently, Articles 10(2) and (7) do not accord MFN treatment with respect to advantages accorded by any double taxation agreement to which a host state is party or resulting from its membership of a Regional Economic Integration Organization[15] (although this exclusion

12 See K. Vogel *et al.*, *Double Taxation Conventions: A Commentary to the OECD, UN and US Model Conventions for the Avoidance of Double Taxation of Income and Capital* (The Hague: Kluwer, 3rd edn, 1997).

13 Enforcement procedures in double taxation conventions are generally much weaker than those in investment treaties, so the avoidance of conflict is very much at the expense of Investors. EU law does, however, place considerable constraints on member states' powers of taxation: see Wälde and Kolo, 'Coverage of Taxation under Modern Investment Treaties', p. 314.

14 Article 2(2) of the OECD Model Tax Convention on Income and on Capital (2010 Revision). See also Article 2(2) of the UN Model Double Taxation Convention between Developed and Developing Countries (1999 Revision), which is in substantially similar terms.

15 As defined in Article 1(3) of the ECT, e.g., the EU.

implies that national treatment must be accorded in such circumstances). Moreover, Articles 10(2) and (7) do not generally apply to 'any Taxation Measure aimed at ensuring the effective collection of taxes'. No further elucidation of this term is given, although similar provisions appear in other investment treaties.[16] One might hazard that it refers to measures relating to the collection of taxes; to the application and enforcement rather than the substance of the tax code. With regard to such measures, however, Articles 10(2) and (7) apply only when such a measure arbitrarily discriminates against an Investor or 'arbitrarily restricts benefits accorded under the Investment provisions of this Treaty'.[17] Arbitrary discrimination would seem to require findings that: (i) the claimant was in a 'like' situation to a national or third-state investor; (ii) the Taxation Measure discriminated against the claimant, that is, it treated him differently from persons in the like situation, and (iii) the discrimination was arbitrary, that is, there was no legitimate reason for the difference in treatment.[18] As for what is required to show that a measure arbitrarily restricted benefits accorded under Part III of the ECT, matters are perhaps less clear. It might seem to require a finding of a breach of a provision of Part III[19] plus a showing that the breach was arbitrary, that is, unjustified by any legitimate governmental interest (although the latter requirement would seem to add little, or nothing, to the former). In such a case, if nationals or third-state investors do not receive the same treatment in like situations, there will be a breach of MFN or national treatment. There is, however, at present no arbitral jurisprudence clarifying the meaning of these provisions.

### 3. Taxation and the prohibition on expropriation (Article 13)

Article 21(5) covers allegations of expropriation under Article 13 of the ECT. It provides that:

> (a) Article 13 shall apply to taxes.
> (b) Whenever an issue arises under Article 13, to the extent it pertains to whether a tax constitutes an expropriation or whether a tax alleged to

16 See Wälde and Kolo, 'Coverage of Taxation under Modern Investment Treaties', p. 327.

17 Although it should be recalled that Article 10(2) does not give rise to any rights enforceable by Investors: see pp. 105–7 above.

18 For discussion of discrimination in the application of tax legislation, see H. Gribnau (ed.), *Legal Protection against Discriminatory Tax Legislation: The Struggle for Equality in European Tax Law* (The Hague: Kluwer, 2006).

19 For example, the requirement to accord fair and equitable treatment in Article 10(1) of the ECT.

constitute an expropriation is discriminatory, the following provisions shall apply:

(i) The Investor or the Contracting Party alleging expropriation shall refer the issue of whether the tax is an expropriation or whether the tax is discriminatory to the relevant Competent Tax Authority. Failing such referral by the Investor or the Contracting Party, bodies called upon to settle disputes pursuant to Article 26(2)(c) or 27(2) shall make a referral to the relevant Competent Tax Authorities;

(ii) The Competent Tax Authorities shall, within a period of six months of such referral, strive to resolve the issues so referred. Where non-discrimination issues are concerned, the Competent Tax Authorities shall apply the non-discrimination provisions of the relevant tax convention or, if there is no non-discrimination provision in the relevant tax convention applicable to the tax or no such tax convention is in force between the Contracting Parties concerned, they shall apply the non-discrimination principles under the Model Tax Convention on Income and Capital of the Organisation for Economic Co-operation and Development;

(iii) Bodies called upon to settle disputes pursuant to Article 26(2)(c) or 27(2) may take into account any conclusions arrived at by the Competent Tax Authorities regarding whether the tax is an expropriation. Such bodies shall take into account any conclusions arrived at within the six-month period prescribed in subparagraph (b)(ii) by the Competent Tax Authorities regarding whether the tax is discriminatory. Such bodies may also take into account any conclusions arrived at by the Competent Tax Authorities after the expiry of the six-month period;

(iv) Under no circumstances shall involvement of the Competent Tax Authorities, beyond the end of the six-month period referred to in subparagraph (b)(ii), lead to a delay of proceedings under Articles 26 and 27.

To an extent, what paragraph 5(a) gives substantively,[20] paragraph 5(b) takes away procedurally. Taxation of an Investment can amount to an expropriation and is covered by Article 13. However, the Investor alleging that an expropriation has taken place or that the expropriation was discriminatory[21] is required to refer the issue to the 'Competent Tax

20 It has occasionally been questioned whether taxation can be expropriatory: see *EnCana Corporation* v. *Ecuador*, LCIA Case No. UN3481, Award, 3 February 2006, para. 177.

21 That an expropriation is not discriminatory is one of the criteria for it to be lawful under Article 13.

Authorities'.[22] Failure to do so, and the initiation of arbitration proceedings under Article 26, will simply result in the arbitral tribunal making the referral itself, as Article 21(5)(b)(i) obliges it to do.

A definition of a 'Competent Tax Authority' is provided in Article 21(7)(c). It means:

> the competent authority pursuant to a double taxation agreement in force between the Contracting Parties or, when no such agreement is in force, the minister or ministry responsible for taxes or their authorized representatives.

The reference to Contracting Parties must mean the Contracting Party of which the claimant is a national and the Contracting Party to the dispute. Bilateral double taxation agreements frequently name the competent tax authorities of the parties to them.[23] In any case, it can be seen that what is envisaged is submission of the issue to an administrative agency for its decision as a pre-condition for it being determined by the tribunal. Indeed, although Article 21(5) and Article 21(7)(c) are not wholly clear, it seems that the procedure envisaged is a referral to the Competent Tax Authorities of both the relevant Contracting Parties for their joint conclusions.[24] This is modelled on the procedure found in double taxation agreements, where the competent tax authorities of the parties to the treaty endeavour to resolve cases by mutual agreement.[25] It also suffers from the same disadvantage, in that both administrative agencies may have interests which differ from those of the complainant.

The Competent Tax Authorities have a period of six months in which to determine whether the tax is an expropriation or is discriminatory. No guidance is given as to the criteria which they should apply in order to decide whether there has been an expropriation. With regard to whether the tax is discriminatory, however, the Competent Tax Authorities are required to apply (i) the non-discrimination provisions of any relevant tax convention or (ii) if there is no such treaty, the non-discrimination

22 Similar, indeed even more stringent, provisions appear in other investment treaties: see Wälde and Kolo, 'Coverage of Taxation under Modern Investment Treaties', pp. 352–4.

23 See Article 3(1)(f) of the OECD Model Tax Convention on Income and on Capital (2010 Revision).

24 See Energy Charter Secretariat, *The Energy Charter Treaty: A Reader's Guide* (Brussels: Energy Charter Secretariat), p. 39.

25 See Article 25 (Mutual Agreement Procedure) of the OECD Model Tax Convention on Income and on Capital (2010 Revision).

principles in the OECD Model Tax Convention on Income and on Capital. These latter, which appear in Article 24 of the Convention, provide that:

> (1) Nationals of a Contracting State shall not be subjected in the other Contracting State to any taxation or any requirement connected therewith, which is other or more burdensome than the taxation and connected requirements to which nationals of that other State in the same circumstances, in particular with respect to residence, are or may be subjected. This provision shall, notwithstanding the provisions of Article 1, also apply to persons who are not residents of one or both of the Contracting States.
>
> ...
>
> (3) The taxation on a permanent establishment which an enterprise of a Contracting State has in the other Contracting State shall not be less favourably levied in that other State than the taxation levied on enterprises of that other State carrying on the same activities ...[26]

Specific provisions concerning the deductibility of interest, royalties and other disbursements appear later in Article 24.[27]

The status of the conclusions of the Competent Tax Authorities depends on two things: first, their subject-matter and, second, whether they were arrived at within the six-month period following the issue's referral to the Tax Authority. As regards conclusions concerning whether a tax is an expropriation (regardless of whether they were issued timeously or not), a tribunal 'may' take them into account; that is, it is permitted but not required to. As to whether a tax is discriminatory, however, providing the Tax Authorities have issued their conclusions within six months, the tribunal must take them into account. If they were issued outside the six-month period, the tribunal is entitled (but not obliged) to take them into account.

In consequence, therefore, the most that a tribunal is required to do is take such conclusions into account; they are persuasive but not determinative of its decision on the issue. The issue is likely to be re-argued in full before the tribunal. Given this, the utility of the procedure might be doubted. Competent Tax Authorities might be seen as better able to interpret and apply provisions of a tax convention than an investment

26 Article 24 (Non-discrimination), *ibid.* It might be noted that despite the limitation of the Model Convention's coverage to taxes on income and on capital, its non-discrimination provisions apply to taxes of every kind and description: see Article 24(6).

27 Article 24(4), *ibid.*

treaty tribunal.[28] However, the same cannot be said as regards whether a tax is expropriatory. Either the Tax Authorities apply Article 13 of the ECT, in which case they are issuing conclusions on a matter which might be seen as rather beyond their expertise, or they do not, in which case their conclusions relate to an issue different from that which the tribunal has to determine. The procedure seems akin to a requirement to exhaust domestic remedies, a requirement which does not, of course, apply in relation to other claims under the Treaty.[29] Its practical effect is likely to be to extend the length and increase the cost of legal proceedings.

Finally, it might be noted that Article 21(5)(b)(iv) provides that an arbitral tribunal is not entitled to delay its proceedings by reason of the failure of the Competent Tax Authorities to report within six months. This, of course, indicates that a tribunal may stay proceedings within that six-month period pending the issuance of the Tax Authorities' conclusions if it deems such a course of action appropriate.

## 4. Transfers related to investments

As regards transfers related to investments, Article 21(7) provides 'for the avoidance of doubt' that Article 14 'shall not limit the right of a Contracting Party to impose or collect a tax by withholding or other means'. Again, although this provision appears simple it is arguably open to abuse. Nothing is said about what is meant by 'other means', nor are any explicit restrictions imposed on the conditions or level of any withholding tax.[30] Such limits might, however, be thought to be implicit. The rule in Article 14(1) is in absolute terms ('Each Contracting Party . . . shall . . . guarantee the freedom of transfer into and out of its Area'), and it might be thought that the exception cannot render the rule ineffective.[31]

28 In which case it might be asked why their decision should not be final.

29 Indeed, the situation may be even less satisfactory for the claimant, as there is no guarantee that it will be permitted to participate in the Competent Tax Authorities' deliberations.

30 See Wälde and Kolo, 'Coverage of Taxation under Modern Investment Treaties', pp. 333–4.

31 A parallel can perhaps be drawn with Article 14(4), which permits Contracting Parties to restrict transfers to protect creditors, and ensure compliance with its securities law and the satisfaction of judgments of its courts, but only 'through the equitable, non-discriminatory, and good faith application of its laws and regulations'.

# Appendix A

## Selected provisions of the Energy Charter Treaty

### FINAL ACT OF THE EUROPEAN ENERGY CHARTER CONFERENCE AS OPENED FOR SIGNATURE IN LISBON ON 17 DECEMBER 1994

UNDERSTANDINGS

IV. By signing the Final Act, the representatives agreed to adopt the following Understandings with respect to the Treaty:

1. With respect to the Treaty as a whole
   (a) The representatives underline that the provisions of the Treaty have been agreed upon bearing in mind the specific nature of the Treaty aiming at a legal framework to promote long-term co-operation in a particular sector and as a result cannot be construed to constitute a precedent in the context of other international negotiations.
   (b) The provisions of the Treaty do not:
      (i) oblige any Contracting Party to introduce mandatory third party access; or
      (ii) prevent the use of pricing systems which, within a particular category of consumers, apply identical prices to customers in different locations.
   (c) Derogations from most favoured nation treatment are not intended to cover measures which are specific to an Investor or group of Investors, rather than applying generally.
2. With respect to Article 1(5)
   (a) It is understood that the Treaty confers no rights to engage in economic activities other than Economic Activities in the Energy Sector.
   (b) The following activities are illustrative of Economic Activity in the Energy Sector:
      (i) prospecting and exploration for, and extraction of, e.g., oil, gas, coal and uranium;
      (ii) construction and operation of power generation facilities, including those powered by wind and other renewable energy sources;

(iii) land transportation, distribution, storage and supply of Energy Materials and Products, e.g., by way of transmission and distribution grids and pipelines or dedicated rail lines, and construction of facilities for such, including the laying of oil, gas, and coal-slurry pipelines;
(iv) removal and disposal of wastes from energy related facilities such as power stations, including radioactive wastes from nuclear power stations;
(v) decommissioning of energy related facilities, including oil rigs, oil refineries and power generating plants;
(vi) marketing and sale of, and trade in Energy Materials and Products, e.g., retail sales of gasoline; and
(vii) research, consulting, planning, management and design activities related to the activities mentioned above, including those aimed at Improving Energy Efficiency.

3. With respect to Article 1(6)

For greater clarity as to whether an Investment made in the Area of one Contracting Party is controlled, directly or indirectly, by an Investor of any other Contracting Party, control of an Investment means control in fact, determined after an examination of the actual circumstances in each situation. In any such examination, all relevant factors should be considered, including the Investor's

(a) financial interest, including equity interest, in the Investment;
(b) ability to exercise substantial influence over the management and operation of the Investment; and
(c) ability to exercise substantial influence over the selection of members of the board of directors or any other managing body. Where there is doubt as to whether an Investor controls, directly or indirectly, an Investment, an Investor claiming such control has the burden of proof that such control exists.

...

6. With respect to Article 5(1)

The representatives' agreement to Article 5 is not meant to imply any position on whether or to what extent the provisions of the 'Agreement on Trade-Related Investment Measures' annexed to the Final Act of the Uruguay Round of Multilateral Trade Negotiations are implicit in articles III and XI of the GATT.

...

9. With respect to Articles 9, 10 and Part V

As a Contracting Party's programmes which provide for public loans, grants, guarantees or insurance for facilitating trade or Investment abroad are not connected with Investment or related activities of Investors from other Contracting Parties in its Area, such programmes may be subject to constraints with respect to participation in them.

10. With respect to Article 10(4)
The supplementary treaty will specify conditions for applying the Treatment described in Article 10(3). Those conditions will include, inter alia, provisions relating to the sale or other divestment of state assets (privatization) and to the dismantling of monopolies (demonopolization).

11. With respect to Articles 10(4) and 29(6)
Contracting Parties may consider any connection between the provisions of Article 10(4) and Article 29(6).

12. With respect to Article 14(5)
It is intended that a Contracting Party which enters into an agreement referred to in Article 14(5) ensure that the conditions of such an agreement are not in contradiction with that Contracting Party's obligations under the Articles of Agreement of the International Monetary Fund.

...

14. With respect to Articles 22 and 23
With regard to trade in Energy Materials and Products governed by Article 29, that Article specifies the provisions relevant to the subjects covered by Articles 22 and 23.

...

16. With respect to Article 26(2)(a)
Article 26(2)(a) should not be interpreted to require a Contracting Party to enact Part III of the Treaty into its domestic law.

17. With respect to Articles 26 and 27
The reference to treaty obligations in the penultimate sentence of Article 10(1) does not include decisions taken by international organizations, even if they are legally binding, or treaties which entered into force before 1 January 1970.

...

## DECLARATIONS

V. The representatives declared that Article 18(2) shall not be construed to allow the circumvention of the application of the other provisions of the Treaty.

VI. The representatives also noted the following Declarations that were made with respect to the Treaty:

. . .

5. With respect to Article 25

The European Communities and their Member States recall that, in accordance with article 58 of the Treaty establishing the European Community:

(a) companies or firms formed in accordance with the law of a Member State and having their registered office, central administration or principal place of business within the Community shall, for the right of establishment pursuant to Part Three, Title III, Chapter 2 of the Treaty establishing the European Community, be treated in the same way as natural persons who are nationals of Member States; companies or firms which only have their registered office within the Community must, for this purpose, have an effective and continuous link with the economy of one of the Member States;

(b) 'companies and firms' means companies or firms constituted under civil or commercial law, including co-operative societies, and other legal persons governed by public or private law, save for those which are non-profitmaking.

The European Communities and their Member States further recall that:

Community law provides for the possibility to extend the treatment described above to branches and agencies of companies or firms not established in one of the Member States; and that, the application of Article 25 of the Energy Charter Treaty will allow only those derogations necessary to safeguard the preferential treatment resulting from the wider process of economic integration resulting from the Treaties establishing the European Communities.

7 With respect to Annex G (4)

(a) The European Communities and the Russian Federation declare that trade in nuclear materials between them shall be governed, until they reach another agreement, by the provisions of article 22 of the Agreement on Partnership and Co-operation establishing a partnership between the European Communities and their Member States, of the one part, and the Russian Federation, of the other part, signed at Corfu on 24 June 1994, the exchange of letters attached thereto and the related joint declaration, and disputes regarding such trade will be subject to the procedures of the said Agreement.

(b) The European Communities and Ukraine declare that, in accordance with the Agreement on Partnership and Co-operation signed at Luxembourg on 14 June 1994 and the Interim Agreement thereto, initialled there the same day, trade in nuclear materials between them shall be exclusively governed by the provisions of a specific agreement to be concluded between the European Atomic Energy Community and Ukraine.

Until entry into force of this specific agreement, the provisions of the Agreement on Trade and Economic and Commercial Co-operation between the European Economic Community, the European Atomic Energy Community and the Union of Soviet Socialist Republics signed at Brussels on 18 December 1989 shall exclusively continue to apply for trade in nuclear materials between them.

(c) The European Communities and Kazakhstan declare that, in accordance with the Agreement on Partnership and Co-operation initialled at Brussels on 20 May 1994, trade in nuclear materials between them shall be exclusively governed by the provisions of a specific agreement to be concluded between the European Atomic Energy Community and Kazakhstan.

Until entry into force of this specific agreement, the provisions of the Agreement on Trade and Economic and Commercial Co-operation between the European Economic Community, the European Atomic Energy Community and the Union of Soviet Socialist Republics signed at Brussels on 18 December 1989 shall exclusively continue to apply for trade in nuclear materials between them.

(d) The European Communities and Kyrgyzstan declare that, in accordance with the Agreement on Partnership and Co-operation initialled at Brussels on 31 May 1994, trade in nuclear materials between them shall be exclusively governed by the provisions of a specific agreement to be concluded between the European Atomic Energy Community and Kyrgyzstan.

Until entry into force of this specific agreement, the provisions of the Agreement on Trade and Economic and Commercial Co-operation between the European Economic Community, the European Atomic Energy Community and the Union of Soviet Socialist Republics signed at Brussels on 18 December 1989 shall exclusively continue to apply for trade in nuclear materials between them.

(e) The European Communities and Tajikistan declare that trade in nuclear materials between them shall be exclusively governed by the provisions of a specific agreement to be concluded between the European Atomic Energy Community and Tajikistan.

Until entry into force of this specific agreement, the provisions of the Agreement on Trade and Economic and Commercial Co-operation between the European Economic Community, the European Atomic Energy Community and the Union of Soviet Socialist Republics signed at Brussels on 18 December 1989 shall exclusively continue to apply for trade in nuclear materials between them.

(f) The European Communities and Uzbekistan declare that trade in nuclear materials between them shall be exclusively governed by the provisions of a specific agreement to be concluded between the European Atomic Energy Community and Uzbekistan.
Until entry into force of this specific agreement, the provisions of the Agreement on Trade and Economic and Commercial Co-operation between the European Economic Community, the European Atomic Energy Community and the Union of Soviet Socialist Republics signed at Brussels on 18 December 1989 shall exclusively continue to apply for trade in nuclear materials between them.

## THE ENERGY CHARTER TREATY (ANNEX 1 TO THE FINAL ACT OF THE EUROPEAN ENERGY CHARTER CONFERENCE)

### *Preamble*

The Contracting Parties to this Treaty,

Having regard to the Charter of Paris for a New Europe signed on 21 November 1990;

Having regard to the European Energy Charter adopted in the Concluding Document of the Hague Conference on the European Energy Charter signed at The Hague on 17 December 1991;

Recalling that all signatories to the Concluding Document of the Hague Conference undertook to pursue the objectives and principles of the European Energy Charter and implement and broaden their co-operation as soon as possible by negotiating in good faith an Energy Charter Treaty and Protocols, and desiring to place the commitments contained in that Charter on a secure and binding international legal basis;

Desiring also to establish the structural framework required to implement the principles enunciated in the European Energy Charter;

Wishing to implement the basic concept of the European Energy Charter initiative which is to catalyse economic growth by means of measures to liberalize investment and trade in energy;

Affirming that Contracting Parties attach the utmost importance to the effective implementation of full national treatment and most favoured nation treatment, and that these commitments will be applied to the Making of Investments pursuant to a supplementary treaty;

Having regard to the objective of progressive liberalization of international trade and to the principle of avoidance of discrimination in international trade as enunciated in the General Agreement on Tariffs and Trade and its Related Instruments and as otherwise provided for in this Treaty;

Determined progressively to remove technical, administrative and other barriers to trade in Energy Materials and Products and related equipment, technologies and services;

Looking to the eventual membership in the General Agreement on Tariffs and Trade of those Contracting Parties which are not currently parties thereto and concerned to provide interim trade arrangements which will assist those Contracting Parties and not impede their preparation for such membership;

Mindful of the rights and obligations of certain Contracting Parties which are also parties to the General Agreement on Tariffs and Trade and its Related Instruments;

Having regard to competition rules concerning mergers, monopolies, anticompetitive practices and abuse of dominant position;

Having regard also to the Treaty on the Non-Proliferation of Nuclear Weapons, the Nuclear Suppliers Guidelines and other international nuclear non-proliferation obligations or understandings;

Recognizing the necessity for the most efficient exploration, production, conversion, storage, transport, distribution and use of energy;

Recalling the United Nations Framework Convention on Climate Change, the Convention on Long-Range Transboundary Air Pollution and its protocols, and other international environmental agreements with energy-related aspects; and

Recognizing the increasingly urgent need for measures to protect the environment, including the decommissioning of energy installations and waste disposal, and for internationally-agreed objectives and criteria for these purposes,

HAVE AGREED AS FOLLOWS:

## Part I
## Definitions and purpose

### *Article 1*
### *Definitions*

As used in this Treaty:

(1) 'Charter' means the European Energy Charter adopted in the Concluding Document of the Hague Conference on the European Energy Charter

signed at The Hague on 17 December 1991; signature of the Concluding Document is considered to be signature of the Charter.

(2) 'Contracting Party' means a state or Regional Economic Integration Organization which has consented to be bound by this Treaty and for which the Treaty is in force.

(3) 'Regional Economic Integration Organization' means an organization constituted by states to which they have transferred competence over certain matters a number of which are governed by this Treaty, including the authority to take decisions binding on them in respect of those matters.

(4) 'Energy Materials and Products', based on the Harmonized System of the Customs Co-operation Council and the Combined Nomenclature of the European Communities, means the items included in Annex EM.

(5) 'Economic Activity in the Energy Sector' means an economic activity concerning the exploration, extraction, refining, production, storage, land transport, transmission, distribution, trade, marketing, or sale of Energy Materials and Products except those included in Annex NI, or concerning the distribution of heat to multiple premises.

(6) 'Investment' means every kind of asset, owned or controlled directly or indirectly by an Investor and includes:

   (a) tangible and intangible, and movable and immovable, property, and any property rights such as leases, mortgages, liens, and pledges;
   (b) a company or business enterprise, or shares, stock, or other forms of equity participation in a company or business enterprise, and bonds and other debt of a company or business enterprise;
   (c) claims to money and claims to performance pursuant to contract having an economic value and associated with an Investment;
   (d) Intellectual Property;
   (e) Returns;
   (f) any right conferred by law or contract or by virtue of any licences and permits granted pursuant to law to undertake any Economic Activity in the Energy Sector.

A change in the form in which assets are invested does not affect their character as investments and the term 'Investment' includes all investments, whether existing at or made after the later of the date of entry into force of this Treaty for the Contracting Party of the Investor making the investment and that for the Contracting Party in the Area of which the investment is made (hereinafter referred to as the 'Effective Date') provided that the Treaty shall only apply to matters affecting such investments after the Effective Date.

'Investment' refers to any investment associated with an Economic Activity in the Energy Sector and to investments or classes of investments designated by a Contracting Party in its Area as 'Charter efficiency projects' and so notified to the Secretariat.

(7) 'Investor' means:

(a) with respect to a Contracting Party:

(i) a natural person having the citizenship or nationality of or who is permanently residing in that Contracting Party in accordance with its applicable law;

(ii) a company or other organization organized in accordance with the law applicable in that Contracting Party;

(b) with respect to a 'third state', a natural person, company or other organization which fulfils, mutatis mutandis, the conditions specified in subparagraph (a) for a Contracting Party.

(8) 'Make Investments' or 'Making of Investments' means establishing new Investments, acquiring all or part of existing Investments or moving into different fields of Investment activity.

(9) 'Returns' means the amounts derived from or associated with an Investment, irrespective of the form in which they are paid, including profits, dividends, interest, capital gains, royalty payments, management, technical assistance or other fees and payments in kind.

(10) 'Area' means with respect to a state that is a Contracting Party:

(a) the territory under its sovereignty, it being understood that territory includes land, internal waters and the territorial sea; and

(b) subject to and in accordance with the international law of the sea: the sea, sea-bed and its subsoil with regard to which that Contracting Party exercises sovereign rights and jurisdiction.

With respect to a Regional Economic Integration Organization which is a Contracting Party, Area means the Areas of the member states of such Organization, under the provisions contained in the agreement establishing that Organization.

(11) (a) 'GATT' means 'GATT 1947' or 'GATT 1994', or both of them where both are applicable.

(b) 'GATT 1947' means the General Agreement on Tariffs and Trade, dated 30 October 1947, annexed to the Final Act Adopted at the Conclusion of the Second Session of the Preparatory Committee of the United Nations Conference on Trade and Employment, as subsequently rectified, amended or modified.

(c) 'GATT 1994' means the General Agreement on Tariffs and Trade as specified in Annex 1A of the Agreement Establishing the World Trade Organization, as subsequently rectified, amended or modified.

A party to the Agreement Establishing the World Trade Organization is considered to be a party to GATT 1994.

(d) 'Related Instruments' means, as appropriate:

(i) agreements, arrangements or other legal instruments, including decisions, declarations and understandings, concluded under the auspices of GATT 1947 as subsequently rectified, amended or modified; or

(ii) the Agreement Establishing the World Trade Organization including its Annex 1 (except GATT 1994), its Annexes 2, 3 and 4, and the decisions, declarations and understandings related thereto, as subsequently rectified, amended or modified.

(12) 'Intellectual Property' includes copyrights and related rights, trademarks, geographical indications, industrial designs, patents, layout designs of integrated circuits and the protection of undisclosed information.

(13) (a) 'Energy Charter Protocol' or 'Protocol' means a treaty, the negotiation of which is authorized and the text of which is adopted by the Charter Conference, which is entered into by two or more Contracting Parties in order to complement, supplement, extend or amplify the provisions of this Treaty with respect to any specific sector or category of activity within the scope of this Treaty, or to areas of co-operation pursuant to Title III of the Charter.

(b) 'Energy Charter Declaration' or 'Declaration' means a non-binding instrument, the negotiation of which is authorized and the text of which is approved by the Charter Conference, which is entered into by two or more Contracting Parties to complement or supplement the provisions of this Treaty.

(14) 'Freely Convertible Currency' means a currency which is widely traded in international foreign exchange markets and widely used in international transactions.

### *Article 2*
### *Purpose of the treaty*

This Treaty establishes a legal framework in order to promote long-term cooperation in the energy field, based on complementarities and mutual benefits, in accordance with the objectives and principles of the Charter.

## Part II
## Commerce

...

### *Article 5*
### *Trade-related investment measures*

(1) A Contracting Party shall not apply any trade-related investment measure that is inconsistent with the provisions of article III or XI of the GATT; this shall be without prejudice to the Contracting Party's rights and obligations under the GATT and Related Instruments and Article 29.

(2) Such measures include any investment measure which is mandatory or enforceable under domestic law or under any administrative ruling, or compliance with which is necessary to obtain an advantage, and which requires:
   (a) the purchase or use by an enterprise of products of domestic origin or from any domestic source, whether specified in terms of particular products, in terms of volume or value of products, or in terms of a proportion of volume or value of its local production; or
   (b) that an enterprise's purchase or use of imported products be limited to an amount related to the volume or value of local products that it exports;

   or which restricts:
   (c) the importation by an enterprise of products used in or related to its local production, generally or to an amount related to the volume or value of local production that it exports;
   (d) the importation by an enterprise of products used in or related to its local production by restricting its access to foreign exchange to an amount related to the foreign exchange inflows attributable to the enterprise; or
   (e) the exportation or sale for export by an enterprise of products, whether specified in terms of particular products, in terms of volume or value of products, or in terms of a proportion of volume or value of its local production.

(3) Nothing in paragraph (1) shall be construed to prevent a Contracting Party from applying the trade-related investment measures described in subparagraphs (2)(a) and (c) as a condition of eligibility for export promotion, foreign aid, government procurement or preferential tariff or quota programmes.

(4) Notwithstanding paragraph (1), a Contracting Party may temporarily continue to maintain trade-related investment measures which were in effect more than 180 days before its signature of this Treaty, subject to the notification and phase-out provisions set out in Annex TRM.

. . .

## Part III
## Investment promotion and protection

*Article 10*
*Promotion, protection and treatment of investments*

(1) Each Contracting Party shall, in accordance with the provisions of this Treaty, encourage and create stable, equitable, favourable and transparent conditions for Investors of other Contracting Parties to make Investments

in its Area. Such conditions shall include a commitment to accord at all times to Investments of Investors of other Contracting Parties fair and equitable treatment. Such Investments shall also enjoy the most constant protection and security and no Contracting Party shall in any way impair by unreasonable or discriminatory measures their management, maintenance, use, enjoyment or disposal. In no case shall such Investments be accorded treatment less favourable than that required by international law, including treaty obligations. Each Contracting Party shall observe any obligations it has entered into with an Investor or an Investment of an Investor of any other Contracting Party.

(2) Each Contracting Party shall endeavour to accord to Investors of other Contracting Parties, as regards the Making of Investments in its Area, the Treatment described in paragraph (3).

(3) For the purposes of this Article, 'Treatment' means treatment accorded by a Contracting Party which is no less favourable than that which it accords to its own Investors or to Investors of any other Contracting Party or any third state, whichever is the most favourable.

(4) A supplementary treaty shall, subject to conditions to be laid down therein, oblige each party thereto to accord to Investors of other parties, as regards the Making of Investments in its Area, the Treatment described in paragraph (3).

That treaty shall be open for signature by the states and Regional Economic Integration Organizations which have signed or acceded to this Treaty.

Negotiations towards the supplementary treaty shall commence not later than 1 January 1995, with a view to concluding it by 1 January 1998.

(5) Each Contracting Party shall, as regards the Making of Investments in its Area, endeavour to:
  (a) limit to the minimum the exceptions to the Treatment described in paragraph (3);
  (b) progressively remove existing restrictions affecting Investors of other Contracting Parties.

(6) (a) A Contracting Party may, as regards the Making of Investments in its Area, at any time declare voluntarily to the Charter Conference, through the Secretariat, its intention not to introduce new exceptions to the Treatment described in paragraph (3).
  (b) A Contracting Party may, furthermore, at any time make a voluntary commitment to accord to Investors of other Contracting Parties, as regards the Making of Investments in some or all Economic Activities in the Energy Sector in its Area, the Treatment described in paragraph (3). Such commitments shall be notified to the Secretariat and listed in Annex VC and shall be binding under this Treaty.

(7) Each Contracting Party shall accord to Investments in its Area of Investors of other Contracting Parties, and their related activities including management, maintenance, use, enjoyment or disposal, treatment no less favourable than that which it accords to Investments of its own Investors or of the Investors of any other Contracting Party or any third state and their related activities including management, maintenance, use, enjoyment or disposal, whichever is the most favourable.

(8) The modalities of application of paragraph (7) in relation to programmes under which a Contracting Party provides grants or other financial assistance, or enters into contracts, for energy technology research and development, shall be reserved for the supplementary treaty described in paragraph (4). Each Contracting Party shall through the Secretariat keep the Charter Conference informed of the modalities it applies to the programmes described in this paragraph.

(9) Each state or Regional Economic Integration Organization which signs or accedes to this Treaty shall, on the date it signs the Treaty or deposits its instrument of accession, submit to the Secretariat a report summarizing all laws, regulations or other measures relevant to:

(a) exceptions to paragraph (2); or

(b) the programmes referred to in paragraph (8).

A Contracting Party shall keep its report up to date by promptly submitting amendments to the Secretariat. The Charter Conference shall review these reports periodically.

In respect of subparagraph (a) the report may designate parts of the energy sector in which a Contracting Party accords to Investors of other Contracting Parties the Treatment described in paragraph (3).

In respect of subparagraph (b) the review by the Charter Conference may consider the effects of such programmes on competition and Investments.

(10) Notwithstanding any other provision of this Article, the treatment described in paragraphs (3) and (7) shall not apply to the protection of Intellectual Property; instead, the treatment shall be as specified in the corresponding provisions of the applicable international agreements for the protection of Intellectual Property rights to which the respective Contracting Parties are parties.

(11) For the purposes of Article 26, the application by a Contracting Party of a trade-related investment measure as described in Article 5(1) and (2) to an Investment of an Investor of another Contracting Party existing at the time of such application shall, subject to Article 5(3) and (4), be considered a breach of an obligation of the former Contracting Party under this Part.

(12) Each Contracting Party shall ensure that its domestic law provides effective means for the assertion of claims and the enforcement of rights with respect to Investments, investment agreements, and investment authorizations.

*Article 11*
*Key personnel*

(1) A Contracting Party shall, subject to its laws and regulations relating to the entry, stay and work of natural persons, examine in good faith requests by Investors of another Contracting Party, and key personnel who are employed by such Investors or by Investments of such Investors, to enter and remain temporarily in its Area to engage in activities connected with the making or the development, management, maintenance, use, enjoyment or disposal of relevant Investments, including the provision of advice or key technical services.
(2) A Contracting Party shall permit Investors of another Contracting Party which have Investments in its Area, and Investments of such Investors, to employ any key person of the Investor's or the Investment's choice regardless of nationality and citizenship provided that such key person has been permitted to enter, stay and work in the Area of the former Contracting Party and that the employment concerned conforms to the terms, conditions and time limits of the permission granted to such key person.

*Article 12*
*Compensation for losses*

(1) Except where Article 13 applies, an Investor of any Contracting Party which suffers a loss with respect to any Investment in the Area of another Contracting Party owing to war or other armed conflict, state of national emergency, civil disturbance, or other similar event in that Area, shall be accorded by the latter Contracting Party, as regards restitution, indemnification, compensation or other settlement, treatment which is the most favourable of that which that Contracting Party accords to any other Investor, whether its own Investor, the Investor of any other Contracting Party, or the Investor of any third state.
(2) Without prejudice to paragraph (1), an Investor of a Contracting Party which, in any of the situations referred to in that paragraph, suffers a loss in the Area of another Contracting Party resulting from
    (a) requisitioning of its Investment or part thereof by the latter's forces or authorities; or

(b) destruction of its Investment or part thereof by the latter's forces or authorities, which was not required by the necessity of the situation,

shall be accorded restitution or compensation which in either case shall be prompt, adequate and effective.

*Article 13*
*Expropriation*

(1) Investments of Investors of a Contracting Party in the Area of any other Contracting Party shall not be nationalized, expropriated or subjected to a measure or measures having effect equivalent to nationalization or expropriation (hereinafter referred to as 'Expropriation') except where such Expropriation is:
   (a) for a purpose which is in the public interest;
   (b) not discriminatory;
   (c) carried out under due process of law; and
   (d) accompanied by the payment of prompt, adequate and effective compensation.

   Such compensation shall amount to the fair market value of the Investment expropriated at the time immediately before the Expropriation or impending Expropriation became known in such a way as to affect the value of the Investment (hereinafter referred to as the 'Valuation Date').

   Such fair market value shall at the request of the Investor be expressed in a Freely Convertible Currency on the basis of the market rate of exchange existing for that currency on the Valuation Date. Compensation shall also include interest at a commercial rate established on a market basis from the date of Expropriation until the date of payment.

(2) The Investor affected shall have a right to prompt review, under the law of the Contracting Party making the Expropriation, by a judicial or other competent and independent authority of that Contracting Party, of its case, of the valuation of its Investment, and of the payment of compensation, in accordance with the principles set out in paragraph (1).

(3) For the avoidance of doubt, Expropriation shall include situations where a Contracting Party expropriates the assets of a company or enterprise in its Area in which an Investor of any other Contracting Party has an Investment, including through the ownership of shares.

*Article 14*
*Transfers related to investments*

(1) Each Contracting Party shall with respect to Investments in its Area of Investors of any other Contracting Party guarantee the freedom of transfer into and out of its Area, including the transfer of:

(a) the initial capital plus any additional capital for the maintenance and development of an Investment;
(b) Returns;
(c) payments under a contract, including amortization of principal and accrued interest payments pursuant to a loan agreement;
(d) unspent earnings and other remuneration of personnel engaged from abroad in connection with that Investment;
(e) proceeds from the sale or liquidation of all or any part of an Investment;
(f) payments arising out of the settlement of a dispute;
(g) payments of compensation pursuant to Articles 12 and 13.

(2) Transfers under paragraph (1) shall be effected without delay and (except in case of a Return in kind) in a Freely Convertible Currency.

(3) Transfers shall be made at the market rate of exchange existing on the date of transfer with respect to spot transactions in the currency to be transferred. In the absence of a market for foreign exchange, the rate to be used will be the most recent rate applied to inward investments or the most recent exchange rate for conversion of currencies into Special Drawing Rights, whichever is more favourable to the Investor.

(4) Notwithstanding paragraphs (1) to (3), a Contracting Party may protect the rights of creditors, or ensure compliance with laws on the issuing, trading and dealing in securities and the satisfaction of judgements in civil, administrative and criminal adjudicatory proceedings, through the equitable, nondiscriminatory, and good faith application of its laws and regulations.

(5) Notwithstanding paragraph (2), Contracting Parties which are states that were constituent parts of the former Union of Soviet Socialist Republics may provide in agreements concluded between them that transfers of payments shall be made in the currencies of such Contracting Parties, provided that such agreements do not treat Investments in their Areas of Investors of other Contracting Parties less favourably than either Investments of Investors of the Contracting Parties which have entered into such agreements or Investments of Investors of any third state.

(6) Notwithstanding subparagraph (1)(b), a Contracting Party may restrict the transfer of a Return in kind in circumstances where the Contracting Party is permitted under Article 29(2)(a) or the GATT and Related Instruments to restrict or prohibit the exportation or the sale for export of the product constituting the Return in kind; provided that a Contracting Party shall permit transfers of Returns in kind to be effected as authorized or specified in an investment agreement, investment authorization, or other written agreement between the Contracting Party and either an Investor of another Contracting Party or its Investment.

*Article 15*
*Subrogation*

(1) If a Contracting Party or its designated agency (hereinafter referred to as the 'Indemnifying Party') makes a payment under an indemnity or guarantee given in respect of an Investment of an Investor (hereinafter referred to as the 'Party Indemnified') in the Area of another Contracting Party (hereinafter referred to as the 'Host Party'), the Host Party shall recognize:
   (a) the assignment to the Indemnifying Party of all the rights and claims in respect of such Investment; and
   (b) the right of the Indemnifying Party to exercise all such rights and enforce such claims by virtue of subrogation.
(2) The Indemnifying Party shall be entitled in all circumstances to:
   (a) the same treatment in respect of the rights and claims acquired by it by virtue of the assignment referred to in paragraph (1); and
   (b) the same payments due pursuant to those rights and claims, as the Party Indemnified was entitled to receive by virtue of this Treaty in respect of the Investment concerned.
(3) In any proceeding under Article 26, a Contracting Party shall not assert as a defence, counterclaim, right of set-off or for any other reason, that indemnification or other compensation for all or part of the alleged damages has been received or will be received pursuant to an insurance or guarantee contract.

*Article 16*
*Relation to other agreements*

Where two or more Contracting Parties have entered into a prior international agreement, or enter into a subsequent international agreement, whose terms in either case concern the subject matter of Part III or V of this Treaty,

(1) nothing in Part III or V of this Treaty shall be construed to derogate from any provision of such terms of the other agreement or from any right to dispute resolution with respect thereto under that agreement; and
(2) nothing in such terms of the other agreement shall be construed to derogate from any provision of Part III or V of this Treaty or from any right to dispute resolution with respect thereto under this Treaty,

where any such provision is more favourable to the Investor or Investment.

*Article 17*
*Non-application of Part III in certain circumstances*

Each Contracting Party reserves the right to deny the advantages of this Part to:

(1) a legal entity if citizens or nationals of a third state own or control such entity and if that entity has no substantial business activities in the Area of the Contracting Party in which it is organized; or
(2) an Investment, if the denying Contracting Party establishes that such Investment is an Investment of an Investor of a third state with or as to which the denying Contracting Party:
   (a) does not maintain a diplomatic relationship; or
   (b) adopts or maintains measures that:
      (i) prohibit transactions with Investors of that state; or
      (ii) would be violated or circumvented if the benefits of this Part were accorded to Investors of that state or to their Investments.

## Part IV
## Miscellaneous provisions

### *Article 18*
### *Sovereignty over energy resources*

(1) The Contracting Parties recognize state sovereignty and sovereign rights over energy resources. They reaffirm that these must be exercised in accordance with and subject to the rules of international law.
(2) Without affecting the objectives of promoting access to energy resources, and exploration and development thereof on a commercial basis, the Treaty shall in no way prejudice the rules in Contracting Parties governing the system of property ownership of energy resources.
(3) Each state continues to hold in particular the rights to decide the geographical areas within its Area to be made available for exploration and development of its energy resources, the optimalization of their recovery and the rate at which they may be depleted or otherwise exploited, to specify and enjoy any taxes, royalties or other financial payments payable by virtue of such exploration and exploitation, and to regulate the environmental and safety aspects of such exploration, development and reclamation within its Area, and to participate in such exploration and exploitation, inter alia, through direct participation by the government or through state enterprises.
(4) The Contracting Parties undertake to facilitate access to energy resources, inter alia, by allocating in a non-discriminatory manner on the basis of published criteria authorizations, licences, concessions and contracts to prospect and explore for or to exploit or extract energy resources.

. . .

*Article 21*
*Taxation*

(1) Except as otherwise provided in this Article, nothing in this Treaty shall create rights or impose obligations with respect to Taxation Measures of the Contracting Parties. In the event of any inconsistency between this Article and any other provision of the Treaty, this Article shall prevail to the extent of the inconsistency.

(2) Article 7(3) shall apply to Taxation Measures other than those on income or on capital, except that such provision shall not apply to:
  (a) an advantage accorded by a Contracting Party pursuant to the tax provisions of any convention, agreement or arrangement described in subparagraph (7)(a)(ii); or
  (b) any Taxation Measure aimed at ensuring the effective collection of taxes, except where the measure of a Contracting Party arbitrarily discriminates against Energy Materials and Products originating in, or destined for the Area of another Contracting Party or arbitrarily restricts benefits accorded under Article 7(3).

(3) Article 10(2) and (7) shall apply to Taxation Measures of the Contracting Parties other than those on income or on capital, except that such provisions shall not apply to:
  (a) impose most favoured nation obligations with respect to advantages accorded by a Contracting Party pursuant to the tax provisions of any convention, agreement or arrangement described in subparagraph (7)(a)(ii) or resulting from membership of any Regional Economic Integration Organization; or
  (b) any Taxation Measure aimed at ensuring the effective collection of taxes, except where the measure arbitrarily discriminates against an Investor of another Contracting Party or arbitrarily restricts benefits accorded under the Investment provisions of this Treaty.

(4) Article 29(2) to (6) shall apply to Taxation Measures other than those on income or on capital.

(5) (a) Article 13 shall apply to taxes.
  (b) Whenever an issue arises under Article 13, to the extent it pertains to whether a tax constitutes an expropriation or whether a tax alleged to constitute an expropriation is discriminatory, the following provisions shall apply:
    (i) The Investor or the Contracting Party alleging expropriation shall refer the issue of whether the tax is an expropriation or whether the tax is discriminatory to the relevant Competent Tax Authority. Failing such referral by the Investor or the Contracting Party, bodies called upon to settle disputes pursuant to Article 26(2)(c)

or 27(2) shall make a referral to the relevant Competent Tax Authorities;

(ii) The Competent Tax Authorities shall, within a period of six months of such referral, strive to resolve the issues so referred. Where non-discrimination issues are concerned, the Competent Tax Authorities shall apply the non-discrimination provisions of the relevant tax convention or, if there is no non-discrimination provision in the relevant tax convention applicable to the tax or no such tax convention is in force between the Contracting Parties concerned, they shall apply the non-discrimination principles under the Model Tax Convention on Income and Capital of the Organisation for Economic Co-operation and Development;

(iii) Bodies called upon to settle disputes pursuant to Article 26(2)(c) or 27(2) may take into account any conclusions arrived at by the Competent Tax Authorities regarding whether the tax is an expropriation. Such bodies shall take into account any conclusions arrived at within the six-month period prescribed in subparagraph (b)(ii) by the Competent Tax Authorities regarding whether the tax is discriminatory. Such bodies may also take into account any conclusions arrived at by the Competent Tax Authorities after the expiry of the six-month period;

(iv) Under no circumstances shall involvement of the Competent Tax Authorities, beyond the end of the six-month period referred to in subparagraph (b)(ii), lead to a delay of proceedings under Articles 26 and 27.

(6) For the avoidance of doubt, Article 14 shall not limit the right of a Contracting Party to impose or collect a tax by withholding or other means.

(7) For the purposes of this Article:

(a) The term 'Taxation Measure' includes:

(i) any provision relating to taxes of the domestic law of the Contracting Party or of a political subdivision thereof or a local authority therein; and

(ii) any provision relating to taxes of any convention for the avoidance of double taxation or of any other international agreement or arrangement by which the Contracting Party is bound.

(b) There shall be regarded as taxes on income or on capital all taxes imposed on total income, on total capital or on elements of income or of capital, including taxes on gains from the alienation of property, taxes on estates, inheritances and gifts, or substantially similar taxes, taxes on the total amounts of wages or salaries paid by enterprises, as well as taxes on capital appreciation.

(c) A 'Competent Tax Authority' means the competent authority pursuant to a double taxation agreement in force between the Contracting Parties or, when no such agreement is in force, the minister or ministry responsible for taxes or their authorized representatives.
(d) For the avoidance of doubt, the terms 'tax provisions' and 'taxes' do not include customs duties.

*Article 22*
*Privileged enterprises*

(1) Each Contracting Party shall ensure that any state enterprise which it maintains or establishes shall conduct its activities in relation to the sale or provision of goods and services in its Area in a manner consistent with the Contracting Party's obligations under Part III of this Treaty.
(2) No Contracting Party shall encourage or require such a state enterprise to conduct its activities in its Area in a manner inconsistent with the Contracting Party's obligations under other provisions of this Treaty.
(3) Each Contracting Party shall ensure that if it establishes or maintains an entity and entrusts the entity with regulatory, administrative or other governmental authority, such entity shall exercise that authority in a manner consistent with the Contracting Party's obligations under this Treaty.
(4) No Contracting Party shall encourage or require any entity to which it grants exclusive or special privileges to conduct its activities in its Area in a manner inconsistent with the Contracting Party's obligations under this Treaty.
(5) For the purposes of this Article, 'entity' includes any enterprise, agency or other organization or individual.

*Article 23*
*Observance by sub-national authorities*

(1) Each Contracting Party is fully responsible under this Treaty for the observance of all provisions of the Treaty, and shall take such reasonable measures as may be available to it to ensure such observance by regional and local governments and authorities within its Area.
(2) The dispute settlement provisions in Parts II, IV and V of this Treaty may be invoked in respect of measures affecting the observance of the Treaty by a Contracting Party which have been taken by regional or local governments or authorities within the Area of the Contracting Party.

*Article 24*
*Exceptions*

(1) This Article shall not apply to Articles 12, 13 and 29.

(2) The provisions of this Treaty other than
 (a) those referred to in paragraph (1); and
 (b) with respect to subparagraph (i), Part III of the Treaty shall not preclude any Contracting Party from adopting or enforcing any measure
  (i) necessary to protect human, animal or plant life or health;
  (ii) essential to the acquisition or distribution of Energy Materials and Products in conditions of short supply arising from causes outside the control of that Contracting Party, provided that any such measure shall be consistent with the principles that
   (A) all other Contracting Parties are entitled to an equitable share of the international supply of such Energy Materials and Products; and
   (B) any such measure that is inconsistent with this Treaty shall be discontinued as soon as the conditions giving rise to it have ceased to exist; or
  (iii) designed to benefit Investors who are aboriginal people or socially or economically disadvantaged individuals or groups or their Investments and notified to the Secretariat as such, provided that such measure
   (A) has no significant impact on that Contracting Party's economy; and
   (B) does not discriminate between Investors of any other Contracting Party and Investors of that Contracting Party not included among those for whom the measure is intended, provided that no such measure shall constitute a disguised restriction on Economic Activity in the Energy Sector, or arbitrary or unjustifiable discrimination between Contracting Parties or between Investors or other interested persons of Contracting Parties. Such measures shall be duly motivated and shall not nullify or impair any benefit one or more other Contracting Parties may reasonably expect under this Treaty to an extent greater than is strictly necessary to the stated end.

(3) The provisions of this Treaty other than those referred to in paragraph (1) shall not be construed to prevent any Contracting Party from taking any measure which it considers necessary:
 (a) for the protection of its essential security interests including those
  (i) relating to the supply of Energy Materials and Products to a military establishment; or
  (ii) taken in time of war, armed conflict or other emergency in international relations;

(b) relating to the implementation of national policies respecting the non-proliferation of nuclear weapons or other nuclear explosive devices or needed to fulfil its obligations under the Treaty on the Non-Proliferation of Nuclear Weapons, the Nuclear Suppliers Guidelines, and other international nuclear non-proliferation obligations or understandings; or

(c) for the maintenance of public order.

Such measure shall not constitute a disguised restriction on Transit.

(4) The provisions of this Treaty which accord most favoured nation treatment shall not oblige any Contracting Party to extend to the Investors of any other Contracting Party any preferential treatment:

(a) resulting from its membership of a free-trade area or customs union; or

(b) which is accorded by a bilateral or multilateral agreement concerning economic co-operation between states that were constituent parts of the former Union of Soviet Socialist Republics pending the establishment of their mutual economic relations on a definitive basis.

*Article 25*

*Economic integration agreements*

(1) The provisions of this Treaty shall not be so construed as to oblige a Contracting Party which is party to an Economic Integration Agreement (hereinafter referred to as 'EIA') to extend, by means of most favoured nation treatment, to another Contracting Party which is not a party to that EIA, any preferential treatment applicable between the parties to that EIA as a result of their being parties thereto.

(2) For the purposes of paragraph (1), 'EIA' means an agreement substantially liberalizing, inter alia, trade and investment, by providing for the absence or elimination of substantially all discrimination between or among parties thereto through the elimination of existing discriminatory measures and/or the prohibition of new or more discriminatory measures, either at the entry into force of that agreement or on the basis of a reasonable time frame.

(3) This Article shall not affect the application of the GATT and Related Instruments according to Article 29.

## Part V
## Dispute settlement

*Article 26*

*Settlement of disputes between an investor and a contracting party*

(1) Disputes between a Contracting Party and an Investor of another Contracting Party relating to an Investment of the latter in the Area of the

former, which concern an alleged breach of an obligation of the former under Part III shall, if possible, be settled amicably.

(2) If such disputes can not be settled according to the provisions of paragraph (1) within a period of three months from the date on which either party to the dispute requested amicable settlement, the Investor party to the dispute may choose to submit it for resolution:
   (a) to the courts or administrative tribunals of the Contracting Party party to the dispute;
   (b) in accordance with any applicable, previously agreed dispute settlement procedure; or
   (c) in accordance with the following paragraphs of this Article.

(3) (a) Subject only to subparagraphs (b) and (c), each Contracting Party hereby gives its unconditional consent to the submission of a dispute to international arbitration or conciliation in accordance with the provisions of this Article.
   (b) (i) The Contracting Parties listed in Annex ID do not give such unconditional consent where the Investor has previously submitted the dispute under subparagraph (2)(a) or (b).
      (ii) For the sake of transparency, each Contracting Party that is listed in Annex ID shall provide a written statement of its policies, practices and conditions in this regard to the Secretariat no later than the date of the deposit of its instrument of ratification, acceptance or approval in accordance with Article 39 or the deposit of its instrument of accession in accordance with Article 41.
   (c) A Contracting Party listed in Annex IA does not give such unconditional consent with respect to a dispute arising under the last sentence of Article 10(1).

(4) In the event that an Investor chooses to submit the dispute for resolution under subparagraph (2)(c), the Investor shall further provide its consent in writing for the dispute to be submitted to:
   (a) (i) The International Centre for Settlement of Investment Disputes, established pursuant to the Convention on the Settlement of Investment Disputes between States and Nationals of other States opened for signature at Washington, 18 March 1965 (hereinafter referred to as the 'ICSID Convention'), if the Contracting Party of the Investor and the Contracting Party party to the dispute are both parties to the ICSID Convention; or
      (ii) The International Centre for Settlement of Investment Disputes, established pursuant to the Convention referred to in subparagraph (a)(i), under the rules governing the Additional Facility for the Administration of Proceedings by the Secretariat of the Centre (hereinafter referred to as the 'Additional Facility Rules'), if

the Contracting Party of the Investor or the Contracting Party party to the dispute, but not both, is a party to the ICSID Convention;

(b) a sole arbitrator or ad hoc arbitration tribunal established under the Arbitration Rules of the United Nations Commission on International Trade Law (hereinafter referred to as "UNCITRAL"); or

(c) an arbitral proceeding under the Arbitration Institute of the Stockholm Chamber of Commerce.

(5) (a) The consent given in paragraph (3) together with the written consent of the Investor given pursuant to paragraph (4) shall be considered to satisfy the requirement for:

(i) written consent of the parties to a dispute for purposes of Chapter II of the ICSID Convention and for purposes of the Additional Facility Rules;

(ii) an 'agreement in writing' for purposes of article II of the United Nations Convention on the Recognition and Enforcement of Foreign Arbitral Awards, done at New York, 10 June 1958 (hereinafter referred to as the 'New York Convention'); and

(iii) 'the parties to a contract [to] have agreed in writing' for the purposes of article 1 of the UNCITRAL Arbitration Rules.

(b) Any arbitration under this Article shall at the request of any party to the dispute be held in a state that is a party to the New York Convention. Claims submitted to arbitration hereunder shall be considered to arise out of a commercial relationship or transaction for the purposes of article I of that Convention.

(6) A tribunal established under paragraph (4) shall decide the issues in dispute in accordance with this Treaty and applicable rules and principles of international law.

(7) An Investor other than a natural person which has the nationality of a Contracting Party party to the dispute on the date of the consent in writing referred to in paragraph (4) and which, before a dispute between it and that Contracting Party arises, is controlled by Investors of another Contracting Party, shall for the purpose of article 25(2)(b) of the ICSID Convention be treated as a 'national of another Contracting State' and shall for the purpose of article 1(6) of the Additional Facility Rules be treated as a 'national of another State'.

(8) The awards of arbitration, which may include an award of interest, shall be final and binding upon the parties to the dispute. An award of arbitration concerning a measure of a sub-national government or authority of the disputing Contracting Party shall provide that the Contracting Party may pay monetary damages in lieu of any other remedy granted. Each Contracting Party shall carry out without delay any such award and

shall make provision for the effective enforcement in its Area of such awards.

. . .

## Part VIII
## Final provisions

. . .

### *Article 45*
### *Provisional application*

(1) Each signatory agrees to apply this Treaty provisionally pending its entry into force for such signatory in accordance with Article 44, to the extent that such provisional application is not inconsistent with its constitution, laws or regulations.

(2) (a) Notwithstanding paragraph (1) any signatory may, when signing, deliver to the Depository a declaration that it is not able to accept provisional application. The obligation contained in paragraph (1) shall not apply to a signatory making such a declaration. Any such signatory may at any time withdraw that declaration by written notification to the Depository.

(b) Neither a signatory which makes a declaration in accordance with subparagraph (a) nor Investors of that signatory may claim the benefits of provisional application under paragraph (1.)

(c) Notwithstanding subparagraph (a), any signatory making a declaration referred to in subparagraph (a) shall apply Part VII provisionally pending the entry into force of the Treaty for such signatory in accordance with Article 44, to the extent that such provisional application is not inconsistent with its laws or regulations.

(3) (a) Any signatory may terminate its provisional application of this Treaty by written notification to the Depository of its intention not to become a Contracting Party to the Treaty. Termination of provisional application for any signatory shall take effect upon the expiration of 60 days from the date on which such signatory's written notification is received by the Depository.

(b) In the event that a signatory terminates provisional application under subparagraph (a), the obligation of the signatory under paragraph (1) to apply Parts III and V with respect to any Investments made in its Area during such provisional application by Investors of other signatories shall nevertheless remain in effect with respect to those Investments for twenty years following the effective date of termination, except as otherwise provided in subparagraph (c).

(c) Subparagraph (b) shall not apply to any signatory listed in Annex PA. A signatory shall be removed from the list in Annex PA effective upon delivery to the Depository of its request therefor.

. . .

## ANNEXES TO THE ENERGY CHARTER TREATY

### *1. ANNEX EM*
### *ENERGY MATERIAL AND PRODUCTS (IN ACCORDANCE WITH ARTICLE 1(4))*

#### *Nuclear energy*

26.12 Uranium or thorium ores and concentrates.

26.12.10 Uranium ores and concentrates.

26.12.20 Thorium ores and concentrates.

28.44 Radioactive chemical elements and radioactive isotopes (including the fissile or fertile chemical elements and isotopes) and their compounds; mixtures and residues containing these products.

28.44.10 Natural uranium and its compounds.

28.44.20 Uranium enriched in U235 and its compounds; plutonium and its compounds.

28.44.30 Uranium depleted in U235 and its compounds; thorium and its compounds.

28.44.40 Radioactive elements and isotopes and radioactive compounds other than 28.44.10, 28.44.20 or 28.44.30.

28.44.50 Spent (irradiated) fuel elements (cartridges) of nuclear reactors.

28.45.10 Heavy water (deuterium oxide).

#### *Coal, Natural Gas, Petroleum and Petroleum Products, Electrical Energy*

27.01 Coal, briquettes, ovoids and similar solid fuels manufactured from coal.

27.02 Lignite, whether or not agglomerated excluding jet.

27.03 Peat (including peat litter), whether or not agglomerated.

27.04 Coke and semi-coke of coal, of lignite or of peat, whether or not agglomerated; retort carbon.

27.05 Coal gas, water gas, producer gas and similar gases, other than petroleum gases and other gaseous hydrocarbons.

27.06 Tar distilled from coal, from lignite or from peat, and other mineral tars, whether or not dehydrated or partially distilled, including reconstituted tars.

27.07 Oils and other products of the distillation of high temperature coal tar; similar products in which the weight of the aromatic constituents exceeds that of the non-aromatic constituents (e.g., benzole, toluole, xylole, naphtalene, other aromatic hydrocarbon mixtures, phenols, creosote oils and others).

27.08 Pitch and pitch coke, obtained from coal tar or from other mineral tars.

27.09 Petroleum oils and oils obtained from bituminous minerals, crude.

27.10 Petroleum oils and oils obtained from bituminous minerals, other than crude.

27.11 Liquified petroleum gases and other gaseous hydrocarbons
- natural gas
- propane
- butanes
- ethylene, propylene, butylene and butadiene (27.11.14)
- other

In gaseous state:
- natural gas
- other

27.13 Petroleum coke, petroleum bitumen and other residues of petroleum oils or of oils obtained from bituminous minerals.

27.14 Bitumen and asphalt, natural; bituminous or oil shale and tar sands; asphaltites and asphaltic rocks.

27.15 Bituminous mixtures based on natural asphalt, on natural bitumen, on petroleum bitumen, on mineral tar or on mineral tar pitch (e.g., bituminous mastics, cut-backs).

27.16 Electrical energy.

### *Other Energy*

44.01.10 Fuel wood, in logs, in billets, in twigs, in faggots or in similar forms.

44.02 Charcoal (including charcoal from shells or nuts), whether or not agglomerated.

## 2. ANNEX NI
## NON-APPLICABLE ENERGY MATERIALS AND PRODUCTS FOR DEFINITIONS OF 'ECONOMIC ACTIVITY IN THE ENERGY SECTOR' (IN ACCORDANCE WITH ARTICLE 1(5))

27.07 Oils and other products of the distillation of high temperature coal tar; similar products in which the weight of the aromatic constituents exceeds that of the non-aromatic constituents (e.g., benzole, toluole, xylole, naphtalene, other aromatic hydrocarbon mixtures, phenols, creosote oils and others).

44.01.10 Fuel wood, in logs, in billets, in twigs, in faggots or in similar forms.

44.02 Charcoal (including charcoal from shells or nuts), whether or not agglomerated.

...

## ANNEX ID
## LIST OF CONTRACTING PARTIES NOT ALLOWING AN INVESTOR TO RESUBMIT THE SAME DISPUTE TO INTERNATIONAL ARBITRATION AT A LATER STAGE UNDER ARTICLE 26 (IN ACCORDANCE WITH ARTICLE 26 (3) (B)(I))

| | |
|---|---|
| 1. Australia | 13. Japan |
| 2. Azerbaijan | 14. Kazakhstan |
| 3. Bulgaria | 15. Mongolia |
| Canada*** | 16. Norway* |
| 4. Croatia | 17. Poland |
| 5. Cyprus | 18. Portugal |
| 6. The Czech Republic | 19. Romania |
| 7. European Communities | 20. The Russian Federation** |
| 8. Finland | 21. Slovenia |
| 9. Greece | 22. Spain |
| 10. Hungary | 23. Sweden |
| 11. Ireland | 24. Turkey |
| 12. Italy | United States of America*** |

* Ratification of ECT pending.

** Announced intention not to ratify ECT.

*** Non-signatories to ECT.

...

## DECISIONS WITH RESPECT TO THE ENERGY CHARTER TREATY (ANNEX 2 TO THE FINAL ACT OF THE EUROPEAN ENERGY CHARTER CONFERENCE)

...

5. <u>With respect to Articles 24(4)(a) and 25</u>

An Investment of an Investor referred to in Article 1(7)(a)(ii), of a Contracting Party which is not party to an EIA or a member of a free-trade area or a customs union, shall be entitled to treatment accorded under such EIA, free-trade area or customs union, provided that the Investment:

(a) has its registered office, central administration or principal place of business in the Area of a party to that EIA or member of that free-trade area or customs union; or

(b) in case it only has its registered office in that Area, has an effective and continuous link with the economy of one of the parties to that EIA or member of that free-trade area or customs union.

# Appendix B

## Signatories to the Energy Charter Treaty

Albania, Armenia, Australia*, Austria, Azerbaijan, Belarus*, Belgium, Bosnia and Herzegovina, Bulgaria, Croatia, Cyprus, Czech Republic, Denmark, Estonia, European Communities, Finland, France, Georgia, Germany, Greece, Hungary, Iceland*, Ireland, Italy, Japan, Kazakhstan, Kyrgyzstan, Latvia, Liechtenstein, Lithuania, Luxembourg, Malta, Moldova, Mongolia, the Netherlands, Norway*, Poland, Portugal, Romania, Russian Federation^, Slovakia, Slovenia, Spain, Sweden, Switzerland, Tajikistan, the former Yugoslav Republic of Macedonia, Turkey, Turkmenistan, Ukraine, United Kingdom, Uzbekistan

* – denotes state in which ratification of the Energy Charter Treaty is still pending

^ – the Russian Federation signed the Energy Charter Treaty and was applying it provisionally until 18 October 2009 inclusive

### Observers to the Energy Charter Conference

Afghanistan**, Algeria, Bahrain, Canada**, China, Egypt°, Indonesia**, Iran, Jordan**, Korea, Kuwait, Morocco, Nigeria, Oman, Pakistan**, Palestinian National Authority, Qatar, Saudi Arabia, Serbia**, Syria**, Tunisia, United Arab Emirates, United States of America**, Venezuela

### International Organisations with Observer Status

ASEAN, BASREC, BSEC, CIS Electric Power Council, EBRD, IEA, OECD, UN-ECE, World Bank, WTO

** – denotes observer state which has signed the 1991 Energy Charter

° – denotes observer state in which signing of the 1991 Energy Charter is pending

# BIBLIOGRAPHY

## Books and Reports


Brownlie, I., *Principles of Public International Law* (Oxford University Press, 7th edn, 2008)

Coop, G. and C. Ribeiro (eds.), *Investment Protection and the Energy Charter Treaty* (New York: JurisNet, 2008)

Dolzer, R. and C. Schreuer, *Principles of International Investment Law* (Oxford University Press, 2008)

Douglas, Z., *The International Law of Investment Claims* (Cambridge University Press, 2009)

Energy Charter Conference, Conclusions of the Review Conducted under Article 34(7) of the Energy Charter Treaty, adopted at 15th meeting, 14 December 2004

Energy Charter Secretariat, *The Blue Book: Making Investments in Energy Charter Member Countries: Exceptions to the Principle of Non-discriminatory Treatment* (Brussels: Energy Charter Secretariat, 2009)

*The Energy Charter Treaty: A Reader's Guide* (Brussels: Energy Charter Secretariat, 2002)

*The Energy Charter Treaty and Related Documents: A Legal Framework for International Energy Cooperation* (Brussels: Energy Charter Secretariat, 2004)

Gaja, G., Fourth Report on Responsibility of International Organizations, Addendum, UN Doc. A/CN.4/564/Add.2

Gribnau, H. (ed.), *Legal Protection against Discriminatory Tax Legislation: The Struggle for Equality in European Tax Law* (The Hague: Kluwer Law International, 2006)

Hart, H. L. A., *The Concept of Law* (Oxford University Press, 2nd edn, 1994)

van Harten, G., *Investment Treaty Arbitration and Public Law* (Oxford University Press, 2007)

Hillion, C. and P. Koutrakos (eds.), *Mixed Agreements Revisited* (Oxford: Hart Publishing, 2010)

Hilpold, P., *Die EU im GATT/WTO-System* (Innsbruck University Press, 3rd edn, 2009)

International Law Commission, Articles on Responsibility of States for Internationally Wrongful Acts (2001) (GA res. 56/83 (2002), Annex)

Draft Articles on the Responsibility of International Organizations, Report of the Sixty-first session, (2009) (UN Dec. A/64/10)

'Draft Articles on the Law of Treaties with Commentaries' (1966) II *Yearbook of the International Law Commission*, 186 at 210

'Draft Articles on Responsibility of States for Internationally Wrongful Acts with Commentaries' (2001) II *Yearbook of The International Law Commission*

'Conclusions of the Work of the Study Group on the Fragmentation of International Law: Difficulties arising from the Diversification and Expansion of International Law' (2006) II(2) *Yearbook of the International Law Commission*

Third Report on Reservations to Treaties by Mr Alain Pellet, Special Rapporteur, UN Doc. A/CN.4/491/Add.4

Klabbers, J., *An Introduction to International Institutional Law* (Cambridge University Press, 2009)

MacLeod, I., I. Hendry and S. Hyett, *The External Relations of the European Communities* (Oxford University Press, 1996)

Madsen, F. (translated R. Ben-Dor), *Commercial Arbitration in Sweden: A Commentary on the Arbitration Act (1999:116) and the Rules of the Arbitration Institute of the Stockholm Chamber of Commerce* (New York: Oxford University Press, 2007)

OECD, *Commentaries on the Articles of the Model Tax Convention*, July 2008 (www.oecd.org/dataoecd/14/32/41147804.pdf)

*International Investment Law: A Changing Landscape* (Paris: OECD, 2008)

*International Investment Law: Understanding Concepts and Tracking Innovations* (Paris: OECD, 2008)

O'Keefe, D. and H. Schermers (eds.), *Mixed Agreements* (Deventer: Kluwer Law & Taxation Publishers and Leiden Europa Instituut, 1983)

McLachlan, C., L. Shore and M. Weiniger, *International Investment Arbitration: Substantive Principles* (Oxford University Press, 2007)

Newcombe, A., and L. Paradell, *Law and Practice of Investment Treaties: Standards of Treatment* (Alphen aan den Rijn: Kluwer Law International, 2009)

Paulsson, J., *Denial of Justice in International Law* (Cambridge University Press, 2005)

Neilsen, F., *American–Turkish Claims Settlement under the Agreement of 24 December 1923* (Washington: US Department of State, 1937)

Reinisch, A. (ed.), *Standards of Investment Protection* (Oxford University Press, 2008)

Ribeiro, C. (ed.), *Investment Arbitration and the Energy Charter Treaty* (New York: JurisNet, 2006)

Schreuer, C., *et al.*, *The ICSID Convention: A Commentary* (Cambridge University Press, 2001)

Schreuer, C., L. Malintoppi, A. Reinisch and A. Sinclair, *The ICSID Convention: A Commentary* (Cambridge University Press, 2nd edn, 2009)

Schrijver, N., *Sovereignty over Natural Resources: Balancing Rights and Duties* (Cambridge University Press, 1997)

Sornarajah, M., *The International Law on Foreign Investment* (Cambridge University Press, 2004)

UNCTAD, *Fair and Equitable Treatment* (UNCTAD Series on issues in international investments) (New York: United Nations, 1999)

*IIA Monitor No. 3 (2009): Recent Developments in International Investment Agreements (2008–June 2009)* (UNCTAD/WEB/DIAE/IA/2009/8)

Voge, K. *et al.*, *Double Taxation Conventions: A Commentary to the OECD, UN and US Model Conventions for the Avoidance of Double Taxation of Income and Capital* (The Hague: Kluwer Law International, 3rd edn, 1997)

Wälde, T. (ed.), *The Energy Charter Treaty: An East–West Gateway for Investment and Trade* (London: Kluwer Law International, 1996)

World Trade Organization, *The Legal Texts: The Results of the Uruguay Round of Multilateral Trade Negotiations* (Cambridge University Press, 1999)

## Chapters in edited books

Acconci, P., 'Most-Favoured-Nation Treatment' in P. Muchlinski, F. Ortino and C. Schreuer (eds.), *The Oxford Handbook of International Investment Law* (Oxford University Press, 2008), p. 363

Bamberger, C., 'Overview' in T. Wälde (ed.), *The Energy Charter Treaty: An East–West Gateway for Investment and Trade* (London: Kluwer International, 1996), p. 1

'The Negotiation of the Energy Charter Treaty' in G. Coop and C. Ribeiro (eds.), *Investment Protection and the Energy Charter Treaty* (New York: JurisNet, 2008), p. xxxix

Bjorklund, A., 'National Treatment' in A. Reinisch (ed.), *Standards of Investment Protection* (Oxford University Press, 2008), p. 29

Blanch, J., A. Moody and N. Lawn, 'Investment Dispute Resolution and the Energy Charter Treaty' in G. Coop and C. Ribeiro (eds.), *Investment Protection and the Energy Charter Treaty* (New York: JurisNet, 2008), p. 8

Coop, G., 'The Energy Charter: More than an MIT' in C. Ribeiro (ed.), *Investment Arbitration and the Energy Charter Treaty* (New York: JurisNet, 2006)

Cordero Moss, C., 'Full Protection and Security' in A. Reinisch (ed.), *Standards of Investment Protection* (Oxford University Press, 2008), p. 131

Doré, J., 'Negotiating the Energy Charter Treaty' in T. Wälde (ed.), *The Energy Charter Treaty: An East–West Gateway for Investment and Trade* (London: Kluwer Law International, 1996), p. 137

Fox, W., 'The United States and the Energy Charter Treaty: Misgivings and Misconceptions', in T. Wälde (ed.), *The Energy Charter Treaty: An East–West Gateway for Investment and Trade* (London: Kluwer Law International, 1996), p. 194

Gaillard, E., 'Identify or Define? Reflections on the Evolution of the Concept of Investment in ICSID Practice' in C. Binder, U. Kriebaum, A. Reinisch and S. Wittich (eds.), *International Investment Law for the 21st Century: Essays in Honour of Christoph Schreuer* (Oxford University Press, 2009), p. 403

Gaja, G., 'The European Community's Rights and Obligations under Mixed Agreements' in D. O'Keefe and H. Schermers (eds.), *Mixed Agreements* (Deventer: Kluwer Law & Taxation Publishers and Leiden: The Europa Instituut, 1983)

Grierson-Weiler, T. and I. Laird, 'Standards of Treatment' in P. Muchlinski, F. Ortino and C. Schreuer (eds.), *The Oxford Handbook of International Investment Law* (Oxford University Press, 2008), p. 259

Hafner, G. 'The "Provisional Application" of the Energy Charter Treaty' in C. Binder, U. Kriebaum, A. Reinisch and S. Wittich (eds.), *International Investment Law for the 21st Century: Essays in Honour of Christoph Schreuer* (Oxford University Press, 2009), p. 593

Heiskanen, V., 'Arbitrary and unreasonable Measures' in A. Reinisch (ed.), *Standards of Investment Protection* (Oxford University Press, 2008), p. 87

Jagusch, S. and A. Sinclair, 'Denial of Advantages Under Article 17(1)' in G. Coop and C. Ribeiro (eds.), *Investment Protection and the Energy Charter Treaty* (New York: JurisNet, 2008), p. 17

Kolo, A., and T. Wälde, 'Capital Transfer Restrictions Under Modern Investment Treaties' in A. Reinisch (ed.), *Standards of Investment Protectian* (Oxford University Press, 2008), p. 205

Konoplyanik, A., 'The Energy Charter Treaty: A Russian Perspective' in T. Wälde, *The Energy Charter Treaty: An East–West Gateway for Investment and Trade* (London: Kluwer Law International, 1996), p. 156

Laird, I., 'A Distinction without a Difference?' in T. Weiler (ed.), *International Investment Law and Arbitration: Leading Cases from the ICSID, NAFTA, Bilateral Treaties and Customary International Law* (London: Cameron May, 2005), p. 201

Lubbers, R., 'Foreword' in T. Wälde (ed.), *The Energy Charter Treaty: An East–West Gateway for Investment and Trade* (London: Kluwer Law International, 1996), p. xiii

Paulsson, J., 'Jurisdiction and Admissibility', in *Liber Amicorum in Honour of Robert Briner, Global Reflections on International Law, Commerce and Dispute Resolution* (Paris: ICC Publishing, 2005), p. 601

Reinisch, A., 'Legality of Expropriations' in A. Reinisch (ed.), *Standards of Investment Protection* (Oxford University Press, 2008), p. 171

Reisman, W., 'The Provisional Application of the Energy Charter Treaty' in G. Coop and C. Ribeiro (eds.), *Investment Protection and the Energy Charter Treaty* (New York: JurisNet, 2008), p. 47

Schlemmer, E., 'Investment, Investor, Nationality and Shareholders' in P. Muchlinski, F. Ortino and C. Schreuer (eds.), *The Oxford Handbook of International Investment Law* (Oxford University Press, 2008), p. 51

Schreuer, C., 'Consent to Arbitration', in P. Muchlinski, F. Ortino and C. Schreuer (eds.), *The Oxford Handbook of International Investment Law* (Oxford University Press, 2008), p. 831

Schreuer, C. and M. Weiniger, 'A Doctrine of Precedent?', in P. Muchlinski, F. Ortino and C. Schreuer (eds.), *The Oxford Handbook of International Investment Law* (Oxford University Press, 2008), p. 1188

Spiermann, O., 'Applicable Law' in P. Muchlinski, F. Ortino and C. Schreuer (eds.), *The Oxford Handbook of International Investment Law* (Oxford University Press, 2008), p. 89

Wälde, T. and A. Kolo, 'Coverage of Taxation under Modern Investment Treaties' in P. Muchlinski, F. Ortino and C. Schreuer (eds.), *The Oxford Handbook of International Investment Law* (Oxford University Press, 2008), p. 305

Waldron, J., 'Legislators' Intentions and Unintended Legislation' in A. Marmor (ed.), *Law and Interpretation: Essays in Legal Philosophy* (Oxford University Press, 1995), p. 329

Yannaca-Small, K. 'Fair and Equitable Treatment Standard: Recent Developments' in A. Reinisch (ed.), *Standards of Investment Protection* (Oxford University Press, 2008), p. 111

Ziegler, A., 'Most-Favoured-Nation (MFN) Treatment', in A. Reinisch (ed.), *Standards of Investment Protection* (Oxford University Press, 2008) p. 59

## Articles and conference papers

Abbott, K., R. Keohane, A. Moravcsik, A. Slaughter and D. Snidal, 'The Concept of Legalization' (2000) 54 *International Organization* 401

Alvarez, J. 'International Organizations: Accountability or Responsibility?', Luncheon Address, Canadian Council of International Law, 35th Annual Conference on Responsibility of Individuals, States and Organizations, 26 October 2006 (www.asil.org/aboutasil/documents/CCILspeech061102.pdf)

Baldwin, E., M. Kantor and M. Nolan, 'Limits to Enforcement of ICSID Awards' (2006) 23 *Journal of International Arbitration* 1

Bamberger, C., J. Lineham and T. Wälde, 'The Energy Charter Treaty in 2000: In a New Phase' (2000) 18 *Journal of Energy & Natural Resources Law* 3

Björklund, M., 'Responsibility in the EC for Mixed Agreements – Should Non-Member Parties Care?' (2001) 70 *Nordic Journal of International Law* 373

Burke-White, W. and A. von Staden, 'Investment Protection in Extraordinary Times: The Interpretation and Application of Non-Precluded Measures Provisions in Bilateral Investment Treaties' (2008) 48 *Virginia Journal of International Law* 307

Chapaev, R. and V. Bradautanu, 'International and Commercial Arbitration in the CIS and Mongolia' (2006) 17(3) *American Review of International Arbitration* 411

D'Allaire, D. 'The Nationality Rules under the Energy Charter Treaty: Practical Considerations', (2009) 10 *Journal of World Investment and Trade* 39

Dolzer, R. 'Fair and Equitable Treatment: A Key Standard in Investment Treaties', (2005) 39 *International Law* 87

Douglas, Z., 'Nothing if Not Critical for Investment Treaty Arbitration: *Occidental, Eureko* and *Methanex*' (2006) 22 *Arbitration International* 27

'The Hybrid Foundations of Investment Treaty Arbitration' (2004) 74 *British Yearbook of International Law* 151

Eilmansberger, T. 'Bilateral Investment Treaties and EU Law' (2009) 48 *Common Market Law Review* 383

Elshihabi, S, 'The Difficulty behind Securing Sector-Specific Investment Establishment Rights: The Case of the Energy Charter Treaty' (2001) 35 *International Lawyer* 137

Fietta, S. 'Most Favoured Nation Treatment and Dispute Resolution under Bilateral Investment Treaties: A Turning Point?' (2005) 8 *International Arbitration Law Review* 131

Heiskanen, V. 'May a State Invoke its Domestic Law to Evade its International Obligations?' (2005) 2(5) *Transnational Dispute Management* 1

Hober, K. and S. Nappert, 'Provisional Application and the Energy Charter Treaty: the Russian Doll Provision' (2007) 10 *International Arbitration Review* 53

Klabbers, J. 'Some Problems Regarding the Object and Purpose of Treaties' (1997) 8 *Finnish Yearbook of International Law* 138

Lipstein, K., 'Conflict of Laws before International Tribunals (ii)' (1949) 29 *Transactions of the Grotius Society* 51

McLachlan, C., 'The Principle of Systemic Integration and Article 31(3)(c) of the Vienna Convention' (2005) 54 *International and Comparative Law Quarterly* 279

von Mehren, R. and P. Kourides, 'International Arbitrations Between States and Foreign Private Parties: The Libyan Nationalization Cases' (1981) 75 *American Journal of International Law* 476

Michie, A., 'The Provisional Application of Arms Control Treaties' (2005) 10 *Journal of Conflict and Security Law* 345

Milanoviç, M. and T Papiç, 'As Bad as It Gets: The European Court of Human Rights' *Behrami and Saramati* Decisions and General International Law' (2009) 58 *International and Comparative Law Quarterly* 267

Mistelis, L. and C. M. Baltag, 'Denial of Benefits and Article 17 of the Energy Charter Treaty' (2009) *Penn State Law Review* 1301

Niebruegge, A., 'Provisional Application of the Energy Charter Treaty: The Yukos Arbitration and the Future Place of Provisional Application in International Law' (2007) 8 *Chicago Journal of International Law* 355

Paasivirta, E., Conference paper delivered at 'Energy Dispute Resolution: Investment Protection, Transit and the Energy Charter Treaty', Brussels, 23 October 2009 (www.encharter.org/index.php?id=472)

Paulsson, J., 'Arbitration without Privity' (1995) 10 *ICSID Review – Foreign Investment Law Journal* 232

Peterson, L., 'ICSID Tribunal will Permit European Commission to File Legal Brief in Energy Charter Treaty Arbitration' (2008) 16(i) *Investment Arbitration Reporter*, 11 December 2008

Polkinghorne, M. and L. Gouiffès, 'Provisional Application of the Energy Charter Treaty: the Conundrum', Conference paper delivered at 'Energy Dispute Resolution: Investment Protection, Transit and the Energy Charter Treaty', Brussels, 23 October 2009 (www.encharter.org/index.php?id=472)

Rubins, N. and A. Nazarov, 'Investment Treaties and the Russian Federation: Baiting the Bear?' (2008) 9 *Business Law International* 100

Schreuer, C., 'Commentary on the ICSID Convention' (1996) 11 *ICSID Review – Foreign Investment Law Journal* 316

'Non-pecuniary Remedies in ICSID Arbitration' (2004) 20 *Arbitration International* 325

'Travelling the BIT Route – Of Waiting Periods, Umbrella Clauses and Forks in the Road' (2004) 5 *Journal of World Investment & Trade* 231

Shore, L., 'The Jurisdiction Problem in Energy Charter Treaty Claims' (2007) 10 *International Arbitration Law Review* 58

Sinclair, A., 'The Origins of the Umbrella Clause in the International Law of Investment Protection' (2004) 20 *Arbitration International* 411

'The Substance of Nationality Requirements in Investment Treaty Arbitration' (2005) 20 *ICSID Review – Foreign Investment Law Journal* 357

Spiermann, O., 'Individual Rights, State Interests and the Power to Waive ICSID Jurisdiction under Bilateral Investment Treaties' (2004) 20 *Arbitration International* 179

'The Other Side of the Story: An Unpopular Essay on the Making of the European Community Legal Order' (1999) *European Journal of International Law* 763

Stein, E., 'External Relations of the European Community: Structure and Process' (1991) 1 *Collected Courses of the Academy of European Law* 115

Swiss Ministry of Foreign Affairs, 'Statement' (1980) 36 *Annuaire suisse de droit international* 178

Thomas, J., 'Reflections on Article 1105 of NAFTA: History, State Practice and the Influence of Commentators' (2002) 17 *ICSID Review – Foreign Investment Law Journal* 21

Tietje, C., 'The Applicability of the Energy Charter Treaty in ICSID Arbitration of EU Nationals vs. EU Member States', (2008) *Institut für Wirtschaftsrecht, Martin Luther Universität Halle-Wittenberg Essays on Transnational Economic Law*, and (2009) 6 *Transnational Dispute Management* 5

Turinov, A., '"Investment" and "Investor" in Energy Charter Treaty Arbitration: Uncertain Jurisdiction' (2009) 26 *Journal of International Arbitration* 1

Vandevelde, K., 'BIT by BIT: A Brief History of International Investment Agreements' (2005) 12 *University of California-Davis Journal of International Law and Policy* 157

Verhoosel, G., 'The Use of Investor–State Arbitration under Bilateral Investment Treaties to Seek Relief for Breaches of WTO Law' (2003) 6 *Journal of International Economic Law* 493

Wälde, T. and P. Wouters, 'State Responsibility in a Liberalised World Economy: "State, Privileged and Sub-National Authorities" under the 1994 Energy Charter Treaty: An Analysis of Articles 22 and 23' (1996) 26 *Netherlands Yearbook of International Law* 143

Wehland, H., 'Intra-EU Investment Agreements and Arbitration: Is European Community Law an Obstacle?' (2009) 58 *International and Comparative Law Quarterly* 297

Wythes, A., 'Investor–State Arbitrations: Can the "Fair and Equitable Treatment" Clause Consider International Human Rights Obligations?' (2010) 23 *Leiden Journal of International Law* 241

Yang, X., 'Thou Shalt not Violate Provisional Measures' (2001) *Cambridge Law Journal* 441

# INDEX

For EU product safety concerns, contact us at Calle de José Abascal, 56–1°,
28003 Madrid, Spain or eugpsr@cambridge.org.

www.ingramcontent.com/pod-product-compliance
Lightning Source LLC
LaVergne TN
LVHW011523200926
848484LV00001B/125

* 9 7 8 0 5 2 1 8 9 9 3 8 3 *